POSTMODERNISM. WHAT MOMENT?

MANCHESTER
1824

Manchester University Press

ANGELAKIHUMANITIES

editors
Charlie Blake
Pelagia Goulimari
Timothy S. Murphy
Robert Smith

general editor
Gerard Greenway

Angelaki Humanities publishes works which address and probe broad and compelling issues in the theoretical humanities. The series favours path-breaking thought, promotes unjustly neglected figures, and grapples with established concerns. It believes in the possibility of blending, without compromise, the rigorous, the well-crafted, and the inventive. The series seeks to host ambitious writing from around the world.

Angelaki Humanities is the associated book series of
Angelaki – journal of the theoretical humanities.

Already published

THE QUESTION OF LITERATURE: THE PLACE OF THE LITERARY
IN CONTEMPORARY THEORY
Elizabeth Beaumont Bissell

ABSOLUTELY POSTCOLONIAL: WRITING BETWEEN THE SINGULAR
AND THE SPECIFIC
Peter Hallward

LATE MODERNIST POETICS: FROM POUND TO PRYNNE
Anthony Mellors

THE NEW BERGSON
John Mullarkey (ed.)

SUBVERSIVE SPINOZA: (UN)CONTEMPORARY VARIATIONS
Timothy S. Murphy

DISCLOSED POETICS: BEYOND LANDSCAPE AND LYRICISM
John Kinsella

ANGELAKIHUMANITIES

POSTMODERNISM.
WHAT MOMENT?

edited by pelagia goulimari

MANCHESTER UNIVERSITY PRESS

MANCHESTER AND NEW YORK

distributed exclusively in the USA by Palgrave

Published by Manchester University Press
Oxford Road, Manchester M13 9NR, UK
and Room 400, 175 Fifth Avenue, New York, NY 10010, USA
www.manchesteruniversitypress.co.uk

Distributed exclusively in the USA by
Palgrave, 175 Fifth Avenue, New York,
NY 10010, USA

Distributed exclusively in Canada by
UBC Press, University of British Columbia, 2029 West Mall,
Vancouver, BC, Canada V6T 1Z2

British Library Cataloguing-in-Publication Data
A catalogue record for this book is available from the British Library

Library of Congress Cataloging-in-Publication Data applied for

ISBN 978 0 7190 7308 3   *hardback*

First published 2007

16 15 14 13 12 11 10 09 08 07   10 9 8 7 6 5 4 3 2 1

Typeset in New Caledonia and Gill Sans Display
by Koinonia, Manchester
Printed in Great Britain
by Bell & Bain Ltd, Glasgow

CONTENTS

pelagia goulimari

INTRODUCTION

Postmodernism – the vast interdisciplinary debate on postmodernism and postmodernity of the 1980s and early 1990s – has been a crossroads for historical descriptions of the latter half of the twentieth century as well as for a variety of new philosophical, ethical and aesthetic perspectives. At the beginning of the twenty-first century, many of the protagonists of the debate have written especially for this collection, together with a younger generation of critics, in order to assess the philosophical, ethical and aesthetic legacies of postmodernism and in order to ask: do we still live in postmodern times? What is the moment – the time, but also the force and significance – of postmodernism?

As this introduction will make clear, the texts assembled in this collection emerge out of multiple, possibly incommensurable, paradigms and genealogies. In varying degrees, they all reflect on their own paradigm and genealogy; they all show awareness of other, "rival," paradigms and attempt to map them; they all mix theoretical concerns with the renewed attempt to engage with actuality. Depending on their particular emphasis, texts are classified under three headings: i. genealogies of the postmodern; ii. mapping the postmodern; iii. the postmodern and the twenty-first century.

All the texts assembled here look upon the beginning of the twenty-first century with a critical eye. However differently understood, they all identify hopeful developments and the means for future reconstruction. The pressure of recent global events seems to have created in these writers austere moods ranging from circumspection, to sobriety, to bleakness. Perhaps accompanying this, there is an emerging consensus around three points: firstly, any triumphal celebration of the postmodern against the modern is out of place; secondly, the relation between the modern and the postmodern is one of continuities as well as discontinuities; thirdly, the postmodern, in its relations of continuity with the modern, is here to stay.

This introduction sets out to present the texts of this collection to an undergraduate interdisciplinary audience, in their full complexity. The emerging picture is indeed a complex one: in the assembled texts we find consensus around certain points; we find incommensurability and disjunction around others.

I. Genealogies of the postmodern

Linda Hutcheon, in "Gone forever, but here to stay: the legacy of the Postmodern," considers postmodernism as a now-established, institutionalised counter-discourse. Postmodernism is now part of the university curriculum, together with postcolonial theory and feminism.

What is distinctively postmodern, according to Hutcheon? Firstly, in the eyes of both subscribers and detractors, postmodernism has a Socratic impulse to question truths; secondly, it has a "both/and" way of thinking and a high tolerance for contradiction. In the eyes of its detractors, postmodernism demolishes without reconstructing and undermines political agency. Hutcheon singles out postmodernism's "both/and" thinking as the most valuable aspect of its legacy. She then demonstrates or performs this thinking by giving us a quick sketch of a "both/and" historical assessment of postmodernism itself.

While historians of postmodernism have tended to be partisan for or against it, Hutcheon argues that a "both/and" assessment would play out like this. Postmodernist demystification might be compromised by postmodernism's institutionalisation and might undermine activist aims. However, postmodernist demystification "may still be considered a crucial first step to action."[1] Postmodernism's ability to tolerate contradiction and to abstain from the role of resolving contradiction, or the role of common ground, may be a first step rather than an impediment to action, in the "brave new world of globalization, [and] diaspora."

Robert Venturi begins "A bas postmodernism, of course" with an ironic denunciation: "I am not now and never have been a postmodernist and I unequivocally disavow fatherhood of this architectural movement." As an architectural style, postmodernism is officially dead. It was replaced by Neomod, a modern-revival style. As a result, an architect's association with postmodernism is now a sign of old-fashionedness, and accepting the label of postmodernism tantamount to professional suicide.

---

1   All quotations are derived from this collection.

Venturi then sloughs off the carapace of institutionalised postmodernism to defend the spirit of his *Learning from Las Vegas* (co-written with Denise Scott Brown), one of the founding texts of postmodernism, and argues for its continuing vitality and relevance. Postmodernism in architecture came to be identified with historical revivalism, but this is not what his work has been concerned with. The two principles of *Learning from Las Vegas* are: firstly, the use of contemporary, "impolite, vital" symbolism; secondly, the use of symbolism, not in order to imitate the "real thing" but in order to engage with the present. Venturi advocates an engagement with contemporary icons that "refers [to these icons] manneristically and incorrectly ... and creates aesthetic tension ... Ultimately our architecture engages mannerism, an architectural approach that accommodates aesthetic ambiguity but also, in our time, creates ambiguity."

Venturi argues that Neomod architecture inherits from modern architecture an industrial iconography which is irrelevant in our post-industrial "Electronic Age, our Multicultural Age, our Information Age dedicated to communication." Describing his position since *Learning from Las Vegas* as a pragmatism, he invites us to "learn from the relevant, if shocking, everyday commercial vernacular of now" and to "acknowledge the relevance of electronic technology for our mannerist-iconographic architecture."

In "On the postmodernism debate," Zygmunt Bauman looks back on his substantial body of work on "postmodernity," in conversation and Keith Tester. Bauman's "postmodernity" was initially a name for several intuitions indebted to Gramsci: "that despite modern ambitions the war against human waywardness and historical contingency is unwinnable, that the resistance of human modality to logic and rule is here to stay, and that the modern crusade against ambivalence and the 'messiness' of human reality only multiplies the targets it aims to destroy." Bauman's early work on postmodernity stressed the *discontinuity* between modernity and postmodernity and elaborated postmodernity's *opportunities* for freedom and responsibility. Bauman initially saw the coming of postmodernity as a "blow against [modern] arrogance" and as "the advance of doubt, scepticism, irony, recognition and acceptance of the perpetuity of ambivalence. I spied in that shift a new *chance* for the free chooser's responsibility." Bauman's later work, firstly, abandoned the polemical juxtaposition of modernity and postmodernity, to point to *continuities* as well as discontinuities between the two: postmodernity or "liquid modernity" is a stage within modernity; it shares in modernity's movement of melting old communities and identities, but it doesn't share in modernity's accompanying counter-movement of solidifying new communities and identities. Bauman's later work, secondly, stressed the ambivalence of postmodernity, the *threats* mixed with the opportunities of this new condition. Bleakly, Bauman points out that the postmodern freedom to choose *temporary* new communities and identities is a "social relation," the pursuit of elites reliant on the unfreedom of others. Further, Bauman summons postmodernity's climate of fear: as membership in elites of every description is now more precarious than ever, dispossession is on every doorstep and "in every heart."

Gianni Vattimo, in "Postmodernity and (the end of) metaphysics," declares that postmodernity is now "our, more or less, universal condition." In his substantial work on postmodernity, Vattimo has defined postmodernity as the historical event of "the dissolution of belief in absolute truth," an event which is our "communal provenance." This definition combines Nietzsche and Heidegger. Vattimo argues that contemporary thought acknowledges this event, in the sense that today "not even potentially foundational theorists employ foundational arguments to argue for their own theses." Today, philosophers justify themselves "not with reference to vital, immediate needs conceived as natural, but to the conditions of existence that characterise a specific society and a specific culture, that of the contemporary world."

Vattimo argues that this situation can be and has been interpreted very differently, with each interpretation projecting us towards a different future. He offers us a map of four interpretations and guides us through them. Firstly, the dissolution of absolute truth can be interpreted as a crisis to be overcome with a reassertion of fundamental values. Vattimo gives the example of the recent war against Iraq, where "a class of 'men of the Enlightenment,' authorised by some kind of absolute metaphysical mission, impose themselves by force." Secondly, the interpretative nature of truth can be viewed as a transhistorical fact finally revealed to us, a temptation to which Nietzsche and Lyotard succumb, according to Vattimo, and which unwittingly returns them to objectivist metaphysics. Thirdly, the dissolution of truth can be viewed as a fact to which we should resign ourselves. Fourthly, there is the interpretation that Vattimo himself champions as the anti-authoritarian possibility for contemporary metaphysics: the dissolution of truth is a "pure eventuality that presents us with open, yet not all equivalent, possibilities."

Assessing those interpretative possibilities requires Nietzschean active nihilism, which Vattimo interprets as "the attitude of the 'most moderate' man who knows how to be ironic even towards himself"; it requires, also, awareness that the task is not descriptive but projective and therefore "empirical" in the original ancient Greek sense of "attempting, trying, without any absolute certainty."

Hugh J. Silverman, in "*Ereignisse* of the postmodern: Heidegger, Lyotard, and Gerhard Richter," explicates Heidegger's *Ereignis* in order to show the difference between the modern – exemplified by Van Gogh as interpreted by Heidegger – and the postmodern – exemplified by Gerhard Richter's task of painting "the appearance of reality" (Richter). The *Ereignis* discloses the world. As the "task of thinking," it is the event of art, creating "a kind of clearing, an opening, a gap … in which the truth happens." The *Ereignis* is a sublime event of "no dimensions at all." It has no substance and is purely differential, happening between the ontological and the ontic – between an unpresentable reality and its presentation, as Lyotard would say. It doesn't belong to the artist: "to be the author of one's own acts, to be one's own and to give place for the event to happen … one must leave 'self' behind." In those senses of *Ereignis*, for Heidegger, Van Gogh was painting reality, not the appearance of reality, when he was painting his famous peasant-boots.

Warhol, already, "had no interest in presenting reality." Silverman argues that Warhol's cows, Mao Tse-tungs, Jackies, Campbell's soup cans, Marilyn Monroes, are *Ereignisse* (in plural) rather than *Ereignis* – the differential between reality and presentation in *Ereignis* is here displaced into a play of images within the art work. In Richter's paintings – for example, in *Uncle Rudi*, showing Richter's uncle Rudi in Nazi uniform; in *48 Portraits*, his portraits of famous men; and in *Die Verkündigung*, his reworking of an Annunciation by Titian – Silverman finds "there may be an *Ereignis*, but the *Ereignis* has an ironic tone, a sense of distance" that has no place in Heideggerian art. Silverman argues that, while in Warhol the differential between reality and its presentation is displaced into a differential between images within the art work, in Richter the differential of the *Ereignis* is displaced between paintings – in Lyotard's terms, the unpresentable is the other painting in Richter. Rather than having a unique style or moving from one style to the next in the heroic manner of modernist painting, Richter paints "in multiple sites at the same time." Richter's postmodern oeuvre is a network linked by its differences, its "multiple *Ereignisse*."

Costas Douzinas, in "Human rights in postmodernity," proposes an alternative philosophy of human rights, inspired by psychoanalysis, Levinas and Nancy. Douzinas argues that globalised human rights are "the fate of postmodernity" in the sense that they are "necessary companions" of the continuing globalisation of capitalism. In an alternative genealogy, Douzinas shows the historical ambiguity of human rights: their increasing adoption has coincided with increased violations; they have served both the powerless and the powerful; proclamations of human rights have combined universalism on the one hand, national sovereignty and cultural relativism on the other. Today, argues Douzinas, the potential for increased conflict inherent in human rights is apparent: on the one hand, the Americans claim to be the authoritative interpreters of human rights while excluding themselves from prosecution by the International Criminal Court; on the other, as the powerless claim "not just formal but material equality," "the unbridgeability of the gap between the missionary statements on equality and dignity and the bleak reality of obscene inequality becomes apparent."

Douzinas sketches out an alternative philosophy of human rights. The "human" of human rights has been and will continue to be constantly redefined with each new declaration or proclamation; it is a floating signifier rather than a pre-existing substance. Human rights can be extended indefinitely, with ambiguous results: "The right to free speech or to annual holidays can be accompanied by a right to love, to party or to have back episodes of *Star Trek* shown daily." In psychoanalytic terms, human rights are the legalisation of the desire to be recognised by others as non-lacking, an insatiable desire because identity is constituted around an inescapable lack. Today, in Western postmodern globalised societies, the legalisation of desire has become the answer to increased existential anxiety and it is now "forbidden to forbid." However, at this moment of triumph of human rights, their limits become visible. Douzinas proposes that "[t]he human rights of the Other" – an other that is "singular and unique" – become "the postmodern principle of justice."

Jane Flax, in "Subjectivity, ethics, politics: learning to live without the subject," returns to a question addressed by Linda Hutcheon: does postmodernism have a theory of agency? In Foucault's last essays, Flax finds a new theory of agency: the subject is engaged in practices that in turn constitute it, in incessant reciprocity. Whereas modern liberalism and identity politics rely on the subject as a substance or an "inside" – abstract universal substance in the case of modern liberalism, concrete universal in the case of identity politics – in order to root the subject's autonomy and freedom, Foucault describes a precarious world of exteriority: practices, power relations, "technologies of the self" that are simultaneously constraining and empowering and that are vulnerable to relations of domination. Foucault thereby allows us to look at problems of justice and politics with "an object-oriented rather than subject-oriented focus" – a focus "not around questions of identity (who are we and what do we require to be or remain us?) but action (what could be done and what are its consequences?)." Adopting this approach, Flax argues that the subject as an autonomous inside is "an effect of particular practices or technologies of the self" which have to be judged by their pernicious consequences: "the *appearance* of stability, autonomy and identity is generated and sustained by practices of domination, denial of contingency and will, and projection of determination onto marked subjects," as, she claims, current global events show. In today's quest for substantive identities, the "resistant leakage of intersubjective and intrasubjective heterogeneity" leads to violence.

According to Foucault, power relations are mobile and reversible; domination freezes power relations and prevents their reversibility. He calls practices resisting domination "care of the self." Flax continues the search for such object-oriented practices today, giving some examples: to multiply ways of life; to "foster a suspicion of uniformity" and an "engaged detachment"; to seek disjunctions rather than consensus; to ensure "the presence of other empowered subjects"; to avoid "fantasies of unambiguous benevolence, redemption or deliverance."

II. Mapping the postmodern

John McGowan, in "They might have been giants," revisits Derrida, Foucault and Habermas, as part of a group of writers who responded to 1968's "incoherent but widespread rebellions." According to McGowan, 1968 opens postmodernism, while 1989's collapse of communism in Eastern Europe announces its end. The year 1968 "was a revolution that had not happened, that was 'to come'" in the form of the desire for a radical critique and transformation of the West. The postmodernists acknowledged Western crimes such as colonialism and the Holocaust and asked whether Western thought and Western political commitments were "root causes of these crimes or a potential source for protesting against or even remedying them."

While Derrida, Foucault and, to a degree, Habermas opposed binary oppositions and generalisations, they are "passionate moral advocates for alternatives to the prevailing social order" – in their work, an "epic struggle between freedom and its opposite ... serves as the grand unifying idea that makes their fine-grained details and sophisticated arguments cohere." They provide us, McGowan claims, with nothing less than "a key to the world we live in." Foucault's and Derrida's last works, on the other hand, in their modesty and sobriety, signal the changed mood of scholarship on the left, after postmodernism. After 1989 and the seeming triumph of the West, "only conservatives ... are thinking big," while capitalism starts "a new round of ruthless exploitation" and the USA turns into a "swaggering bully." McGowan argues that while postmodernism failed to transform the West, while its "heightened rhetoric and oversimplifications are easy to mock," and while scholarship is now more pluralistic and egalitarian, postmodernism's passion for a better world is a lasting legacy.

Douglas Kellner, in "Reappraising the postmodern: novelties, mapping and historical narratives," argues that accounts of the postmodern provide us with valuable maps of important historical developments. However, these accounts must show an awareness of different fields – for example, postmodernity as an historical period marked by global capitalism; postmodern science and technology, in the service of capitalism but also resisting it; postmodernism as an aesthetic phenomenon; postmodern theory, etc. Accounts of the postmodern must also elaborate clear and full distinctions between the modern and the postmodern specific to each field.

Kellner suggests we see our world "holistically," as a complex and "conflict-ridden" *system*, in transition between modernity and postmodernity. The complexity of the system can only be conveyed in a "transdisciplinary and multiperspectivist" approach, aiming to synthesise chosen elements in accounts of the modern and the postmodern. Concurring with other contributors to this collection, Kellner suggests that "[r]ather than pursuing the modern logic of the either/or (for example, either the modern or the postmodern), one can pursue a postmodern logic of both/and, drawing on both modern and postmodern traditions."

In relation to historical change, in each field a clear distinction between the modern and the postmodern allows us to analyse emerging phenomena – such as the new technoculture and the "life online" brought about by personal computers, or the current revolution in warfare – with an eye to continuities as well as discontinuities, to the hopeful as well as the menacing. In relation to scholarship, postmodern metacartography recognises that maps are not objective representations but "rhetorical and political devices." Hence the great variety of maps: quantitative and qualitative; scientific, theoretical, aesthetic, religious; for or against a ruling order; descriptive, normative, utopian; experiential and abstract. Each new situation puts pressure on our techniques of representation and invites new kinds of mapping, and each map is a perspective with its own blind spots. This is why Kellner advocates a multiperspectivist – whether dialectical or Nietzschean – approach. Assessing contemporary work in the humanities, he identifies lack of substantial knowledge and engagement with science and technology as its major blind spot and declares an interest in synthesising "critical social theory, cultural studies, science and technology studies, race theory, postcolonial analysis, feminism, and environmental concerns."

In "The Postmodern: after the (non-)event," Mike and Nicholas Gane advocate a postmodernist sociology of postmodernism. Whereas a modernist sociology of postmodernism embraces "clarity, consensus and convergence" and searches for "the truth of *the* postmodern," a postmodernist sociology of postmodernism is open to "plurality [and] dissensus," experiments with new styles, explores a more nominalistic position, questions the "hierarchy of different genres of knowledge" and mixes them up. This is not a new kind of modern "grand narrative" but "an ironic or agonistic perspective" that avoids modern closure. The Ganes duly affirm that "the postmodern has meant many things, none of which are 'correct' in the modern sense," but explore one particular version of the postmodern: Lyotard's well-known story that the postmodern and the modern follow each other in a cycle.

The Ganes ask whether postmodern episodes are linked to political defeat – in the case of the recent postmodern episode which is now over, "the historic defeat of the socialist and communist projects." They pursue the argument that, in postmodern episodes, social thought moves away from past hierarchies and truths; this *can* be followed by a return of "repressed" or subjugated forms of knowledge – for example, the revelation in the latest postmodern episode that "racism and sexism underpinned institutional structures and even the basic structures of philosophical knowledge" – or by new values.

How, then, can the latest postmodern episode be assessed? The Ganes explore two arguments. Firstly, we now live in a transversal world, a world of incessant connections across right and left, East and West, man and woman, human and machine – a world of Deleuzian rhizomatics. The new order of things is one of "chaos and confusion." Secondly, in the latest postmodern episode, sections of the left adopted a vacuous "loser's tolerance," but no new values emerged. The left's welcoming of "multiculturalism and radical institutional pluralism" ought to have been entwined with a new "radical move within the spirit of postmodernism to define a practice of intolerance" towards key targets. But the opportunity was missed, and today the right and sections of the left return to old fundamentalisms.

III. The postmodern and the twenty-first century

Akbar S. Ahmed in "Postmodernism and Islam: where to after September 11?" argues that, after September 11, postmodernism became the shared enemy of George W. Bush and Osama bin Laden and was attacked by both. Ahmed defines postmodernism as the "[i]deas and practice of multicultural harmony, eclecticism and juxtapositions, ... the mingling of diverse sources, a juxtaposition of the high and the low, the use of irony and humor and an ambiguity toward, if not outright rejection of, any monolithic ideology" or grand narrative. After September 11, we have been suddenly transported back to a world of grand narratives, a world where my narrative is true and good, the other's narrative "false and evil."

For Ahmed, postmodernism still holds the promise of understanding between the West and Islam. Islam's encounter with postmodern scepticism has been tense and difficult. Yet the version of Islam that Ahmed embraces can bear this strain because it shares with postmodernism an inclusivism, an "acceptance of others" and human compassion. Understanding Islam will be an equally difficult process for the postmodern West.

In "Goodbye to all that" McKenzie Wark tells a neo-Marxist story of the present as a new stage of the commodity economy and as the site of a new class struggle. "What if the commodity economy had already had two quite distinct historical phases, of which 'capitalism' was only one?" and what if we are now in transition to a third phase? If the first stage was marked by the privatisation of land and class antagonism between land owner and tenant farmer; if the second stage was marked by the privatisation of the means of industrial production (capitalism) and class antagonism between capitalist and worker; the new stage is marked by the privatisation of information and class antagonism between those who produce information (the "hacker" class) and those who "own the vectors along which information moves" (the "vectoralist" class). Wark claims that this is the "postmodern" class relation. Artists, scientists, intellectuals, who were peripheral to previous class antagonisms, suddenly find themselves at the centre of the postmodern commodity economy and the postmodern class relation, as de facto members of the hacker class. While Wark argues that older forms of class antagonism persist outside the "overdeveloped" world, he turns his attention to the struggle over information and the utopian possibilities of the hacker class. When the hacker class meets electronic technology, file sharing and peer-to-peer networks point towards a world of free intellectual production. Computer programming has already had its hacker visionaries. "The mission of the hacker class as a class might be to hack into existence practices by which information can be extracted from the commodity form and returned to the realm of the gift."

Arthur and Marilouise Kroker, in "Suspicion of thought," describe the "second-order" postmodernism of the beginning of the twenty-first century. The war on terrorism, "confronted with the fluidity, indeterminacy, and mobility of postmodern capitalism," responds with a "high-security realism" and by resurrecting old binaries: good and evil, reality and representation, nature and technology. "It is now forbidden to destabilize this framework of understanding. It is now criminal to create unlikely juxtapositions … to speak on behalf of the hyperreality of parody, irony and indeterminacy," as recent incidents of criminalisation of postmodern performance art show. The Krokers argue that the war on terrorism prepares the coming of the new "biometric state." The rising use of biometric identifiers and database surveillance point to a systematic deployment of new technologies to trigger "primitive collective emotions of fear and anxiety" and a *state of suspicion.*"

The "first-order" or "negative" postmodernism of Baudrillard, Barthes, Irigaray and Lyotard fights high-security realism with "the specter of the unrepresentable ... the creative aporias of a poetry of silence" in texts that are themselves unrepresentable and singular. Their insights and, the authors claim, the insights of Einsteinian science find today a new "experimental confirmation" in postmodern performance art – an ironic and singular "art of the impossible and the ineffable." They also find experimental confirmation in the "second-order" or "positive-postmodern" remix aesthetic of contemporary electronic culture – "from remix music and streamed video to the cut-ups of 'turntabilism' and the explosion of recombinant imagery in arts and entertainment" – and the "second-order" postmodern body. Now that "the virtual helmets of fighter pilots have come inside us" and now that our perception and subjectivity are vacated of interiority, exteriorised and ersatz, "the lament of first-order postmodernism of the 1980s implodes into the creative resistance of the remix culture of twenty-first-century second-order postmodernism."

Lawrence Grossberg, in "Affect and postmodernity in the struggle over 'American modernity,'" presents postmodernity as a new lived experience of dissociation between meaning and affect, an ironic awareness that no source of meaning can justify the affect we invest in it. Grossberg calls this new popular sensibility "ironic nihilism" or "authentic inauthenticity" and argues that it has led to two antithetical responses, "cynical inauthenticity" and "sentimental inauthenticity," constructing a frontier that cleaves America into two camps. Cynical inauthenticity withdraws all affective investments and leads to political disengagement, whereas sentimental inauthenticity affectively over-invests a source of meaning to compensate for its groundlessness, leading to the dominance of a purely affective politics, or, a depoliticised politics where serious debate has no place. Grossberg argues that the new right has been successful in using this postmodern popular frontier in order to fight the "liberal modernity" of the first half of the twentieth century and to construct a new American modernity. On the side of sentimental inauthenticity, the right has reorganised Americans' affective lives, disinvesting old liberal sites and over-investing "affective magnets" – such as the child and the family – "affective epidemics" – such as the war on drugs and, more recently, the war on terrorism – and a new "affective discipline" revolving around the avoidance of humiliation rather than the old liberal "freedom, happiness and pleasure." On the side of cynical inauthenticity, Grossberg insists that, on the one hand, political apathy is systematically produced by the new right; on the other hand, existing forms of a vibrant political culture of protest have been systematically misrecognised in a variety of ways: either trivialised, or demonised, or presented as unrealistic dreaming, or presented as self-interested.

Ernesto Laclau, in "Heterogeneity and post-Modernity," argues that the distinction between modern homogeneity and postmodern heterogeneity is simplistic and misleading. Yes, postmodernity is the time of a "systematic degrounding"; yes, today heterogeneity is our starting point, is primary. However, on this primary terrain of heterogeneity, a number of language games and logics are possible, including homogenising or totalising or universalising ones, so that Lyotard was wrong to announce the end of grand narratives and to describe contemporary reality as a pure multiplicity of non-communicating islands and "irreducible differends." Instead of a break between modernity and postmodernity, there has been a displacement whereby homogeneity is now not the assumed ground but the never-reached destination or the horizon of political activity. Out of heterogeneity, political alliances are built as chains of equivalence between elements which have no common content – with one of the elements, the hegemonic element, taking on the task of representing a totality-to-come, a fullness of being which is not there. The *name* of the hegemonic element, rather than a pre-existing content, given to a whole chain of elements in a "primal baptism," initiates a homogenising logic and announces the totality-to-come. In this sense, the name "presents the unpresentable," as Laclau comments in an original rewriting of Lyotard. In other words, the name of the hegemonic element is a figurative meaning taking the place of a non-existing literal meaning – what classical rhetoric calls catachresis. Catachresis is now exemplary of rhetoric and rhetoric constitutive of collective political identities. Which element will give its name to a chain of equivalence and function as the hegemonic element? This, Laclau argues, cannot be predicted because it is a matter of affect – one of the elements will just happen to be libidinally invested or cathected (to use Freud's language), as the name of the futural political totality.

Fredric Jameson, in his Postscript to this collection, asserts: "we can be sure that the third stage of capitalism, as it is expressed in globalization and postmodernity alike, will still be with us for a bit longer." Outlining directions for future work, he argues that, if indeed we are faced with an emerging new system, those who focus exclusively on postmodernism or postmodernity either as a philosophical stance or as a social phenomenon or as an artistic phenomenon, risk missing the "dynamics of the totality." Jameson suggests we distinguish between three concepts: postmodernism as a stance or style, postmodernity as an historical period, and postmodernisation as the role of "cybernetic production" in the postmodern labour process. He calls for descriptions of the new system, especially of finance capitalism in the globalised "informational age."

Reviewing the present collection, Jameson is especially sceptical of what he sees as a widespread "slippage in which we move insensibly from a historical description to something closer to an ethical judgment or a moral choice." Any enthusiastic endorsement of a postmodern ethics, coupled with revulsion towards a modern ethics, strikes Jameson as an instance of the "waning of affect" which he identified as a symptom of postmodernity in the early 1980s. Further, any slippage from description to ethics risks underestimating the degree to which large populations – including ourselves, our philosophies and our ethics – are determined by the new system, and risks creating a "mirage of autonomy." Jameson therefore calls for constant vigilance – openness to the possibility that our thinking on postmodernism and postmodernity might not be "cognitive" but "symptomatic" of the new system – coupled with a "restless search for fuller descriptions."

Now that postmodernism is no longer a bandwagon, now that postmodernism, postmodernity, the postmodern are no longer buzzwords, after the welter of anthologies, followed by the definitive compendia, this collection seeks to plot the ways in which a number of leading exponents of postmodern theory see the theoretical matrices of ten, fifteen, twenty years ago transmuting to address the new contemporary, the contemporary now; transmuting to serve new imaginations of our global present, of our ongoing intellectual and political work, and of a possible global future radically different from the present.

GENEALOGIES OF THE POSTMODERN

linda hutcheon

GONE FOREVER, BUT HERE TO STAY: THE LEGACY OF THE POSTMODERN

Two opposing impulses clashed in the late twentieth-century writing of the cultural history of the postmodern. On the one hand, as John Frow asked so presciently in 1990, "what was postmodernism?" Terry Eagleton and Christopher Norris were among the many who confirmed the past-ness of the tense by declaring the postmodern not only over but also a failure. On the other hand, in 1998 Charles Altieri forcefully articulated the sense many others retained of the astounding plural-ness and abiding present-ness of the phenomenon in his title *Postmodernisms Now*.[1] At the century's end, this position suggested, postmodernism was still alive and indeed thriving.

What about now, in the twenty-first century, in the brave new world of globalization, diaspora, electronic technology? Is any kind of helpful or even heuristic historical perspective possible yet? With the benefit of hindsight, we can certainly look back and watch the usage of the word "postmodern" spread across domains, from architecture to literature and philosophy, and from there to other art forms and other "human sciences." We can see that the final decades of the last century witnessed the institutionalization of the postmodern in the academy, the publishing and movie industries, the art gallery, and the theatre, concert, and opera stage. With this institutionalization came what can only be called a generalization of postmodernism into a kind of generic counter-discourse, but paradoxically one well on its way to becoming a discourse, a *doxa*.

At this point we can observe that other competing counter-discourses – those of identity politics, in particular – clearly sensed trouble. Fearing the absorption of their own specific interventionary oppositional agendas into those of some generic category called postmodernism and deeply suspicious of the postmodern's apparent lack of a theory of political agency, feminists in the 1980s were among the first to attack postmodernism's complicitous form of critique, its tendency to deconstruct cultural monoliths but never to reconstruct. As Seyla Benhabib put it, postmodernism "in its infinitely skeptical and subversive attitude toward normative claims, institutional justice and political struggles, is certainly refreshing. Yet it is also debilitating."[2] Ajay Heble took up this critique to argue that, for oppositional critics, the value of postmodern theory's suspicion of truth-claims and its denaturalizing and demystifying impulses had been compromised by its very institutionalization.[3] Postmodernism's deliberate open-endedness, its "both/and" thinking, and its resolute lack of resolution risked immobilizing oppressed people, he argued. As postcolonial theorists insisted (echoing feminists before them), it can be hard to achieve activist ends (with firm moral values) in a postmodern world where such values are not permitted to be grounded, where no utopian possibility is left unironized.

Where does this leave the postmodern politically today? Is it dead or alive? The answer is: "yes." In other words, "both/and" is more appropriate than "either/or" in addressing this issue. In the twenty-first century too, all evidence points to the realization that it is no longer enough simply to focus attention on ex-centricity, marginality, and difference as part of a demystifying process – though that may still be considered a crucial first step to action. Nevertheless, there are others – Elizabeth Ermarth, among them – who wish to remind us of the *potential* that still lies in what she calls the "generous impulses of postmodernity" in the political arena:

> the postmodern condition re-opens political options that the culture of modernity has increasingly suppressed by its search for unity, rationality, and non-contradiction. Postmodernity acknowledges and even features precisely the inescapability of contradiction, of unmediatable difference; it shifts emphasis from rational resolution to negotiated contradiction in ways that have profoundly political implications.[4]

Le postmodernisme est mort; vive le postmodernisme!

Notes

1 John Frow, "What was Postmodernism?" in *Past the Last Post: Theorizing Post-Colonialism and Post-Modernism*, eds Ian Adam and Helen Tiffin (Calgary: U of Calgary P, 1990) 139–59; Terry Eagleton, *The Illusions of Postmodernism* (Cambridge, MA and Oxford: Blackwell, 1996); Christopher Norris, *What's Wrong with Postmodernism* (Baltimore: Johns Hopkins UP, 1990); Charles Altieri, *Postmodernisms Now: Essays on Contemporaneity in the Arts* (University Park: Pennsylvania State UP, 1998).

2 Seyla Benhabib, *Situating the Self: Gender, Community, and Postmodernism in Contemporary Ethics* (New York: Routledge, 1992) 15.

3 Ajay Heble, "New Contexts of Canadian Criticism: Democracy, Counterpoint,

Responsibility" in *New Contexts of Canadian Criticism*, eds Ajay Heble, Donna Palmateer Pennee and J.R. (Tim) Struthers (Peterborough, ON: Broadview, 1996) 78.

4 Elizabeth Ermarth, "Agency in the Discursive Condition," *History and Theory* 40 (2001): 39.

robert venturi

A BAS POSTMODERNISM, OF COURSE[1]

I am not now and never have been a postmodernist and I unequivocally disavow fatherhood of this architectural movement. The reaction against it by the architectural and critical establishment in the early 1990s I can understand; however, I disagree with Neomod, the modern-revival or modern-dramatique style that has replaced it.

I first heard the term "postmodernism" in the late 1940s when I was a student at Princeton. Its author was said to be my professor, Jean Labatut, and/or Walter Gropius. I rather liked the sound of it but hardly thought about it again, although I did mention it once while talking to Robert Stern in the 1960s. Soon after that Philip Johnson took it up. There was no promotion of postmodernism in *Complexity and Contradiction in Architecture*, published in 1966, but ironically, accusations abound that that book started it. A lack of any kind of prescription in *Complexity and Contradiction* is noted by Alan Chimacoff and Alan Plattus in their September 1983 essay in *Architectural Record*:

> ... Venturi's book challenged, in certain significant ways, the entire tradition of architectural theory since the Renaissance. From Alberti and the Quattrocento rediscovery of Vitrivius on, the principal thrust of the theoretical enterprise, with a few isolated exceptions, has been normative – concerned with the establishment and polemical propagation of rules, or systems thereof, according to which the "right" kind of architecture could be built, taught, and, of course, understood. Venturi, however, was not concerned with the substitution of one set of rules for another but rather sought to question, and even to undermine, the uncritical acceptance of any supposedly universal system of rules and the purity of style or taste they supported.

The revivalism characteristic of postmodernism cannot, in my view, be derived from *Complexity and Contradiction*. Such an interpretation would constitute a profound misunderstanding of my ideas. The book did not "give architects license to draw once again on the historical styles," as Herbert Muschamp asserted in a 1997 *New York Times* article. *Complexity and Contradiction* employed a well-established method of analysis, the comparative method, using architectural analogy and comparison, not as sources for architectural vocabularies but as methods for understanding and clarification – just as Sigfried Giedion did not refer to the spatial characteristics of baroque architecture in order to promote it as a style. I feel it helps to know where you've been in order to know where you are and to learn how to evolve or revolt as you progress as an architect. But such references to history seem to create fear among architects and critics educated in our era.

A further irony: postmodernism, as a style involving historical revivalism, was engaged with symbolism in architecture, while *Complexity and Contradiction* was essentially about form in architecture. Our next book, *Learning from Las Vegas* (1972), was about symbolism but it involved impolite, vital commercial iconography – i.e., signage – rather than historical style, as an element of architecture.

A further misunderstanding: historical reference in our architecture unambiguously involves reference; it is not intended to convey "maybe the real thing," nor to cover the whole building form, nor to create overall motific consistency. It does involve representation – representation as explicit ornament, as applied two-dimensional signage – and in the end it deals in iconography rather than style. For example, the front façade of the Sainsbury Wing of the National Gallery in London is not a postmodern-revivalist, historically correct copy of the historical façade beside it: it is a plane, a sign, a very large billboard; it refers manneristically and incorrectly to that other façade and thereby accommodates the context of Trafalgar Square and creates aesthetic tension.

Ultimately our architecture engages mannerism, an architectural approach that accommodates aesthetic ambiguity but also, in our time, creates ambiguity: in our time the critics don't get it – i.e., mannerism.

The issue here is the fundamental relevance of iconography in architecture – symbolic, graphic, informative, persuasive/didactic iconography that embraces a human dimension that was lost in twentieth-century modern architecture and is lost once again in revival modernism where abstract-expressionist form predominates. The unacknowledged industrial symbolism that accompanies modern formalism is as historical now as the symbolic classical vocabulary of Renaissance architecture would be now. Everyone except architects and critics knows we are in the Post-Industrial Age. Let us learn from the relevant, if shocking, everyday commercial vernacular of now, as the modernists learned from the relevant and, we tend to forget, shocking everyday industrial vernacular vocabulary of the early twentieth century. And let us in our Post-Industrial Age, in our Electronic Age, our Multicultural Age, our Information Age dedicated to communication, acknowledge the relevance of electronic technology for our mannerist-iconographic architecture, where the famous building with the Nasdaq sign incorporated into its façade and Times Square equate with the Doge's Palace and its ornamental façade and with St. Mark's Square.

Remember it's not about Space any more, it's about Communication. A *bas* Space and Structure of then; viva Symbolism and Iconography of now!

Other criticisms of postmodernism that are explicit abound in our later writings, such as my assertion in the June 1982 *Architectural Record*: "The Postmodernist, in supplanting the Modernist, has substituted for the largely irrelevant universal vocabulary of heroic industrialism another largely irrelevant universal vocabulary – that of parvenu Classicism, with its American manifestation, a dash of Deco, and a whiff of Le Doux." More recently, in a 1992 edition of *Lotus International*, Denise Scott Brown has further differentiated our approach: "Contextual borrowings should never deceive; you should know what the real building consists of beneath the skin. For this reason our allusions are representations rather than copies of historical precedents. The deceit is only skin-deep."

Ultimate irony, I promise: at this moment our position is not so much misunderstood as unacknowledged – when, ironically, pragmatism is all the rage at MoMA and Columbia. Yet my book *Iconography and Electronics upon a Generic Architecture*, of 1996, which is essentially about pragmatism, is ignored – and MoMA's new design for its Queens, New York, satellite is like our Basco building of 1976!

And then there's our mannerism!

Note

1 This text was originally published in *Architecture* (May 2001). It is reprinted here with the kind permission of *Architecture* and of Robert Venturi.

zygmunt bauman and keith tester

ON THE POSTMODERNISM DEBATE

Keith Tester: Starting with the publication of Legislators and Interpreters *in 1987, you wrote a series of books that played a very significant part in making postmodernity a key part of sociological discourse.*[1] *But if your approach to the matter is compared with that of others, it is possible to identify a very distinctive way of thinking. For many people the question of postmodernity was conflated with postmodernism, and so there was a turn by sociologists to aesthetics, architecture, social geography and so on; all of this might be summed up in the phrase "the cultural turn." Meanwhile your approach focused on questions of morality and ethics. Did you ever feel part of a wider debate, or was it more like writing in hope of finding readers?*

Zygmunt Bauman: If I ever took a "cultural turn" it must have been in the early 1960s, and it was Antonio Gramsci and his *Prison Notebooks*, hardly a postmodern or even a proto-postmodern tract, that took me along that path.[2] *Culture versus Society* marked the breakthrough.[3] I wrote it just after the publication in 1964 of my *Introduction to Marxist Sociology*, which was still a very orthodox piece by both Marxist and Parsonian standards.[4] The *Introduction* presented society as a sort of recycling contraption, a mechanism that bribes or forces ordinary humans to do willingly what they must do, and which discharges fully "patterned" humans at the far end of the assembly line and then uses that recycled product to go on reproducing itself so that further recycling may be done endlessly. Between the two diametrically different books stood my discovery of Gramsci.[5]

From Gramsci I learned about culture being a thorn in the flesh of "society" rather than a handmaiden of its monotonous order-reproducing routine; an adamantly and indefatigably mutinous agent, culture as propulsion to oppose and disrupt, a sharp edge pressed obstinately against what-already-is. Culture became shorthand for the human propensity to set apart the "is" from "can be," the "ought" from the "is," and for the inclination to rebel against the "is" in the name of the "can be" and/or "ought." The concept of "culture" refers to the lifting of the human mode of being-in-the-world above and beyond the site which "society" tried and goes on trying to ensconce and fence off. I came to Britain with such a view fully formed and operational. It was a time when the notion of culture, despite Mathew Arnold's Herculean efforts, was only beginning to be recalled from its protracted exile, thanks mostly to Stuart Hall's pioneering, formidable labours.

To cut a long story short: your guess is correct. I seem to have entered the "postmodernist" discourse through a different door than most of its participants. Well before the word "postmodernity" was coined, and much before it became the badge of belonging to an exclusive company of the chattering classes, I desperately sought a generic name for a large set of intuitions: that despite modern ambitions the war against human wayward-ness and historical contingency is unwinnable, that the resistance of human modality to logic and rule is here to stay, and that the modern crusade against ambivalence and the "messiness" of human reality only multiplies the targets it aims to destroy. "Postmodernity" fit the bill nicely. I first spotted the term in the context of architecture, where Charles Jencks put it. That helped me to invest all my concerns in it and so adopt the term in good conscience. After all, architecture was the very epitome of, simultaneously, the modern pilgrimage to finitude and the war of attrition which modernity waged against contingency. When applied to architecture, "postmodernity" suggested most vividly a castrated modernity admitting its own impotence, a disempowered modernity, stripped of the confidence that the end is round the next corner or the corner after the next. "Postmodernity" also seemed noncommittal and open-ended. It spoke about what no longer could be held to be true, but it wisely refrained from any alternative syntheses, which would be inevitably premature and half-baked.

Or at least this is what seemed to me to be the case at the time. Alas, I should have known better. Entering a discourse bent on becoming the talk of the town (of the urban salons, to be precise) meant giving hostages to fate from the start. Soon all my efforts to protect the intended meaning turned out to be hopeless. I had been "filed away," and, having read the label on the file's cover, who would care to contemplate the subtleties inside?

Now if anyone pressed me, I would argue that running through the entire body of your sociological work is a commitment to human being as free possibility. That is clear from what you have just said about culture. But modernity was a condition in which that free possibility was identified as a problem to be overcome; instead of free possibility, the institutions of modernity were concerned to impress upon humanity the rationalism, the utilitarianism and the managerialism that is required by the pursuit of security. Modernity held out the promise of security to men and women who were encouraged to believe that freedom is to be feared. That security meant the imposition of designs of order or the pursuit of the perfect future. And with that imposition, human being was reduced to what must be done rather than what could be done.

In these terms, the questioning of modernity that postmodernity represents could be embraced and supported. As soon as the cage of modernity was questioned, human possibility could be released and, so, there emerged the possibility of a rehumanization of the otherwise ossified world. Consequently, I would propose that what the postmodernity debate was about, at least in its initial phases in your work, in Intimations of Postmodernity *and* Postmodern Ethics, *was an attempt to narrate these new possibilities.[6] Is that a fair statement of your position?*

Not just fair; you have clarified for me what, once you'd stated it, struck me as obvious, but had to be spelled out to me first.

In *The Rebel*, Albert Camus pointed out that the epoch that was arrogant enough to think of itself as a rebellion against "what is" did no more than offer to replace one worn-out conformism with another, which was promised to be wear-and-tear resistant. He concluded that the passion of the twentieth century was serfdom.[7] As I saw it, the guiding motif of the modern adventure was to deploy human freedom in the construction of a world that would make freedom redundant (in a perfect state all further change can be only for the worse), and so to rebel in the name of a world that renders all further rebellion inconceivable. Modernity was also a theatre of a massive and ubiquitous cruelty, cold-blooded since no longer dependent on unleashing the passions. I've traced that second attribute to the first. And so I welcomed the advent of "postmodernity" first and foremost as a blow against arrogance, as an act of debunking and disavowing the replacement of the urge to transcendence and redemption with the marching orders towards a managed history and the thousand-year kingdom of Reason. If the replaced urge was, at least potentially, a push to moral decency, the orders that replaced it were in theory and in deed a licence to kill. The result? Camus again: There is more impulse to destroy than to build – contrary to the officially approved story, which duplicitously reverses the priorities.[8]

In "the initial phase," as you put it, postmodernity meant to me mostly the retreat of arrogance, and the advance of doubt, scepticism, irony, recognition and acceptance of the perpetuity of ambivalence. I spied in that shift a new *chance* for the free chooser's responsibility, that prime scene of morality. Only a *chance*, mind you. From the start the "chances" were supplemented by "threats." Both the chances and the threats were of a new kind, however. Both clamoured for exploration. That was another valid reason to look beyond "modernity as we know it," as it has sedimented, through training, in our conceptual net.

I believe that from the beginning I viewed the triumphant return of ambivalence from its modern exile as itself an ambivalent affair. If something in my views has changed over the years, primarily it has been the estimate of the *proportions* of chances and threats inside that ambivalent condition. And perhaps (so I hope) more insight was gained into the tricky ways in which chances are forfeited, threats magnified, while the chances are sometimes harnessed to the chariot of the threats.

Certainly, if we look at publishers' catalogues, it is immediately clear that in the early to mid-1990s piles of books were published with the word "postmodernity" in their title, but that around 1997 or so the tide started to turn. Nowadays postmodernity has almost become a love that dare not speak its name. There are three obvious reasons why the debate might be in the past rather than the present tense: first, perhaps the social world stopped being amenable to analysis as postmodern. Second, the debate might not have disappeared at all. Rather, it has now seeped out to cover everything, so that now the word "postmodernity" is obsolete – we are all postmodernists nowadays. Third, it was a publishing phenomenon and the academic publishers pulled the plug on titles with the word because the profit margin could not be guaranteed.

All three of your hypotheses have a lot going for them. I guess that the third hypothesis offers a hint to what has indeed happened. Consumer society works through excess and currently favoured targets tend to be overshot. But I trust the publishers to have learned (if only the hard way) when to pull the plug. They have by now become good judges of the admittedly shifty consumer moods, and above all they are well aware of the brevity of the consumers' attention span. Boredom is the sequel and consequence of any hype, and seasoned publishers, like prudent generals, do not commence any action without an exit scenario. The trick is to spot in time when the hype has reached its limit, targets are no longer met and the time to dismantle the unused missiles or remainder (or shred) the unsold books has arrived.

Boredom was bound to come. We get tired of buzzwords. To this general factor add a specific one: the purely negative function of the "postmodernity" concept. It said what social reality was *no longer* but it kept silent or sounded neutral about what it was instead. How long can you go on listing the has-been traits? The term "cleared the site," but once ground-clearing jobs are done the bulldozers need to be removed lest they block the start of building works (by the way, in my view this applies to other contemporary and apparently alternative terms as well, notably "late" and "second" modernity). It is high time to arrive at more "positive" concepts, referring to what our realities *are*, instead of what they have ceased to be. For me, *liquid modernity* is such a concept.[9]

The postmodernity debate may have been a "fleeting affair," but in its time it was indispensable. Like many other good intentions, it went astray. The earth that was taken away from the future building site was dumped over the rocks on which the foundations of the new building should have rested. Or, to paraphrase the cliché, the baby has been drowned in the muddy bathwater …

For me, at least, one of the most important consequences of the postmodernity debate was that it raised in a contemporary way questions about the responsibility of intellectuals. The bottom line is this: however difficult the intellectual vocation might have become thanks to the destruction of higher education, people like us remain privileged. We have time to think, read, engage in conversation; time to nurture our own human being in the world, in a way that is not so easily available to those who have been made into the "wretched of the earth." The postmodernity debate was an opportunity hesitantly and stumblingly to think about the whys and wherefore of what it is that we do. And yet it is hard not to conclude that the postmodernity debate proceeded in a way that made that particular debate impossible; a lot of the debate seemed to collapse into variations of grand theory (led by fashion not passion) and the empiricism of certain cultural pursuits and signs. Quite simply: was the postmodernity debate a feast in the time of locusts?

Or I may say "fiddling when Rome is burning" since I have already resorted to clichés. "Postmodernism" was for a time a darling of the "Left" or whatever part of it scrambled out of the debris of the Berlin Wall. The timing was perfect – bereaved minds on one side, an all-smiling chirpy toddler yelling for adoption on the other. The toddler's vocabulary was colourful and naturally limited, and the few words it mastered were yet to be composed into meaningful sentences. For the would-be foster parents, the adoption was like being born again. The toddler's babbling that politics is a sham, even though everything is political, was particularly endearing. It was exactly the kind of soothing balm that fingers singed to the bone in hot, fiery and yet shamefully lost political battles badly needed.

Richard Rorty's verdict is spot on: "that the Left is unable to engage in national politics" and cannot "be asked to deal with the consequences of globalization." He told the Left that: "After reading Jameson, you have views on practically everything except what needs to be done." That "everything," to be sure, is also highly selective. The Left "prefers not to talk about money. Its principal enemy is a mind-set rather than a set of economic arrangements." Rorty says that in order to become relevant to national politics or fit to confront the consequences of globalization the Left "should put a moratorium on theory" and "would have to talk much more about money, even at the cost of talking less about stigma."[10]

I thought I spotted a potential for lifting critical theory to the level of the new challenges in what I had provisionally called the "postmodern condition."[11] That was one thing. The "really existing postmodernism" (that is, talking about the postmodern condition) was something else. The latter developed as a wholesale absolution for the critics bereaved of a vision of the "good society" and as a consolation for the intellectuals, wardens deserted by their wards. Rorty noted six years ago that nobody was "setting up a programme in unemployed studies, homeless studies, or trailer-park studies, because the unemployed, the homeless, and residents of trailer parks are not 'other' in the relevant sense," in the sense relevant for the postmodern academic Left.[12]

Let us turn to the question of postmodernity and the value of sociology. For you sociology is meaningful and valuable if it helps men and women make sense of their lives through engaging in a dialogue with one another. Through that dialogue they will appreciate that their personal troubles are not simply amenable to personal remedy and thus begin to move towards a politics of the ethical rehumanization of the world.[13] Was the postmodernity debate any help in that task?

Let me put it this way: what have we learned from the "postmodernism episode" that sociologists should not (and I hope *would* not) forget when struggling to come to grips with the social issues of our times? And what, on the contrary, should be sorted out as erroneous and removed from the legacy?

Like in its first stage, modernity in its present-day "liquid" phase remains the era of disembedding.[14] No longer, though, is the disembedding followed by "re-embedding." At no point of an individuals' life-itinerary can they be correctly described as "embedded" (even if only temporarily and "until further notice"). The boundaries of the flowerbeds are now unclear, if not washed out altogether. Instead of seeking their proper, pre-fabricated locations, individuals must conjure up the locations as they go along, and the only roads in sight are the lines of footprints they've left behind. We all seem to be Penelopes now – ripping up by night the canvasses we have woven during the day.[15] Society no longer looks like a garden. It seems to have returned to a state of wilderness, or rather a "secondary wilderness," a frontier-land, where locations need to be carved out and fenced off in order to be fit for settlement.[16]

Alberto Melucci was most emphatic in his description of the seminal change in the conditions of life and the life-strategies that they require:

> We can no longer conceive of our needs as compelling and instinctual urges, or as transparent manifestations of a benevolent nature that guides us. But nor can we continue to labour under the illusion that nature can be substituted by a society to which we assign the task of instructing us or which we accuse of repression. Needs are a signal of something that we lack, and it is up to us to recognize these needs and to give them cultural expression.[17]

We can skip the "needs" word; the important thing, whatever it is called, is the sense of *lack*: of un-finishedness, of un-accomplishment, of something continually, harrowingly missing and missed, of a road ahead stubbornly refusing to shorten, let alone promising to reach its (vexingly invisible) destination. That eerie feeling – that the world around and the world inside are both, to deploy the never bettered expression of Ernst Bloch, *noch nicht gevorden* ("not yet made" or "not yet to hand").[18] It is the sense of lack so understood (or rather so experienced) that makes us all compulsive and obsessive identity-seekers, but which also prevents us from ever finishing the search. We are, so to speak, bound to remain the "also-runs" in the life-long chase after identity.

The freedom to choose identity, like all freedoms, has its positive and negative aspects. What is celebrated in most postmodernist literature is the positive aspect: freedom to choose at will the difference of one's liking and to "make it stick," however temporarily, come what may. But such *positive* freedom is today a privilege of the global elite and off limits for a great majority of the planet's residents. A substantial part of that majority, though, have not as yet come anywhere near obtaining and securing their *negative* freedom: freedom to refute and reject the differences imposed by others and to resist being "socially recognized," against their will, for what they resent being compelled to be and would actively refuse to be were it in their power.

Freedom to choose and keep an identity is, like all freedoms, a social relation. The freedom of some *presumes* the un-freedom of some others, and more often than not is enjoyed as a *privilege* – no privilege being conceivable unless coupled with someone else's deprivation. Like most new departures in history, the liquid-modern version of the "identity problem" and of self-formation is not a blessing uniformly enjoyed by all. It only augurs a new mechanism of redistribution of blessings and banes and a new method of counting gains and losses.

Anthony Elliott attempted to grasp the dual nature of the present-day transformations and the duality of reactions they prompt by suggesting the co-presence of two sharply distinct "object-relational configurations." The first, "modern," "suggests a mode of fantasy in which security and enjoyment are derived by attempting to control, order and regulate the self, others, and sociopolitical world." The second, "postmodern," "suggests a mode of fantasy in which reflective space is more central to identity and politics, the creation of open spaces to embrace plurality, ambiguity, ambivalence, contingency and uncertainty." Elliott's main point, though, is that in contemporary society *both* "reveries," modern and postmodern, are deployed, inevitably with a considerable amount of tension and contradiction.[19]

The two "reveries" (manifested in two diametrically opposed life-strategies, or two mutually contradictory political predilections/impulses, or both) are indeed present in a liquid-modern context, but they are not, let me comment, *class-ascribed*. Neither is there class-ascription of the two actual, feared or desired social conditions (of freedom and un-freedom) with which they correlate. The two "reveries" and the two social contexts in which they tend to arise are, rather, the ideal-typical extreme points of a continuum along which the perceived condition, as well as the strategies deemed appropriate to such conditions, are plotted, and along which they vacillate.

Regarding the identity-related issues, both freedom and un-freedom are realistic prospects for *each and any* resident of a liquid-modern society. None of the currently privileged and enjoyable situations is guaranteed to last, while most of the currently handicapped and resented positions in principle can be re-negotiated using the rules of the liquid-modern game.[20] There is, accordingly, a mixture of hope and fear in every heart. It is spread over the whole spectrum of the emergent planetary stratification. And so is the perpetual ambivalence about the life-strategy that is most appropriate in a stubbornly ambiguous world. Intermittently actors and victims, torn between joyful bouts of self-confidence and sinister premonitions of vulnerability and doom, the denizens of the planet may be excused for their volatile moods, schizophrenic demeanour, inclination to panic and lust for witch-hunting.

Notes

1 See the following books by Bauman: *Legislators and Interpreters: On Modernity, Post-Modernity and Intellectuals* (Cambridge: Polity, 1987); *Intimations of Postmodernity* (London: Routledge, 1992); *Postmodern Ethics* (Oxford: Blackwell, 1993); *Life in Fragments: Essays in Postmodern Morality* (Oxford: Blackwell, 1995); *Postmodernity and its Discontents* (Cambridge: Polity, 1997). Keith Tester prepared this and the following notes and, where an opinion is expressed, it is his and not Zygmunt Bauman's.

2 Antonio Gramsci, *Selections from the Prison Notebooks*, eds and trans. Quintin Hoare and Geoffrey Nowell Smith (London: Lawrence, 1971).

3 Zygmunt Bauman, *Kultura a spoleczenswo: Preliminaria* (Warsaw: Panstowe Wydawnictwo Naukowe, 1966).

4 Zygmunt Bauman, *Zarys marksistowskiej teorii spoleczenstwa* (Warsaw: Panstowe Wydawnictwo Naukowe, 1964).

5 See Zygmunt Bauman, "Antonio Gramsci – czyle socjologia w dzialaniu," *Kultura i Spoleczenstwo* 7.1 (1963): 19–34.

6 It is possible to identify three phases in Bauman's postmodernity books. First there is the hesitant, cautious and measured welcoming that is represented in *Legislators and Interpreters* and *Intimations of Postmodernity*. There then follow *Postmodern Ethics* and *Life in Fragments* which explore the personal responsibilities and troubles of postmodernity and, in the third stage, *Postmodernity and its Discontents* focuses on the threats that are associated with postmodernity. Since 1997, Bauman's discussions of postmodernity have tended to focus much more on its threats than its possibilities; see, for example, Bauman's *In Search of Politics* (Cambridge: Polity, 1999). Of course, changing shades of grey represents these "phases" rather than sharp divisions; to argue that there are sharp classificatory divisions would actually be contrary to the development and spirit of Bauman's thought.

7 Albert Camus, *The Rebel*, trans. Anthony Bower (London: Hamish, 1953).

8 For a discussion of the influence of Camus on Bauman's thought, see Keith Tester, "Paths in Zygmunt Bauman's Social Thought," *Thesis Eleven* 70 (2002): 55–71.

9 See Zygmunt Bauman, *Liquid Modernity* (Cambridge: Polity, 2000).

10 These references to Rorty draw on Richard Rorty, *Achieving Our Country: Leftist Thought in Twentieth-Century America* (Cambridge, MA: Harvard UP, 1998).

11 Bauman discusses the "postmodern condition" in his paper "A Sociological Theory of Postmodernity," where it is established that, for him: "The term *postmodernity* renders accurately the defining traits of the social condition that emerged throughout the affluent countries of Europe and of European descent in the course of the twentieth century" (*Intimations of Postmodernity* 187). By this definition, when Bauman talks about the postmodern condition he is, then, attempting to provide a sociological conceptualization, and he is not primarily concerned with questions of aesthetics or knowledge production. See Bauman, *Intimations of Postmodernity* 187.

12 Rorty, *Achieving Our Country*.

13 See Zygmunt Bauman, *Hermeneutics and Social Science. Approaches to Understanding* (London: Hutchinson, 1978).

14 Bauman has explained that he introduced the concept of liquid modernity in order to overcome the problem that the word "postmodernity" implies that the contemporary condition is *after* modernity: "But this is blatantly untrue. We are as modern as ever, obsessively 'modernizing' everything we can lay our hands on." He continues: "Hence my own proposition: *liquid modernity* which points to what is continuous (melting,

disembedding) and discontinuous (no solidification of the melted, no re-embedding) alike." See Zygmunt Bauman and Keith Tester, *Conversations with Zygmunt Bauman* (Cambridge: Polity, 2001) 97–8.

15 This comment, "we all seem to be Penelopes now," is an allusion to the Greek myth of Penelope. When her husband Ulysses was away besieging Troy, suitors besieged Penelope. She promised to choose one of them as soon as she had finished weaving a shroud for her father-in-law. Every night she undid the work she had done during the day.

16 This paragraph summarizes key aspects of Bauman's understanding of liquid modernity, as explored in greater detail in *Liquid Modernity*. See also: *Society under Siege* (Cambridge: Polity, 2002); *Liquid Love: On the Frailty of Human Bonds* (Cambridge: Polity, 2003).

17 See Alberto Melucci, *The Playing Self: Person and Meaning in the Planetary Society* (Cambridge: Cambridge UP, 1996).

18 This sensibility, which emphasizes the ongoing incitement to action in the present that is constituted by the destination that is always "not yet" reached, is important in Bauman's work and derived from Ernst Bloch. See Bloch, *The Principle of Hope*, vol. 1, trans. Neville Plaice, Stephen Plaice and Paul Knight (Oxford: Basil Blackwell, 1986); *The Spirit of Utopia*, trans. Anthony A. Nassar (Stanford: Stanford UP, 2000). This is the key to understanding Bauman's approaches to culture and socialism as utopias: see *Culture as Praxis* (London: Routledge, 1973) and *Socialism: The Active Utopia* (London: Allen, 1976).

19 See Anthony Elliott, *Subject to Ourselves: Social Theory, Psychoanalysis and Postmodernity* (Cambridge: Polity, 1996) 4.

20 The rules of this game are ones in which "Things are obtained to be consumed, not kept. They are not expected nor desired to last, lest they clutter the site where other 'new and improved' things could be enjoyed." Those "things" include other people; friends, lovers, partners: "duration has been devalued, while the value of transience is rapidly climbing" (Bauman and Tester, *Conversations with Zygmunt Bauman* 127).

gianni vattimo
trans. david rose

POSTMODERNITY AND (THE END OF) METAPHYSICS

The concept of postmodernity is now said by many to be "superseded" (by something more (post)modern?) and even the Heideggerian discourse on the end of metaphysics is considered to be worn out. Perhaps this is "true" – not because someone has "refuted" either the discourse on the postmodern or the Heideggerian vision of (the end of) metaphysics – but only due to some kind of historical process of ageing. If there are no true and real refutations of Heidegger, it is because he is – even for his critics – paradoxically right. If he is "superseded" and so on, it means that one is arguing using historical reasons. The reason for reminding ourselves of this is not just to show the performative contradiction of the critics, according to the logic of the famous argument (which never persuaded anyone) used against the Sceptics, but it is rather to be aware that not even potentially foundational theorists employ foundational arguments to argue for their own theses.

All this shows – at least it seems to me – is that the postmodern is our, more or less, universal condition. To deny it would be to revoke a doubt, a large part of the philosophical and cultural *auctoritates* of which our culture is made; that is to leave us, in some sense, "without words," unable to use the conceptual vocabulary in which we were brought up and which makes our communication possible. Also, and above all, the neo-pragmatism that has largely replaced the neo-positivist position of analytic philosophy "proves" itself or, to put it better, recommends itself as the reasonable and preferable philosophical position, not with reference to vital, immediate needs conceived as natural, but rather to the conditions of existence that characterise a specific society and a specific culture; that of the contemporary world.

Even the fundamental notion of human rights, which is so central to the social and political life of today, has clearly been revealed not to be grounded in metaphysical essences. Moreover, where such an attempt is made, the authoritarian inspiration of those who think in this way becomes immediately obvious. It is anything but an academic question since one must face it each time a group, a church, a country claims to be the bearer of rights based on human nature itself, in the name of which they want to impose some kind of law, hierarchy and discipline. No one, I believe, will deny that this is the crucial issue of today's world: in international relations, as the example of the Iraq war demonstrates, where the American super-power claims the right for itself to impose "democracy," as America under-stands and practises it, on other populations of the world (and what is most serious, often does so in good faith).

Yet this is true even for the internal politics of many other democratic countries within which the Church or churches claim to speak in the name of natural right. The situation in non-secular Muslim countries is even worse, as we know, and constitutes one of the threats of war with which we find ourselves faced (the collision of civilisations). I want to stress strongly that this does not mean that the "natural law" claims of governments, churches and groups should not also be interpreted as ideological positions that express well-defined material interests (once more the example of the Iraq war and the interests of oil and industry in general that motivated it come to mind). Yet, even in examples such as this, the idea of being able to empty the claims of right and of natural law of their persuasive and historically effective force, and of displaying their purely ideological character, does not appear capable of resolving conflicts unless, once again in the name of "truth" (for example, in the name of the "species being" [*Gattungwesen*] of which Marx spoke), a class of "men of the Enlightenment," authorised by some kind of absolute metaphysical mission, impose themselves by force. In the final analysis, this is the "philosophical" meaning of the failure of the twentieth-century's revolutions, beginning with the Russian one, which seemed, in the beginning, to best conform to the human ideals of equality and distributive justice. Even more obvious is the inhuman and authori-tarian character of every "naturalist" foundation of the fascist movements that easily develop from social Darwinism (each according to his "natural" abilities) to explicit racism (promoting the "naturally" superior humanity).

Would it make sense to talk of contemporary world politics without bearing in mind this conceptual but primarily practical "impossibility" of natural law? A similar thing occurs in philosophy and in science, confirming, in the broadest sense, the ideas of Thomas Kuhn. We have not demon-strated scientifically the non-existence of witches and vampires; they are just no longer terms belonging to our vocabulary, and whosoever talks about them isolates himself definitively from the community of contemporary speakers. To recognise such "impossibilities" – that are basically neither logical nor conceptual but actually practico-political – means ultimately to take account of our postmodern condition, whatever one then wants to call it.

Yet even the name we choose to describe, interpret and react to this situation is, without it, of course, becoming an issue of metaphysical essences, not purely an arbitrary affair. If, however, what I here call the postmodern condition is defined, for example, in terms, common in all circles, of the "crisis of values," we immediately see that there is a massive difference between the interpretations expressed by these two phrases: "postmodern condition" and "crisis of values." Here, it seems to me, the significance of the reference to the Heideggerian theory of the end of metaphysics arises. Whoever speaks of a crisis of values seems to consider our condition as a moment of loss of foundations that we must mourn and, possibly, recover, leaving the negative state of loss behind. It would therefore be necessary to regain some sort of absolute metaphysics.

Nietzsche spoke in this very respect of negative or reactive nihilism. When "God is dead," that is when the interpretative character of every (assumed) absolute truth becomes explicit, the negative or reactive version of nihilism offers itself as the escape route for those who cannot overcome the mourning for that death, and in fact refuse to realise it, attempting to recover some absolutism that may replace the lost one. This attitude repeats the mechanism of the will to power in its worst sense: even if Nietzsche does not define it so, it is obvious for him – for example in a fragment like that of the summer of 1887 on "European Nihilism" – that active nihilism, that of the *Übermensch*, is the attitude of the "most moderate" man who knows how to be ironic even towards himself; who did not mourn for that God (neither did Pascal).[2] "God is dead, and we now want many gods to live," Nietzsche wrote elsewhere.

The interpretation of Nietzsche's thought, as one well knows, is nowhere near a finished task, even more so than in the case of almost all other authors who have had an impact on European culture in recent centuries. Even the possible "Nazi" reading seems to me determined by the lack, in both Nietzsche himself and his interpreters, of a more precise and explicit connection with that which Heidegger calls the end of metaphysics as the history of Being. Put more clearly, if the death of God and the advent of nihilism as awareness of the interpretative character of every "truth" are not understood as the history of Being or, we could even say, as the history of God himself, what results for the existence of man and for his historical projects is only the realisation of violence as the insuperable substance of the world. The advent of nihilism is not the unveiling of the essence of nothingness of Being itself. Even Nietzsche ends up interpreting it in these terms since he has not completely liberated himself from the metaphysical vision of truth as correspondence. The affirmation "we want many gods to live" surely seems to open the way to a project; that, however, in its indeterminacy, rather has the character of the irresponsible game, made possible by the awareness that Being is nothingness. This would be a completely relativistic Nietzsche, always on the point of merging with the Nazi Nietzsche and the theorist of violence as the essence of history.

To speak of the end of metaphysics as the history of Being means, according to me, to free the postmodern from every restorative temptation (the "return to values") as well as from the impression of relativism or scepticism. I insist on the fact that positions such as these are intrinsically metaphysical since they think of themselves like the realisation – sometimes resigned or sometimes desperately playful – of the death of God and the end of absolute truth. That is, these positions still believe that they affirm a true structure of Being conceived in terms of (temporary) absence or total, absolute negativity. There is no projection in these positions and it is this, above all, that characterises them as metaphysical. What needs to be stressed in the idea of the end of metaphysics as the history of Being – in keeping with the meaning of Heidegger's thought – is the term history. Only by seeing Being as (endowed with) history, can one open the way to the project; and projection is freedom itself. Certainly, even here one can think that it is a question of descriptively articulating the "truth" of human existence, in the same terms in which the existential analytic of *Being and Time* illustrates it. Yet once again – let us allow ourselves this pragmaticist approach – we clearly understand that we are no longer on the level of objectivist metaphysics if we look at the results. To think Being in historical terms and existence as "thrown project" [*geworfener Entwurf*][3] makes a difference, it is not just a choice of another type of "description" of the human condition. Here I wish tentatively to develop the consequences of such an approach.

First, the reference to Heidegger and the history of Being resolves an ambiguity that had been left unresolved with respect to the original use of the term postmodern in philosophy by Lyotard. Metanarratives, according to him, were out of date, "denied" as false by events (Stalinism for the Marxist metanarrative; the ecological crisis for the positivist metanarrative). Once again, we account for these events on the basis of narrations constructed according to an interpretative scheme. Lyotard thought, or gave the impression that he thought, according to an objectivist perspective: the true, though not recognised as such, metanarrative ended up being his; which is to say, the dissolution of modern metanarratives only appeared as the (metaphysical) discovery of a state of things finally unveiled in its truth ("there are" objectively no metanarratives).

But as long as postmodernity is recognised as a result of a process, it places us before a provenance, naturally interpreted but for this very reason also directed towards a development. At a certain point in his work, Wittgenstein writes that to find oneself on a path means to already know more or less where one is going. Provenance is the term with which one can, with licence, translate both this intuition of Wittgenstein and the Heideggerian terminology that stresses the suffix *kunft: Zu-kunft*, future, *An-kunft*, arrival, advent, *Her-kunft*, provenance. If provenance is meant in this sense of a history of a past that directs, and not simply a past that opens in a vague and purely negative way (remember Nietzsche's thesis that to construct it is necessary to destroy; but in terms of pure arbitrary play), then provenance can also translate the crucial word *Er-eignis*.

The end of metaphysics, as the death of God and the dissolution of belief in absolute truth, is our common provenance which philosophy has to think through. It is not a fact, a closed and objectively describable past to which one resigns oneself, or an eternal structure that is unveiled to us in a specific instant; it is the pure eventuality that presents us with open, yet not all equivalent, possibilities. It shows us, more or less, the direction in which to go. Provenance is, in this sense, as vague as experience itself, to which philosophies have always expressed their wish to conform.

The Greek etymology of the term *empeiria*, in fact, refers to attempting, trying, without any absolute certainty; the Aristotelian difference between empirical and technical is not, at least it seems in the *Nicomachean Ethics*, a difference of degree, as if the culmination of *empeiria* were necessarily science, *techne* or *episteme*. (Note that *empeiria* is connected with tempt, try, *peirazo* – from which even the term *peirates*, pirate, is derived.) In this perspective, it is not coincidental that the affirmation of twentieth-century hermeneutics is accompanied by the rediscovery of practical philosophy of an Aristotelian origin; which itself is an ensemble of "empirical" ideas, without dictatorial imperatives, but more tied to *Verstehen* in the sense of being an expert in something – the empirical person, in Greek, is in fact he who is an expert in, has practical knowledge of something, "is good at something," *versteht sich (auf etwas)*. At least for certain connotations of the term –notwithstanding the meaning analogous to *empeiria* that it has often – the *episteme* is more closely tied to the past, to the having seen and to knowledge (*oida*), and therefore it becomes the word for science itself.

Stories of words? Certainly, but, even without going too far with adventurous etymologies – which have been, amongst other things, a resource of philosophy from Vico to Heidegger and Derrida – these stories can help us to understand the meaning of philosophy after the end of metaphysics. And such a meaning is projective rather than descriptive, and in so far as it is projective, it is more "empirical," uncertain, like the interpretation that applies to "objects" (texts, institutions, artefacts of the past or of something else) but always only to speak of it with someone.

Seen in this light, the postmodern is anything but a post-; not at all an epigonical awareness, as if it were only a question of contemplating that which has been, cataloguing it, wandering like a curious tourist in the garden of history (the image is Nietzsche's from the second Untimely Meditation). As can be seen, we are moving in a circle here, or in many circles that spiral: postmodern and end of metaphysics; end of metaphysics and projection of philosophy; project and provenance; in the final analysis, the pervasiveness of hermeneutics. Or, as Nietzsche writes, there are no facts, "only interpretations ... [E]ven this is interpretation."[4] The observation from which I began is that, no matter what one does, one cannot "leap outside" these circles. Not because these are logically constricting, apodictic evidence; but rather because deliberately leaving them out of our consideration would mean to no longer speak the language of our culture, to put to one side the *empeiria*, experience – to speak in the void and not talk to anyone.

Of course, already (deciding to) realise this condition means to accept the discourse of postmodernity and the end of metaphysics. One cannot, I cannot, see the meaning of any other decision. I once more make playful reference to Wittgenstein: a language is a form of life, but just as there is no universal meta-language which allows us to move between the languages and perhaps choose that in which to place ourselves, the same is true for the way of life that is ours, with respect to which our liberty is certainly not nullified, but consists in the possibility to meet diverse ways of life and to enter into dialogue with them.

The task of philosophy, once it is aware of the postmodern condition, consists in articulating this pre-comprehension; attempting, or better inventing, starting from this very condition (projecting) a guiding thread for choices and plans, from individual ethics to politics. In place of the nostalgic effort, characteristic of reactive nihilism, to go back to "values," it is a question of actively continuing the "active nihilistic" work of the destruction of absolutes. For what reason? For an individual ethics or a political society explicitly grounded in the free choice of that which, of course always starting from the path where we already find ourselves, most certainly appears capable of liberating us from idols; a further Wittgenstinian expression: philosophy can only free us from idols. When Heidegger says, discussing Hölderlin, that "we are a *Gespräch*" (we are a conversation) he offers us in these "social" terms the way to clarify his thesis according to which Being is language.[5] Being is not some arcane word to be sought only in the poets; or only in the sacred sayings of the pre-Socratics; or only – going beyond Heidegger (or perhaps not) – in

37

effective social dialogue; or only in the constructions of majorities and minorities around "values" that become such only because they are historically grounded in acts of freedom. And if today we commit ourselves with regard to Being, in order to welcome its announcement, its event, beyond the metaphysics of presence, does it mean that philosophy draws nearer to politics – continuing the dissolution of objectivist metaphysics in the sense of an always more greatly emphasised affirmation of liberty and of projection? Being is not the *to ti en einai* – that which was (and will always be). It is that which happens, with the active participation of the thrown project that man (not since always, but today) is.

Notes

1 The translator wishes to acknowledge the help of Laura Leonardo and Enzo Rossi in the preparation of the English version.
2 Friedrich Nietzsche, *Will to Power*, ed. Walter Kaufmann, trans. Walter Kaufmann and R.J. Hollingdale (New York: Vintage, 1968), Book 1, sect. 55 (summer 1887) 38.
3 See Martin Heidegger, *Being and Time*, trans. J. Macquarrie and E. Robinson (Oxford: Blackwell, 1962) translator's footnote, 185.
4 Nietzsche, *Will to Power*, Book 3, sect. 481 (1883–88) 267.
5 Martin Heidegger, "Hölderlin and the Essence of Poetry," trans. Douglas Scott, in *Existence and Being*, 3rd ed. (London: Vision, 1968) 277.

hugh j. silverman

EREIGNISSE OF THE POSTMODERN: HEIDEGGER, LYOTARD, AND GERHARD RICHTER

In a 2002 interview with Robert Storr, the German painter Gerhard Richter commented: "I never wanted to capture and hold reality in a painting. Maybe at a weak moment I did, but I don't remember. However, that was never my intention. But I wanted to paint the appearance of reality."[1] What is the difference between capturing and holding reality in a painting and painting the appearance of reality?

I. Capturing reality in painting: a weak moment

The project of capturing and holding reality in a painting is a bold and adventurous enterprise. Of course, in one sense, paintings are already part of reality – they are not as such imaginary. They are material. They have a shape. They can be picked up, moved, altered, damaged. In this sense, they partake of the everyday world of concrete objects. But when a painter says that he wants to "capture and hold reality in a painting" he is proposing something much more adventuresome. Somehow, the mistaken assumption that there is an "external reality" can be brought into the "internal space" of the painting – capturing reality. But Richter says that such a desire would appear at best in a "weak moment" – a gap in his overall task.

A weak moment. Why "weak"? Is it weak because he really would like to achieve such a task and because he in fact knows that such a task is an impossible desire? Or is it "weak" because, as Gianni Vattimo has shown, weak thought happens in the interstices, at the moments when strong thought, bold and daring, dynamic and energetic, demanding and assertive, cannot hold on, cannot control everything, cannot achieve full and absolute knowledge. Weak thought is getting over the idea that the Faustian goals cannot be fully achieved, but even more crucially that they are not even worth striving after. Richter's weak moment, however, is an inverted weakness. For him, the weak moment occurs when the Faustian desire comes into play center stage, when he imagines that he could for a moment "capture reality." But this weak moment is just that – a momentary whim, one that interrupts Richter's genuine Apollonian self-image – the artist capable of achieving all there is to achieve as an artist. But the strength of this weak (Dionysian, excessive) moment is an insistence that is quickly overcome. He can then return to his more sober, controlled, balanced attitude.

So if it is a weak moment in which he tenders the idea of actually capturing reality, this event would be nevertheless an *Ereignis* of grand proportions – should he be able to achieve it. But, in all modesty, could a painter really be able to capture or hold reality? Would it not be like "owing another painter the truth in painting, and saying it!"[2]

Imagine the grandeur of the event: capturing reality in a painting, in a work of art, in one single artistic flourish. That would be an *Ereignis* to write home about. Indeed, Heidegger's conception of *Ereignis* is something of this order. The Heideggerian *Ereignis* is an event, a happening, an occurrence, an advent even of grand proportions. It is a colossus that is bigger than can be conceived, and yet it has no dimensions at all, no content, no shape, no materiality, no substance. So how can it be so big if it lacks all these crucial features of content, shape, materiality, substance? It would take a "weak moment" to even think that it could be grasped, captured, held in one place. And yet the Heideggerian *Ereignis* does happen, if it is indeed to be an *Ereignis*.

The Heideggerian *Ereignis* happens in the ontico-ontological difference. It does not belong to beings. It does not characterize beings, entities that are. An *Ereignis* is not even an "it," for it has no substantial features, nothing to hold onto, nothing to grasp. So to appeal to the Heideggerian *Ereignis* is to invoke an event so grand as to be like capturing reality in a painting. Would Heidegger consider it a "weak moment" were an *Ereignis* to be grasped, understood, captured in thinking? Vattimo's *schwache Denkens* or *pensiero debole* (weak thought) would indeed be the success and achievement of the Heideggerian *Ereignis*. But Heidegger would hardly consider such an event to be weak, for this is the very task of thinking (*die Sache des Denkens*).[3] How could it be "weak"? Weakness, as we know from Nietzsche, is hardly to be admired – the herd, those who are unable to think for themselves, those who live in *ressentiment*, who are unable to will themselves, who cannot will to live the eternal return – they are the weak ones. And Heidegger would surely agree – and yet what does he mean in his Nietzsche lectures of the late 1930s when he states that the will to power is the Being of beings?

If the "will to power" is the Being of beings (*Seiendes Sein/Sein des Seiendes*),[4] then this grand, strong moment is the event of all time, an *Ereignis* that is unlike any other occurrence (unlike any other *Geschehen*). The will to power, Heidegger says, is Art. Art, then, is the event in which the Being of beings happens. It is the moment in which not just any stroke of the brush, line of poetry, chink of sculpture, bite of music, corner of a building carves its little space but in which Art itself happens. This is not the happening, then, of an aspect of Art, a feature of Art, a sample of Art, an instance of Art, a piece of Art. It is the happening of Art itself. The will to power is the Being of beings as Art. And in this place where the will to power happens, that is where the eternal return happens in the Being of beings. But what does this all mean? It means that the will to power is very strong. It is forceful, powerful, energetic, but it also opens up a space where something other than the strong, powerful, forceful, energetic happens. This space is a kind of clearing, an opening, a gap (occupied by nothing) in which the truth happens.

As we know all too well from Heidegger's many pronouncements, the truth (*aletheia*) is the coming out of concealment, the unhiddenness, the non-closure, the disclosure of what has been hidden for a very long time, of what has been forgotten for ages, of what most merits being thought. Given such grand dimensions, it would hardly be a moment of weakness that would give way to Art, that would be the Truth of Art, that would open up a space of disclosure in which the meaning of the Being of beings is at issue.

The Heideggerian *Ereignis* is in no way trivial, in no way insignificant, in no way false. Indeed, it cannot be false. It must be what it is, namely the disclosure that is named "truth" – *die Wahrheit*. The truth happens in the disclosure, for that is where there is to be understanding. For Heidegger, the will to power is the Being of beings, namely the place where understanding takes place, where the break or dif-ference marks out the between of the relation of beings to Being. What gives here? And Heidegger answers: "it gives." "What gives?" (*Was gibt?*) might be asked again. "*Es gibt*" – it gives in the giving.[5] What gives in the giving? Could this be as grand as "capturing reality"? Presumably not, since the very idea of capturing reality remains – even for Gerhard Richter – a frivolous yet daring act.

And if one claims that "*das Es*" "*gibt*," then an entirely different dimension appears out of the woodwork. *Das Es* – the Freudian id – gives. But what does it give? It gives libidinal desire – often forbidden desires, passions that have to be controlled, that have to be placed under careful supervision by the ego (*das Ich*). But Heidegger has no place for *das Es* in the *es gibt*, in the giving of the event of the Being of beings. Richter's moment of weakness would be more like *das Es* shining through in his properly German, appropriately controlled conception of the limits of painting, the limits to his art, the scope of his enterprise. And yet, and yet, the ego, *das Ich*, also dares sometimes to allow the passion to escape, to enter into the Open, to happen in the Being of beings.

Even in Heidegger, it has been shown again and again, *Ereignis* has something of the *Eigen* in it. There is something of one's own that happens there. Emad and Maly sought to capture this element in their translation of *Ereignis* as "Enowning" – the new American name for *Ereignis* in the 1936–38 *Beiträge zur Philosophie (Vom Ereignis)*.[6] And the link with Hofstadter's earlier translation of "Eigentlichkeit" as "ownliness" makes a similar point about the appearance of the "Eigen" in both *Eigentlichkeit* (authenticity, responsibility, doing what is most one's own) and *Ereignis*. But the subject does not appear here, only its "ownness." *Das Ich* cannot find its "own" in the Being of beings, in the ontico-ontological difference, in the event of *Ereignis*. There is no "ego" there in *Ereignis*. And "ego" is precisely what Richter needs to leave by the wayside before he can properly think his own proper task, one that surely cannot presume to capture reality in painting. To be authentic, to be the author of one's own acts, to be one's own and to give place for the event to happen, for beings to invoke Being, for all this, one must leave "self" behind. And the project of leaving self behind is what momentarily failed when Richter considered that he might capture reality in painting. An act of hubris, of overweening self-esteem, an attempt to think the will to power as the Being of beings otherwise, that is what would permit a painter such as Richter to think that he can (in a moment of weakness) render reality in painting, in his paintings.

But then when Richter appeals to this moment of "weakness" of weakness of will, he then says that he does not "remember." Not remembering. For a German not to remember is a dangerous thing to do. *Er-innerung* – whether in Hegel, or in Heidegger – whether remembering everything that the Spirit had traversed in its path to Absolute Knowledge, or trying to remember with Heidegger the forgetting of Being throughout the ages – there will nevertheless be a "turn," an "inward turn," an "er"-*inner-ung*, a turning inward, a making one's own. And imagine – Richter came from East Germany but got to the West in time – not remembering to remember – as in not remembering the Holocaust. That would be un-thinkable. Richter, trying to right himself, states: "I never wanted to capture and hold reality in a painting. Maybe at a weak moment I did, but I don't remember." Not remembering those weak moments is also convenient. And what of those moments in Richter? For weak moments, moments in between, moments that have no space, moments that cannot even be remembered, these are the moments of another *Ereignis*, moments that never achieve the Being of beings, but moments in which painters paint, artists carry out their work as artists, events happen without motive or motivation …

II. Painting the appearance of reality

Plato would never let anyone forget that reality is somewhere other than appearance, that what appears is radically different from reality. Indeed, the only relation between the two is either a formal one (one is a copy of the other) or an epistemological one (from the position in one the other can be known). Knowing reality, comparing appearance to reality, this is the job for specially trained technicians of knowledge – namely philosophers. And painters, artists, they are the last people one should ever ask for an account of reality (or so Plato ventured to have Socrates say in the *Republic*). So what could Gerhard Richter possibly have up his sleeve when he says that he "wanted to paint the appearance of reality"?

There is an enormous difference between painting the appearance of reality and painting reality, just as there is an enormous difference between painting the appearance of reality and painting appearances. Richter is not interested in painting reality – except perhaps in those weak moments we have already addressed. In fact, he has already forgotten about any such attempts. They belong to the past, to the unsuccessful, to the impossible. But he is also not interested in painting "appearances."

What are "appearances?" They are *phainomena*, appearings which phenomenologically speaking are the meanings that are given in acts of intentionality, which are interpreted as essences, which happen in meaning-giving acts. Can painters paint them? There are good reasons why Heidegger does not subscribe to the Husserlian account of intentionality as acts of consciousness. However, Heidegger replaces the study of appearances in acts of consciousness taken as meanings (*noemata*) with the ontico-ontological difference of the place of interpretation as the site of thinking (*Denken*), even poetizing (*Dichtung*). What is Hölderlin doing when he asks "what are poets for in a destitute time?" (*Wozu Dichter in eine dürftige Zeit?*)[7] Hölderlin is trying to figure out what he, as poet, can accomplish when things are so bad (or when they are as bad as he perceives them to be). The question is a penetrating one, a question that calls for some careful examination of the task of the poet. But our concern here is with the painter. Certainly Heidegger, when he took up the Van Gogh painting of shoes in 1935–36, just before he turned to the question of *Ereignis* in the *Beiträge*, just before he challenged himself to understand Nietzsche's will to power as Art, he was trying to see what kind of world a painter could construe. He sought to give an account of a world disclosed by the shoes that Van Gogh has so adeptly painted. But would the answer tell what painters are for in a destitute time? In part, yes.

For Heidegger, these shoes disclosed a world of German peasant women, desperately trying to make ends meet nearly a century after Van

Gogh painted them. So the painter, for Heidegger, was not trying to paint the appearance of reality, for him, the painter was disclosing the world of the present reality, a reality that called out for interpretation and understanding. But would such painting provide a task? Would the painter have a "calling" (a *Ruf*) in the way in which Hölderlin had a calling? And Hölderlin's calling was to an extent filled out by Rilke in that he could show the way out of the destitute time, or even Trakl who could (later in the early 1950s) show that language speaks in the most proximate zone – i.e., in the Being of beings, in the ontico-ontological difference, in the place of the Heideggerian *Ereignis*.

If the painter takes as his or her task the painting of the appearance of reality, what good would this do? After all, if a painter could really paint reality – which Plato thought was not possible, but which effectively Heidegger thought was what the painter was doing when disclosing a world, opening up the place of truth in the conjuncture of artwork, artist, and art … Surely Heidegger thought that this would be a space of reality that was being disclosed. But when the painter says that he is painting the appearance of reality, this is very different from saying that he is disclosing reality.

Consider now some of Richter's paintings. Early on, he took up some themes that would have shocked a Germany trying desperately to place in the past a recent history of war and atrocity. In 1965, Richter paints his Uncle Rudi, wearing a Nazi uniform. Already in these early paintings, Richter offers fuzzy, blurred, out-of-focus images – as if a camera had been used at the incorrect aperture. Even in his most photorealist paintings of years later, there is still a hazy, glazed-over sheen to the images. Uncle Rudi standing there all by himself, as if posing for a camera, smiling uncomfortably, looking ahead and shown from head to foot in the center of the painting. Is Richter painting reality? Surely not – although reality is treated ironically here. Rudi is not demonstrated as if he were Maximilian Schell playing the most earnest Nazi officer. Rudi is standing there awkwardly, as if wondering how he ever ended up wearing a Nazi uniform, as if he had made a mistake, and yet as if he were half-proud of who he is and who he had become. The "as if" (*als ob*) is important here. Rudi is not disclosing a genuine world as Van Gogh's shoes would have to do, nor even recounting a destitute time as in Hölderlin's poetry. Uncle Rudi is at best one of those family members whom one is not sure one really wants to claim as one's own, as one's own relative. And yet there is something endearing about him. He obviously tried to be someone and tried hard to do it right.

Now Richter often paints from photographs and it is likely that this 1965 painting was done after a photo of Uncle Rudi. But Richter has taken the photograph and translated a direct snapshot of reality into an appearance of reality. A world may be disclosed here, there may be an *Ereignis*, but the *Ereignis* has an ironic tone, a sense of distance that has no place in the Being of beings. Uncle Rudi is distant – he is not close up – certainly nothing like the gallery of painted photographs of famous European scientists, philosophers, writers, musicians, etc. which Richter produced in 1971–72 for the 1972 Venice Biennale. Rudi keeps his distance. What if Richter had painted Rudi's shoes – close up? What world would they disclose? What *Ereignis* would be worth telling about? But Richter takes up his uncle, whom Robert Storr describes as a German commonplace: "The Nazi in the family." Storr cites Richter remembering his Uncle Rudi: "He was young and very stupid, and then he went to war and was killed during the first days" (*Gerhard Richter* 40).

There is something compelling about Richter's portraits of famous intellectuals, writers, musicians, scientists (*48 Portraits*). They are all men – no women. There are no painters. There are no controversial figures. They are all intensely serious. Indeed, they all look like a row of defunct Enron executives at a Senate hearing, all wearing suits, all dressed for a very serious formal event. Unlike the painting of Uncle Rudi, only the head is displayed, only a few actually looking forward as if in a mirror, most looking partially away for an almost side view. They look like photographs – indeed, like most of Richter's paintings they are painted from photographs in an old encyclopedia. From a distance, and if placed high near the ceiling around a staircase as they were at the 2002 Museum of Modern Art retrospective in New York, they look acutely "real," almost like photographs. But they are not photographs, and that is what is important here. They are paintings. Benjamin's "work of art in the age of mechanical reproducibility" has been turned on its head – the aura returns in the image of the photograph.

And what of his efforts at reproducing a Titian Annunciation (*Die Verkündigung*) in 1973? The characteristic fuzziness is there, but the theme is that of a classical late Renaissance painting. Mary does not really look serious as she should, and Gabriel looks more like Peter Pan than an angel. Most significant is the blast of light that is supposed to be sending the word to Mary, typically with actual writing accompanying the flash of light, but here it looks as though the light is going the other way – from Mary upward rather than coming to Mary. There is a ghostlike atmosphere here. It is an event of grand proportions. The Annunciation is just about always portrayed as an *Ereignis*! Announcing to Mary that she will bear the child of God. What more significant an *Ereignis* could one want? And there is clearly a difference between the ontic life of Mary and the *deus absconditus* who should have sent the blast of light. But there is the hint of a telecommunication going in the opposite direction as Gabriel offers witness to the event rather than transmitting it. He gestures to Mary and even carries a feather presumably hoping to offer a writing event, or signature event in her book that she holds open before her. But in the haze it is difficult to see, the visibility (*Sichtbarkeit*) is low, and there is at best the "appearance" (*Erscheinung/Erscheinen*) of reality.

Who speaks here? Well, as Heidegger announces in the Language essay, *"die Sprache spricht."*[8] Language speaks, and it is the language of Richter's painting that is speaking here, not the absent God, not Gabriel, and certainly not Mary who hardly looks as dumbfounded as she ought to. The dramatic structure of a Leonardo Annunciation is missing here.[9] This is hardly something that is to be taken seriously. Irony once again settles upon the scene and if the figures were different it would look more like Hamlet's father's ghost appearing to Horatio, Bernardo, and Marcellus at the ramparts. Richter calls for the "appearance of reality." But although there are figures here, the reality is neither that of theological earnestness nor the lightheartedness of a Rogers and Hammerstein musical, and yet there is something of both in the appearances. The painting speaks in its own name, in its own style, in its own theme – and the citations are out of joint. The *Ereignis* is displaced …

III. Displaced *ereignisse*

When Jean-François Lyotard defined the postmodern in an interview with Régis Durand, he said that it involves the "presentation of the unpresentable in presentation itself."[10] And he later asks, in connection with Barnett Newman's account of the sublime: "is it happening?"[11] It could be said that these two formulations are the same, but with a difference.

The presentation of the unpresentable in presentation itself is nevertheless a "presentation." An *Ereignis* is effectively a "presentation" in Lyotard's sense. The presentation happens, it occurs, it is an event, and it appropriates that which is appropriated in the appropriation itself. Each presentation in the modern is an *Ereignis* of sorts. Andy Warhol's cows, his Mao Tse-tungs, his Jackies, his Campbell's soup cans, his Marilyn Monroes, etc. – they are all events, but multiple events. In Warhol the multiplicity of the events – the repetition of the events – marks the displacement of the centering of the Heideggerian *Ereignis*. Differential as in Heidegger but displaced to the next image, repeated chiasmatically in the painting, Warhol's silkscreen paintings are presentations that repeat in multiple sites. They are *Ereignisse* rather than a constitution of an *Ereignis*. Gerhard Richter remembers some of Warhol's repetitions, but never of the same image. His 48 portraits recall the Warhol repetitions, but each image is different. They are presentations, but not repetitions. Warhol had already done that …

Already done that … The modern requires that if it has already been done, already been presented, already been experienced, already happened, then it is not worth repeating – except, of course, the repetition itself is new (as it was in Warhol). Warhol had no interest in presenting reality, nor did he care about appearances – except perhaps how he himself looked to his male lovers. Warhol wanted to reiterate what is already culturally charged. His events turned culture back on itself – like a mirror held up (not to nature but) to society and culture itself. Richter has an element of this sort of presentation. By taking photographs and painting them, Richter also aestheticizes the cultural technologies of his age. But Richter's presentations also happen in many different places. He has no unique style. There are impressionist-type paintings (his 1967 *Olympia*), Degas-like nudes (e.g. the *Small Nude* of 1967), Kirchner-like aerial views of a city (*Townscape PL*, 1970), Turner-like open ocean scenes (*Seascape (Cloudy)*, 1969; *Seascape (Cloudy)*, 1998), but also photorealist paintings of his daughter Betty (1998), abstract paintings (1979–80, 1997), even a fuzzy self-portrait – a cross between a Munch and a Francis Bacon (1996), his paintings on aluminum panels (1999) and on and on. Each time the style is radically different, with some recursions back to similar topoi and styles. Except perhaps for the hazy look to many of his paintings, if one does not know them, or had not seen them before, it would be difficult to identify them as Richters. Indeed, he operates in many different stylistic modalities and sites. None belong to him, none carry his signature, none make his work unmistakable. It may be that what is characteristically Richter is its diversity of presentations, its multiple *Ereignisse*, its interruptions of stylistic integrity, its disseminations into unexpected themes. The return of the photograph behind the paintings might give him away, but then one could say that as a "modern" painter the endless return of the photograph behind the painted image is his presentation of the previously unpresentable – the hallmark of the modern.

But there is also a presentation of the unpresentable in all these presentations, and that is what is happening between the paintings. Between each and every painting is a difference, but this difference is not really the difference between the photograph and the painting, for that would be a simple representational issue. Were that the whole story, his attempts to paint appearances of reality would have to do with attempts to render photographs in painting. Important and admirable as that might be, then each and every painting that has a photograph behind it would be a question of fidelity or infidelity, accuracy or inaccuracy, interpretation or representation, etc. But when Richter says that he is painting appearances of reality, the key is the "of." "Is it happening?" we might ask with Lyotard. For what is this "of" that takes place between the reality of the photography or the reality imaged in the photography and the appearance of these realities? The genitive, as we have learned to think with Heidegger when he interrogates the ontico-ontological genitive in the Being of beings, in Richter's appearance of reality is the site of difference that displaces each particular painting metonymically to another Richter painting. For precisely by the multiplicity of styles, topoi, and themes, each particular presentation of the unpresentable in the presentation (and the whole of this formulation is an *Ereignis* for Lyotard) is disseminated to the next painting that also has a photo behind it. The unpresentable is not the photograph, however. The unpresentable is the next or last or other painting that is endlessly made other and related at the same time. Against the concept of an oeuvre, Richter's oeuvre is linked by the differences.

When you have seen one Rubens you have seen them all, one might say in a derogatory tone. But one could also make that claim of a Van Gogh, a Kandinsky, or a Warhol. Stylistic integrity binds the various paintings of each of these painters. Picasso changed styles but in chronological sequence. Richter continues to paint in multiple sites at the same time. The differences link the paintings into a network of extraordinary virtuosity, but the multiple *Ereignisse* are what make Richter's paintings of appearances of reality in fact neither paintings of appearances nor of reality. Richter's *Ereignisse* are postmodern sites constituted by their deferrals and displacements. Richter's *Ereignisse* of the·appearances *of* reality are Lyotard's postmodern sublime in action.

Notes

1 See Robert Storr, "Interview with Gerhard Richter" in *Gerhard Richter: Doubt and Belief in Painting* (New York: Museum of Modern Art, 2003) 172.

2 See Jacques Derrida, *The Truth in Painting* [1978], trans. Geoff Bennington and Ian McLeod (Chicago and London: U of Chicago P, 1987). See in particular "Passe-Partout" (2) where Derrida cites Cézanne as writing (to the painter Emile Bernard): "I owe you the truth in painting and I will tell it to you" (*"je vous dois la vérité en peinture et je vous la dirai"*).

3 See Martin Heidegger, *The End of Philosophy and the Task of Thinking* [1964], trans. Joan Stambaugh, in *Basic Writings*, ed. David Farrell Krell (New York: Harper, 1993). German title: *Zur Sache des Denkens* [1969] (Tübingen: Niemeyer, 1988).

4 See Martin Heidegger, *Nietzsche I: The Will to Power as Art*, ed. and trans. David Farrell Krell (New York: Harper, 1979). Originally published in German as *Nietzsche: Band I und II* [1961] (Pfullingen: Neske, 1998).

5 See Martin Heidegger, *Sein und Zeit* [1927] (Tübingen: Niemeyer, 1986). See two English translations: *Being and Time*, trans. John Macquarrie and Edward Robinson (New York: Harper, 1978) and Joan Stambaugh (Albany: State U of New York P, 1996).

6 See Martin Heidegger, *Beiträge zur Philosophie (Vom Ereignis)* (1936–38). Translated as *Contributions to Philosophy. From Enowning*, trans. Parvis Emad and

Kenneth Maly (Bloomington: Indiana UP, 1999).

7 See Martin Heidegger, "What Are Poets For?" [*Wozu Dichter?*] [1946] in *Holzwege* [1950] (Frankfurt: Klostermann, 1994) and in *Poetry, Language, Thought*, trans. Albert Hofstadter (New York: Harper, 1971) 91.

8 See Martin Heidegger, "Language" [*Die Sprache*] [1946] in *Unterwegs zur Sprache* (Pfullingen: Neske, 1959) and in *Poetry, Language, Thought*, trans. Albert Hofstadter (New York: Harper, 1971) 189–210.

9 See Leonardo da Vinci's *Annunciation* in the Uffizi Gallery (Florence, Italy).

10 See "Answering the Question: What is Postmodernism?," trans. Régis Durand, in Jean-François Lyotard, *The Postmodern Condition: A Report on Knowledge*, trans. Geoff Bennington and Brian Massumi (Minneapolis: U of Minnesota P, 1984) 81. For another version, see Jean-François Lyotard, *The Postmodern Explained: Correspondence 1982–1985*, trans. Julian Pefanis and Morgan Thomas (Minneapolis: U of Minnesota P, 1993) 15.

11 See Jean-François Lyotard, "The Sublime and the Avant-Garde [1983] in *The Inhuman*, trans. Geoff Bennington and Rachel Bowlby (Stanford: Stanford UP, 1991) 89–107.

costas douzinas

HUMAN RIGHTS IN POSTMODERNITY

I. Introduction

A new ideal has trumped on the global world stage: human rights. It unites left and right, the pulpit and the state, the minister and the rebel, the developing world and the liberals of Hampstead and Manhattan. Human rights started their life as the principle of liberation from oppression and domination, the rallying cry of the homeless and the dispossessed, the political programme of revolutionaries and dissidents. But their appeal is not confined to the wretched of the earth. Alternative lifestyles, greedy consumers of goods and culture, the pleasure-seekers and playboys of the Western world, the owner of Harrods, a former managing director of Guinness plc, as well as a former king of Greece, have all glossed their claims in the language of human rights.[1]

Human rights were initially linked with specific class interests and were the ideological and political weapons in the fight of the rising bourgeoisie against despotic political power and static social organisation. But their ontological presuppositions – the principles of human equality and freedom – and their political corollary – the claim that political power must be subjected to the demands of reason and law – have now become part of the staple ideology of most contemporary regimes and their partiality has been transcended.

Internationally, the New Times after the collapse of communism have elevated human rights as the central principle. Humanitarian interventions, war crimes tribunals and domestic prosecutions of heads of states for violations of human rights are all part of the new order. Human rights are the fate of postmodernity, the energy of our societies, the fulfilment of the Enlightenment promise of emancipation and self-realisation. Human rights are the ideology after the end, the defeat of ideologies, or, to adopt a voguish term, the ideology of globalisation at the "end of history."[2]

And yet many doubts persist.[3] The record of human rights violations since their ringing declarations at the end of the eighteenth century is quite appalling. "[I]t is an undeniable fact," writes Gabriel Marcel, "that human life has never been so universally treated as a vile and perishable commodity than during our own era."[4] If the twentieth century was the epoch of human rights, their triumph is, to say the least, something of a paradox. Our era has witnessed more violations of their principles than any of the previous and less "enlightened" epochs. The twentieth century was the century of massacre, genocide, ethnic cleansing – the age of the Holocaust. At no point in human history has there been a greater gap between the poor and the rich in the Western world or between the North and the South globally. No degree of progress allows one to ignore the fact that never before, in absolute figures, have so many men, women and children been subjugated, starved or exterminated. It is this paradox of triumph and disaster that I want to explore.

A second paradox characterises the theory of human rights. While rights are one of the noblest liberal institutions, liberal political and legal philosophy appears unable to grasp fully their operation. Part of the problem must be attributed to the woefully inadequate historical sense and philosophical awareness of the liberals. The world they inhabit is an atomocentric place that is constituted by social contracts, motivated by blindness and veils of ignorance, attributed to ideal speech situations and harking back to the pre-modern certainty of single right answers to moral and legal conflicts. Similarly, the model of the person populating this world is that of the self-certain individual, knowledgeable and reflective – a Kantian autonomous subject, who does not belong to class or gender, has no unconscious or traumatic experiences and who stands towards the world in a position of perfect control. Indeed, it is striking that our most acclaimed theorists of rights forget two hundred years of social theory and philosophy and act as if they have never heard the names of Marx, Freud, Nietzsche or Weber.

Let me offer, in seven inevitably condensed epigrammatic theses, an alternative genealogy and philosophy of rights:

1. Nature and natural right were the creations of revolutionary thought, acts of Promethean rebellion.

2. Natural rights and sovereignty, the two opposing principles, which permeate the law of human rights, are two sides of the same coin. Ethnic cleansing is the descendant of the great declarations of the eighteenth century.

3. Ideals start their careers in conflict with the police. They end when they call in the police and the air force for their protection. An angel protected by the police: that's how ideals die.

4. To defend human beings, we must attack humanism – a banal combination of classical and Christian metaphysics. Human rights do not belong to humans but they construct humans.

5. Universalism and cultural relativism, rather that being fatal enemies, are totally dependent on one another.

6. Human rights are the public proclamation or legalisation of individual desire. Their action expands the boundaries of the social and introduces undecidability, but it also dismembers the subjected subject.

7. The human rights of the Other could become the postmodern principle of justice.

II. Nature and natural rights

Ancient Greece did not distinguish between law and convention or right and custom. Custom is a strong cement: it binds families and communities firmly, but it can also numb. Without external standards, the development of a critical approach towards traditional authority is impossible: the given goes unchallenged and the slaves stay in line. Originally, the root of all authority is the ancestral.

But the discovery, or rather the invention, of the concept of nature challenged the claim of the ancestral. Philosophy could now appeal from the ancestral to the good – to that which is good intrinsically, by nature. Nature as a critical concept acquired philosophical currency in the fifth century BCE when it was used by the sophists against custom and law, and by Socrates and Plato in order to combat the moral relativism of the sophists and to restore the authority of reason.[5] Turning nature into norm or into the standard of right was the greatest early step of civilisation, but it was also a cunning trick against priests and rulers. To this day, when knowledge and reason are subjected to authority, they are called "theology" or "legal learning" but they cannot be the philosophy practised by the Greeks.[6] Nature (the most cultured of concepts), the idea of the good and political philosophy were all born together in an act of rebellion.

This critical function of nature was in evidence in the appeal to natural rights by the great revolutions of the eighteenth century and again in the popular rebellions in Eastern Europe in the 1980s. Indeed, the symbolic foundation and starting point of modernity can be located at the passing of the great revolutionary documents of the eighteenth century. They returned to the critical function of classical natural law, which had been concealed by successive layers of Christian theology. But victorious revolutionaries turned rulers can become as oppressive as their predecessors. The popularity of natural rights declined dramatically after the great declarations and the revolutions of the 1980s ended up in the mafia governments of the 1990s and the destruction of whole cultures and populations through the discipline of the market.

III. Sovereignty and human rights

Let me now turn to the relationship between power and morality or between sovereignty and human rights. We can explore the strong internal connection between these two superficially antagonistic principles in three key periods of national and international construction: the late eighteenth century, the post-Second World War international system and, finally, the New Times emerging after the collapse of communism.

The great eighteenth-century declarations pronounced natural rights inalienable because they were independent of both governments and temporal and local factors and they expressed, in legal form, the eternal rights of man. Rights were declared on behalf of the universal "man." Yet the French Declaration is quite categorical as to the real source of universal rights.[7] Let us follow briefly its strict logic. Article 1 states that "men are born and remain free and equal in their rights"; Article 2 that "the final end of every political institution is the preservation of the natural and imprescriptible rights of man" and Article 3 proceeds to define this association: "The source of all sovereignty lies essentially in the Nation. No corporation or individual may exercise any authority not expressly derived therefrom."[8]

It was the act of enunciation which established the power of a particular type of political association, the nation-state, to become the sovereign law maker and, second, of a particular "man," the national citizen, to become the beneficiary of rights. First, let us consider national sovereignty. The declarations set out the universality of rights but their immediate effect is to establish the boundless power of the state and its law. It was the declaration of rights which established not only those rights but also the power of the constituent assemblies to legislate. In a paradoxical fashion, these declarations of universal principle "perform" the foundation of local sovereignty. If the declarations ushered in the epoch of the individual, they also launched the age of the state – the mirror of the individual. Human rights and national sovereignty – the two antithetical principles of international law – were born together, their contradiction more apparent than real.

The legislator of the proclaimed universal community was none other than the historical legislator of the French or American nation. From that point – statehood, sovereignty and territory – followed a national principle. If the Declaration inaugurated modernity, it also started nationalism and all of its consequences: genocide, ethnic and civil wars, ethnic cleansing, minorities, refugees, the stateless. Citizenship introduced a new type of privilege which was protected for some by excluding others. Since the revolutions, nation-states have been defined by territorial boundaries and have shifted exclusion from class to nation: the modern formal class barrier.

One could argue that the French National Assembly notionally split itself into two parts: a philosophical and a historical. The first legislated on behalf of "man" for the whole world, the second for the only territory and people it could – France and its dependencies. The gap between the two is also the distance between the universality of the law (eventually of human rights) and the generality of state legislation. From that point onwards, it remains unknown, as Lyotard put it:

> whether the law thereby declared is French or human, whether the war conducted in the name of rights is one of conquest or one of liberation, … whether those nations which are not French ought to become French or become human by endowing themselves with Constitutions that conform to the Declaration.[9]

We can substitute "American" for "French" and have the perfect contemporary position: the discourse of the universal needs a unique subject to pronounce it. But this particular enunciator of the universal should remain unaffected by its demands, as the current American hostility towards the creation of an International Criminal Court proves.[10]

On the subjective side, the separation between human and citizen is the main characteristic of modern law. The modern subject reaches its humanity by acquiring political rights of citizenship. The alien is not a citizen. Aliens do not have rights because they are not part of the state and they are lesser human beings because they are not citizens. One is a human to greater or lesser degree because one is or is not a citizen to a greater or lesser degree. The alien is the gap between human and citizen. We become human through citizenship, and subjectivity is based on the gap, the difference between universal man and state citizen. Modern subjectivity is based on those Others whose existence is evidence of the universality of human nature but whose exclusion is absolutely crucial for concrete personhood, in other words, for citizenship.

We can observe the same internal linking between human rights (the moral perspective on politics) and national sovereignty in the great enterprise of international standard-setting since 1945. A huge process of international legislation and codification has been taking place on the world stage, but also regionally, and even at the national level as the inexorable pressure to introduce a Bill of Rights in Britain has shown.[11] Why has so much energy been placed on this attempt to codify what is a human being? Because "it is quite conceivable," according to Arendt, "that one fine day a highly organized and mechanized humanity will conclude quite democratically – namely by majority decision – that for humanity as a whole it would be better to liquidate certain parts thereof."[12] The "market" of human dignity and equality did not conceal a "hidden hand," and people voted and still vote for regimes and parties determined to violate all human rights, as the examples of Hitler's Germany and Milosevic's Yugoslavia show.

III.i. Globalised human rights

An endless process of international and humanitarian law making has been put into operation, aimed at protecting people from the putative assertions of their sovereignty. To paraphrase Nietzsche, if God, the source of natural law, is dead, he has been replaced by international law. But there are many problems with these globalised rights.

First, this huge enterprise of legislation and codification has become the safest haven of a *sui generis* positivism. Codification, from Justinian to the *Code Napoléon*, has always been the ultimate exercise of legislative sovereignty, the supreme expression of state power. In the same way that the early declarations of rights helped to bring about the absolute, indivisible and illimitable power of the sovereign, so too the post-Second World War expansion of international human rights turned the principle of non-intervention in the domestic affairs of states into the cornerstone of the law and founded the power of the new international institutions. The major powers unanimously agreed that human rights could not be used to pierce the shield of national sovereignty. Human rights became a major tool for legitimating, nationally and internationally, the post-Second World War order, at a point at which all principles of state and international organisation had emerged from the war seriously weakened. The principles of human rights and national sovereignty, both paramount, paradoxically served two separate agendas of the great powers: the need to legitimise the new order through their commitment to rights, without exposing the victorious states to scrutiny and criticism about their own flagrant violations.

Second, law making in the huge business of human rights has been taken over by government representatives, diplomats, policy advisers, international civil servants and human rights experts. But priests, princes and prime ministers are the enemy against whom nature, natural rights and human rights were conceived as a defence. The business of government is to govern, not to follow moral principles. Governmental actions in the international arena are dictated by national interests and political considerations, and morality enters the stage always late, when the principle invoked happens to condemn the actions of a political adversary. Government-operated international human rights law is the best illustration of the poacher turned gamekeeper.

This leads us to a crucial distinction between globalisation and universalisation, which has been almost totally elided in the debate on human rights. The variable universalism of classical natural law or the Kantian normative universalisation both acted as regulative principles: they gave a perspective from which each particular action could be judged, in theory at least, in the name of the universal.[13] The empirical universality of human rights, on the other hand, is not a normative principle. It is a matter of counting how many states have adopted how many and which treaties, or how many have introduced which reservations or derogations from treaty obligations. When normative universality becomes a calculable globalisation, it turns from a lofty, albeit impossible, ideal into the lowest common denominator of state interests and rivalries. Every state and power comes under the mantle of the international law of human rights, every government becomes civilised as the "law of the princes" has finally become the "universal" law of human dignity. But this is an empirical universality, based on the competitive solidarity of sovereign governments and on the pragmatic concerns and calculations of international politics. The community of human rights is universal but imaginary: universal humanity does not exist empirically and cannot act as a transcendental principle philosophically.

IV. Universal morality and political conflict

Let me turn to the world order that emerged at the turn of the twentieth century. After the collapse of communism, a new global arrangement is being established which follows moral principles of universal applicability. International human rights are the most common form of universal morality, and their task is to impose moral principles on the exercise of (domestic and international) power – to moralise politics. The moralisation of politics is evident at a number of levels. The most important and violent is the use of force for "humanitarian intervention" by the USA or an American-led coalition with or without UN authorisation. The usual justification for the gross violation of sovereignty is that atrocities and other flagrant violations of human rights allow the overriding of the cardinal principle of the international order of modernity.

The moralisation of international politics and the accompanying weakening of the principle of sovereignty are taken further with the tendency to criminalise politics and to pursue, through the courts, leaders who have committed human rights violations.[14] The international criminal justice system appears unstoppable. The early feeble efforts of the ad hoc criminal tribunals for Yugoslavia and Rwanda are now coming to maturity with the extradition of Milosevic and his trial at The Hague. At the same time, the creation of a permanent war crimes tribunal with its own charter has recently become a reality.[15]

However, the various versions of moralism, whether they are presented as cosmopolitanism or universal morality or human rights, express and promote the quasi-imperial configuration of the power of the New Times. Its signs are everywhere. At the ideological level, the collapse of communism signalled the victory of the principles of mass capitalist democracy and human rights, the main Western weapon in the ideological Cold War. In the same way that the victory of the Christian Roman Emperor Constantine over pagan opponents in the Eastern Empire led to the spread of Christianity around the known world, the American triumph over the "evil empire" has led to the global dissemination of the principles of universal morality.

But these principles and the attempt to disseminate them are not simply the result of the liberal or charitable disposition of the West. Global moral and civic rules are the necessary companion of the universalisation of economic production and consumption, of the creation of a world capitalist system. Over the last twenty years we have witnessed, without much comment, the creation of global legal rules regulating the world capitalist economy, including rules on investment, trade, aid and intellectual property. These are being gradually supplemented by moral and civic regulations and directives which prepare the individual of the new order, a world citizen, highly moralised, highly regulated but also highly differentiated materially, despite the common human rights that everyone enjoys, from Helsinki to Hanoi and from London to Lahore.

We can find parallels with the emergence of early capitalism. The legal system first developed the rules necessary for the regulation of capitalist production, including rules for the protection of property and contract and the development of legal and corporate personality. Only later did civic rules emerge, mainly with the creation of civil and political rights, which led to the creation of the modern subject and citizen. These rules gave the man of the classical declarations the legal tools and public recognition necessary to cut his traditional ties, abandon any residual ideas of virtue and duty and organise his activities and life-plan according to a calculation of interest borne by the institution of rights.

Similarly today, the universalisation of morality follows the gradual unification of world markets. As economic practices and legal rules and conventions become standardised, unified ethics, semiotics and law become the international lingua franca. The universalism of human rights cannot work in the abstract. It can only operate as an instrument of the leading powers of the New Times or by the citizens claiming not just formal but material equality. While human rights appear to be universal and uninterested in the particularities of each situation, their triumph means that they will soon become tools in political conflict, thus undermining their claim to universality. The common reference to values will not stop their polemical use, as the Milosevic trial clearly indicates.

The universalism of rights was invented by the West, but will now be used by the South and East to make claims on the distribution of the world product. The recent converts to universal values are led to believe that improvement of domestic human rights will strengthen their claim against world resources. Milosevic was extradited to The Hague for a few hundred million dollars in aid to Serbia, and the new Afghan regime is promised a few more million if they police the orders of America. Aid agreements routinely impose privatisation, market economics and human rights as the new gospel of liberation. Neo-liberal economic policies and human rights appear to promise an inexorable process of equalisation between East, South and West.

Indeed, we know from our Western histories that formal liberties cannot be contained in their formalism for too long. Soon, the workers with the vote and freedom of speech will demand the income and resources needed to make their new-found freedoms real: they will ask for the material preconditions of equality. Lecturers in China and farmers in India will demand to earn as much as those in Helsinki or Southern France, something that can be achieved only through a substantial reduction in the Western standard of living. But the (implicit) promise that market-led home-based economic growth will inexorably lead the South to Western economic standards is fraudulent. Historically, the Western ability to turn the protection of formal rights into a limited guarantee of material, economic and social rights was based on huge transfers from the colonies to the metropolis. While universal morality and rights now militate in favour of reverse flows, Western policies on development aid and Third World debt, and American policies on oil pricing, gas emissions and defence spending, indicate that this is not politically feasible. When the unbridgeability of the gap between the missionary statements on equality and dignity and the bleak reality of obscene inequality becomes apparent, human rights – rather than the elimination of war – will lead to new and uncontrollable types of tension and conflict. Spanish soldiers met the advancing Napoleonic armies, shouting "Down with freedom!" It is not difficult to imagine people meeting the "peacekeepers" of the New Times with cries of "Down with human rights!"

Universalist morality claims to muster agreement about the content of its prescriptions. It follows that as human rights become the lingua franca of the New Times but are unable to eliminate conflict, the formal struggle over human rights will revolve predominantly around their interpretation and application. As always, the universal is placed at the service of the particular: it is the prerogative of a particular to announce the universal.

The enunciating particular can place itself towards the universal in two positions: either it can attach an opt-out clause and exclude itself from the applicability of the universal or it can arrogate itself the exclusive power and right to offer the correct interpretation of the universal. France was the enunciator of the universal in early modernity, the USA in the New Times, and they have adopted both practices. The opt-out clause is most apparent when the Americans denounce the universal jurisdiction of the new International Criminal Court and declare that under no circumstances will they allow American personnel to be tried by it. But they also claim the power of the sole authoritative interpreter. During the Afghan campaign, President Bush declared that, despite the unanimous view of international lawyers to the contrary, his interpretation of the Geneva Conventions was the only valid one and, accordingly, the Taliban prisoners held in the Guantanamo Bay camp would not be designated as prisoners of war, but would instead fall into the novel category of "unlawful combatants."[16]

V. Humanism and "human" rights

Who or what is a human? Even if we had the answer, when does the existence of a human being (and its associated rights) begin and when does it end? What about foetuses, children, the mentally or terminally ill or prisoners? Are they fully human, entitled to all the rights that belong to humanity, or are they only partially human, since their rights are severely restricted? Do they enjoy fewer rights because they are lesser humans or on account of some other quality? What about animals? The animal rights movement, from deep ecology and anti-vivisection militancy to its gentler green versions, has placed the legal differentiation between human and animal firmly on the political agenda and has drafted a number of bills of animal entitlements. Important philosophical and ontological questions are involved here. How did we arrive at the concept of human nature and humanity?

The concept of humanity is an invention of modernity. Both Athens and Rome had citizens but not "men," in the sense of members of the human species. Free men were Athenians or Spartans, Romans or Carthaginians, but not persons; they were Greeks or barbarians but not humans. The word *humanitas* appeared for the first time in the Roman Republic. It was a translation of *paideia*, the Greek word for education, and meant *eruditio et institutio in bonas artes*.[17] The Romans inherited the idea of humanity from Hellenistic philosophy, in particular Stoicism, and used it to distinguish between the *homo humanus*, the educated Roman, and *homo barbarus*. The first humanism was the result of the encounter between Greek and Roman civilisation, and the early modern humanism of the

Italian Renaissance retained the two characteristics of nostalgia for a lost past and exclusion of others who are not equal to this Edenic period. It was presented as a return to Greek and Roman prototypes and was aimed at the barbarism of medieval scholasticism and the gothic north.

A different conception of *humanitas* emerged in Christian theology, superbly captured in the Pauline assertion that there is no Greek or Jew, free man or slave. All men are equally part of spiritual humanity, which is juxtaposed to the deity. They can all be saved through God's plan of salvation. Universal equality – albeit of a spiritual character – a concept unknown to the classics, entered the world stage. But the religious grounding of humanity was undermined by the liberal political philosophies of the eighteenth century. The foundation of humanity was transferred from God to (human) nature. By the end of the eighteenth century, the concept of "man" came into existence and soon became the absolute and inalienable value around which the whole world revolved. Humanity, man as species existence, entered the historical stage as the peculiar combination of classical and Christian metaphysics.

For humanism, there is a universal essence of man and this essence is the attribute of each individual who is the real subject.[18] As species existence, man appears without differentiation or distinction in his nakedness and simplicity, united with all others in an empty nature deprived of substantive characteristics except for his free will, reason and soul – the universal elements of human essence. This is the man of the rights of man, someone without history, desires or needs, an abstraction that has as little humanity as possible, since he has jettisoned all those traits and qualities that build human identity. A minimum of humanity is what allows man to claim autonomy, moral responsibility and legal subjectivity. At the same time, he who enjoyed the "rights of man" was a man all too man – a well-off, heterosexual, white male – who condensed the abstract dignity of humanity and the real prerogatives of belonging to the community of the powerful. Indeed, one could write the history of human rights as the ongoing and always failing struggle to close the gap between the abstract man and the concrete citizen; to add flesh, blood and sex to the pale outline of the "human."

The existence of "non-humans," the "vermin" of older and more recent concentration camps, the potential of world annihilation by nuclear weapons, recent developments in genetic technology and robotics indicate that even this most banal and obvious of definitions is neither definite nor conclusive. Humanity's mastery, like God's omnipotence, includes the ability to redefine who or what counts as human and even to destroy itself. From Aristotle's slaves to designer babies, clones and cyborgs, the boundaries of humanity have been shifting. What history has taught us is that there is nothing sacred about any definition of humanity and nothing eternal about its scope. Humanity cannot act as the a priori normative principle and is mute in the matter of legal and moral rules. Its function lies not in a philosophical essence but in its non-essence, in the endless process of redefinition and the continuous but impossible attempt to escape fate and external determination.

We can conclude that the "human" of rights, and humanity, is a floating signifier. As a signifier, it is just a word, a discursive element that is neither automatically nor necessarily linked to any particular signified or meaning. On the contrary, the word "human" is empty of all meaning and can be attached to an infinite number of signifieds. As a result, it cannot be fully and finally pinned down to any particular conception because it transcends and overdetermines them all.[19] But the "humanity" of human rights is not just an empty signifier; it carries an enormous symbolic capital, a surplus of value and dignity endowed by the revolutions and the declarations and augmented by every new struggle that adopts the rhetoric of human rights. This symbolic excess turns the "human" into a floating signifier, into something that combatants in political, social and legal struggles want to co-opt to their cause, and explains its importance for political campaigns.

From a non-essentialist perspective, rights are highly artificial constructs, a historical accident of European intellectual and political history. The concept of rights belongs to the symbolic order of language and law, which determines their scope and reach with scant regard for ontologically solid categories, like those of man, human nature or dignity. From a semiotic perspective, rights do not refer to things or other material entities in the world but are pure combinations of legal and linguistic signs, words and images, symbols and fantasies. No person, thing or relation is in principle closed to the logic of rights. Any entity open to semiotic substitution can become the subject or object of rights; any right can be extended to new areas and persons, or, conversely, withdrawn from existing ones. Civil and political rights have been extended to social and economic rights, and then to rights in culture and the environment. Individual rights have been supplemented by group, national or animal rights. The right to free speech or to annual holidays can be accompanied by a right to love, to party or to have back episodes of *Star Trek* shown daily. If something can be put into language, it may acquire rights and can certainly become the object of rights.

The only limits to the ceaseless expansion or contraction of rights are conventional: the effectiveness of political struggles and the limited and limiting logic of the law. Human rights struggles are symbolic and political: their immediate battleground is the meaning of words, such as "differ-ence" and "equality" or "similarity" and "freedom," but, if successful, they have ontological consequences – they radically change the constitution of the legal subject and affect people's lives. If we accept the psychoanalytic insight that people have no essential identities outside of those constructed in symbolic discourses and practices,[20] a key aim of politics and of law is to fix meanings and to close identities by making the contingent, historical linkings between signifiers and signifieds permanent and necessary. But such attempts can succeed only partially because identities are always open to new symbolic appropriations and articulations within different discourses and practices, and every – partially – fixed identity is always overdetermined by the surplus value of the floating signifier.

Human rights do not belong to humans and do not follow the dictates of humanity; they construct humans. A human being is someone who can successfully claim human rights.

VI. Cultural relativism

The continuing pathos of the universalism/relativism debate coupled with its repetitive and rather banal nature indicates that the stakes are high. The universalist claims that all cultural value and, in particular, moral norms are not historically and territorially bound, but should pass a test of universal consistency. As a result, judgements which derive their force and legitimacy from local conditions are morally suspect. But as all life is situated, an "unencumbered" judgement based exclusively on the protocols of reason goes against the grain of human experience – unless, of course, universalism and its procedural demands have become the cultural tradition of some place: the USA would be a prime candidate. The counter-intuitive nature of universalism can lead its proponent to extreme individualism: only I, as the real moral agent or as the ethical alliance or as the representative of the universal, can understand what morality demands. Moral egoism easily leads to arrogance, and universalism to imperialism: if there is one moral truth, which it is incumbent upon its agents to impose on others, there remain many errors. What started as rebellion against the absurdities of localism ends up legitimising oppression and domination.

Cultural relativism and communitarianism are potentially even more murderous, because they have privileged access to community and neighbourhood, the places where people are killed and tortured. Relativists start from the obvious observation that values are context bound, and use it to justify atrocities against those who disagree with the oppressiveness of tradition. But the cultural embeddedness of self is an unhelpful sociological truism; the context, as history, tradition and culture, is malleable – always under construction rather than given and unchanging. History does not teach anything; it is historians and journalists, intellectuals and politicians, academics and ideologues who turn historical events into stories and myths and, in so doing, construct ways of seeing the present through the lens of the past.

Kosovo and Rwanda are good example of this process. It was only after Milosevic withdrew Kosovo's autonomy in 1994 and declared that it would remain forever in the Yugoslav state, as the cradle of the Serb nation, that Serb oppression started and the Kosovo Liberation Army became active. The fratricidal nationalism which took hold of the two communities was created and fanned by the respective power holders. This process was even more evident in Rwanda. The genocide there was committed not by monsters but by ordinary people who were coaxed, threatened and deceived by bureaucrats, the military, politicians, the media, intellectuals, academics and artists into believing that killing was necessary to avoid their own extermination at the hands of their victims. The tribal rivalry between the Hutu and Tutsi was redefined, fanned and exaggerated to such a point that the "action" eventually became inevitable.

In Kosovo, Serbs massacred in the name of threatened community, while the Allies bombed in the name of threatened humanity. Both principles, when they become absolute essences and define the meaning and value of culture without remainder or exception, can find everything that resists them expendable. Both positions exemplify, perhaps in different ways, the contemporary metaphysical urge: each side has made an axiomatic decision as to what constitutes the essence of humanity and follows it, like all metaphysical determinations, with a stubborn disregard of opposing strategies or arguments. They both claim to have the answer to the question "What is human value?" and to its premise "What is (a) human?," and both take their answers to be absolute and irrefutable. Universalism then becomes an aggressive essentialism, which has globalised nationalism and has turned the assertiveness of nations into a world system. Community, on the other hand, is the condition of human existence, but communitarianism can become even more stifling. When the supposed opponents become convinced about their truth and the immorality of their demonised opponents, they can easily move from moral dispute to killing. At that point, all differences disappear. From the position of the victim, the bullet and the "smart" bomb kill equally, even if the former travels only a few yards from the gun of the ethnically proud soldier, while the latter covers a huge distance from the aircraft of the humanitarian bomber.

The individualism of universal principles forgets that every person is a world and comes into existence in common with others; that we are all in community. Being in common is an integral part of being self: self is exposed to the other, it is posed in exteriority, and the other is part of the intimacy of self. "[M]y face [is] always exposed to others, always turned toward an other and faced by him or her, never facing myself."[21] Being in community with others is the opposite of common being or of belonging to an essential community. Most communitarians, on the other hand, define community through the commonality of tradition, history and culture; the various past crystallisations, the inescapable weight of which determines present possibilities. The essence of the communitarian community is often to compel or "allow" people to find their "essence"; its success is measured by its contribution to the accomplishment of a common "humanity." But this immanence of self to itself is nothing other than the pressure to be what the spirit of the nation or of the people or the leader demands, or to follow traditional values and exclude what is alien and other. This type of communitarianism destroys community in a delirium of incarnated communion. A solid and unforgiving essence, be it that of nation, class, tribe or community, turns the subjectivity of man into totality. It completes subjectivity's self-assertion, which refuses to yield. Community, as communion, accepts human rights only to the extent that they help submerge the "I" into the "we" all the way till death, the point of absolute communion. As the French philosopher Jean-Luc Nancy puts it, this attitude is catastrophic because "it assigns to community a *common being*, whereas community is a matter of something quite different, namely, of existence inasmuch as it is *in* common, but without letting itself be absorbed into a common substance."[22]

Both universal morality and cultural identity express different aspects of human experience. Their comparison in the abstract is futile and the differences between the two are not pronounced. When a state adopts "universal" human rights, it will interpret and apply them, if at all, according to local legal procedures and moral principles, making the universal the handmaiden of the particular. The reverse is also true: even those legal systems which jealously guard traditional rights and cultural practices against the encroachment of the universal are already contaminated by it. All rights and principles, even if parochial in their content, share the universalising impetus of their form. In this sense, rights carry the seed of dissolution of community and the only defence is to resist the idea of right altogether – something impossible in the global capitalist world. Developing states that import Hollywood films, Big Macs and the Internet also import human rights willy-nilly. The claims of universality and tradition, rather than standing opposed in mortal combat, have become uneasy allies, the fragile liaison of which has been sanctioned by the World Bank.

What are the stakes in the debate? Postmodern mass societies and the globalisation of economics, politics and communications increase existential anxiety and create unprecedented uncertainty and insecurity about life prospects. In this climate, the desire for simple life instructions and legal and moral codes, with clearly defined rights and duties, becomes paramount. Codification transfers the responsibility of deciding ethically to legislators and moralists, to false prophets and fake tribes. In an over-legalised world, rules and norms discourage people from thinking independently and discovering their own relation to themselves, others, language and history. The proliferation of human rights treaties and the mushrooming of legal regulation are part of the same process, which aims to relieve the burden of ethical life and the anxiety, or – in Heidegger's terms – the "homelessness" of postmodern humanity. International human rights law promises to set all that is valuably human on paper and hold it before us in triumph: the world picture of humanity will have been finally drawn, and everyone will be free to follow his or her essence as defined by world governments and realised by technologies that will dismember and reassemble the prosthetic human.

VII. Identity and desire

The twin aims of the Enlightenment were emancipation and self-realisation; domination and oppression the two evils it attacked. The struggle against tyranny and dictatorship is still the first priority in many parts of the world. But in Western, postmodern societies, self-realisation and self-fulfilment have become central aspirations of self and polity. In a society in which every desire is a potential right, it is forbidden to forbid.

Self-realisation is a process of shaping the self, an aesthetic poiesis and care, which can be carried out only in relations with others and within a community. Other people, groups, and the law are aspects of our identity, the supports and constraints of our radical openness to the world. Being is being together, being with others. Human rights acknowledge the radical intersubjectivity of human identity, they involve the Other and the law in the construction of self. The Hegelian tradition explains how rights are involved in the struggle for recognition, and psychoanalysis adds that such recognition passes through the desire of the Other, as symbolic order or as other person.[23] The desire for integrity projects the Other as non-lacking, but this gesture misfires: the Other is as lacking as self. Let us examine this dialectic of lack as expressed in rights.

A right-claim involves two demands addressed to the other: a specific request in relation to one aspect of the claimant's personality or status (to be left alone, not to suffer in one's bodily integrity, to be treated equally), but, second, a much wider demand to have one's whole identity recognised in its specific characteristics. In demanding recognition and love from the other person we also ask the Big Other, the symbolic order represented by the law, to recognise us in our identity through the other. When a person of colour claims, for example, that the rejection of a job application amounted to a denial of her human right to non-discrimination, she makes two related but relatively independent claims: that the rejection amounts both to an unfair denial of the applicant's need for a job but also to the denigration of her wider identity with its integral racial component. Every right therefore links a need of a part of the body or personality with what exceeds need, the desire that the claimant be recognised and loved as a whole and complete person.

But the attainment of identity through the desire and recognition of the other fails in different ways, even in those cases in which human rights are successful on the surface and succeed in legalising desire. The subject of rights tries incessantly to find in the desire of the other the missing object that will fill her lack and turn her into a whole being. But this object does not exist and cannot be possessed. The impossibility of fulfilling desire leads into ever-increasing demands for recognition, and every acknowledgement of right leads to a spiralling escalation of further claims. In this sense, the promise of self-realisation becomes the impossible demand to be recognised by others as non-lacking, and so too all human rights become expressions of the unattainable "right to be loved." Right-claims proliferate because legalised desire is insatiable. It looks as though the more rights and recognition we get, the more "in the deepest recesses of one's egocentric fortress a voice softly but tirelessly repeats 'our walls are made of plastic, our acropolis of papier-mâché.'"[24]

But the progressive legalisation of existence, in which many aspects of life become rights, keeps undermining the unity of self. Human rights break down the body into functions and parts and replace its unity with rights, which symbolically compensate for the denied and barred bodily wholeness. Encountering rights nihilates and dismembers the body: the right to privacy isolates the genital area and creates a "zone of privacy" around it; the mouth is severed and reappears "metonymised" as free speech which protects its communicative, but not its eating, function. Free movement does the same with legs and feet, which are allowed to move in public spaces while the whole person is not given a right of abode.[25] Similarly, the debate over abortion places the woman's body in the hands and imaginings of others who deny her coherence by separating her womb from her self. In the process of constructing legal subjects and of making humans, rights split and rebind body and self in a way analogous to the technological – whether biological, genetic or cybernetic – manipulation of bodies and selves.

But each new and specialised right, the right to same-sex marriage, for example, exposes the artificiality of the ego by increasingly colonising its intimate parts. New rights remove activities and relations from their communal habitat and make them calculable, exchangeable, cheap. While rights are a compensation for the lack of wholeness, the more rights I get, the more I need to claim, and, paradoxically, the greater the sense of disjunction of self. Rights are self-devouring; the "rights culture" turns everything into a legal claim and leaves nothing to its "natural" integrity. Desire and fear increasingly dominate all relationships and the action of community changes from being-in-common into beings attacking others and defending themselves. There is a great paradox at the heart of rights culture. The more rights I have, the smaller my protection from harms; the more rights I have, the greater my desire for even more but the weaker the pleasure they offer.

In our global world of rights, subjects – following their desire – fight for more and more effective rights, political power comes under increasing pressure to acknowledge and codify them, and their protection has become the mark of the civility of a society. But the success will always be limited, since no right can earn me the full recognition and love of the other and no bill of rights can complete the struggle for a just society. Indeed, the more rights we introduce, the greater the pressure to legislate for more, to enforce them better, to turn the person into an infinite collector of rights and humanity into an endlessly proliferating mosaic of laws.

We can conclude that the positivisation and globalisation of human rights marks the end of political modernity in the same way that a globalised economy marks the end of Leviathan. Their triumph is the recognition of the lack that constitutes human identity. Desire is moved by lack, by the desire and fear of the other. The sovereign and human rights are the twin causes and objects of legalised desire. The sovereign, built on the principle of unlimited individual desire, but assuming the mantle of the party, the class or the nation, can turn its desire into murderous rage and the denial of all right.

The globalisation of the principle of sovereignty and the aggressive legitimation of state power by reference to morality and human rights leave no one and nothing untouched. Human rights have become the *raison d'être* of the state system as its main constituents are challenged by economic, social and cultural trends. It is no coincidence that human rights "triumphed" at a point of maximum angst about life chances and malaise about the collapse of moral certitudes and political blueprints. The enormous potential for diversity released by the demise of communism was accompanied by an unprecedented desire for unity and order. If modernity created the moral panic, in postmodernity it is moral to panic. Its signs are apparent all over the Western world: as despair about the loss of state authority, national virility and parental – specifically paternal and male – power; as grave concern about the increase of broken and non-standard families, of "scroungers" and "welfare mothers"; as hatred of "bogus" refugees and criminal children, muggers and corrupt policemen; as fear about nationalist warlords, ex-communist mafias and juvenile thugs; or as millenarian angst, identity crisis and *fin de siècle* blues.

As institutional practice, human rights often express the imagination of the one and homogeneous world society, in which the extension of formal equality and negative freedom and the globalisation of Western capitalism and consumerism will equate society with its "ideal" picture drawn by governments and international law experts. Individually, they are the mechanism for shaping identity and life according to the dictates of the desire of the other and the trauma of a lacking self. Human rights are fissured; they both offer limited protection against the society of desire, against the threatening state and the fearsome other, but they also express the way in which identity is arranged in shifting relations of fear and affection and care towards the other. There is no guarantee that affection will win over fear. Experience tells us, however, that when the fear of the other – the foreigner, the Jew, the refugee – wins out, human rights lose all protective value against the state. An alternative, already visible in the politically liberal part of our globalised world, is that the devouring potential of fearsome desire in its legal form will go on colonising the social world. The final outcome will be the fracturing of community and of the social bond into a monadology, in which some people will be able to assert their final and absolute sovereignty, while others will be reduced to the status of the perpetually oppressed underclass. But a fully sovereign individual is a delusionary and rather farcical simulacrum of Leviathan. In both instances, positivised human rights and legalised desire – based on the fear of the other – coincide, and their world- and self-creating potential are extinguished. Human rights, rather than being the ideology of the end, are the postmodern *pharmakon*, the disease of an all-devouring desire (of the sovereign or the individual) and its partial cure when the old sovereign or the new order becomes delirious.

VIII. A postmodern principle of justice?

Rights exist only in relation to other rights; right-claims involve the acknowledgement of others and their rights and of trans-social networks of mutual recognition and arrangement. There can be no freestanding, absolute right, because such a right would violate the freedom of everyone except its bearer. There can be no positive right, because rights are always relational and involve their subjects in relations of dependence on others and responsibility to the law. Rights are a formal recognition of the fact that before my (legal) subjectivity always and already has come another. Linked with that is the recognition that human rights have the ability to create new worlds by continuously pushing and expanding the boundaries of society, identity and law. They continually transfer their claims to new domains, fields of activity and types of (legal) subjectivity; they ceaselessly construct new meanings and values; and they bestow dignity and protection to novel subjects, situations and people. Human rights come to institutional existence in their performative declaration, which declares what it creates and creates the ground upon which it stands. A human rights society turns this experience into a main principle of organisation and legitimation. Human rights are the recognition of the world-making power of groundlessness which turns the experience of ontological freedom into a principle of law and politics.

Human rights do not "belong" only to the citizens of states which explicitly, even if ineffectively, recognise them. After their ideological and rhetorical triumph, postmodern human rights define the fluid relation between power blocs and the contested identities of individuals and groups. In a strange, almost metaphysical, way human rights "exist," even when they have not been legislated. When the American civil rights activists asserted the right to equality, when torture victims all over the world claim the right to be free in their bodily integrity, when gays and lesbians in homophobic cultures proclaim the dignity of their identity, or when an abandoned lover demands his "right to love," they acted, or are acting, strictly within the human rights tradition, even though no such legal rights existed, or currently exist, or would have been or are likely to be accepted. The protester, the rebel, the melancholic lover or the new age traveller belong to a long and honourable lineage; the eighteenth-century revolutionaries, the nineteenth-century political reformers and the twentieth-century economic, social and cultural protesters share the common determination to proclaim and thus to bring into being new types of entitlements against received wisdom and the law. The absence of legislative approval, often the legislator's opposition to the new claims, is their structural characteristic. In this sense, human rights have a certain independence from the context of their appearance. Legal procedures, political traditions and historical contingencies may be part of their constitution, but human rights retain a critical distance from law and stretch its boundaries and limits. Indeed, their rhetorical nature, proclamatory enunciation and regular defiance of state law are aspects of their ability to transcend and redefine their contextual boundaries. Legal and social contexts are part of the definition of concrete rights, but it is also in the "essence" of right to suspend any reference to the vagaries of time and the exigencies of place.

The persistence of the gap between humanity and (legal) rights or between the utopian moment in human rights and law indicates that their force and rebelliousness may be related to a metaphysical or redemptive urge which lay dormant, but which has acquired renewed significance in postmodernity. Following the end of the most atrocious century, it is too late in history to return to the concepts of human nature and free will of classical liberalism. The universalism of rights and the historicism of cultural relativism share with Western philosophy and ethics a common characteristic: they reduce the distance between self and other and return the different to the same. As Heidegger argued, philosophy has put the meaning of Being at the centre of its concerns since classical Greece and has claimed that the question of Being is governed by the protocols of reason. Universal logos reflects and reveals the structure of reality since the ontological realm follows the demands of theoretical necessity. The traces of this ontological totalitarianism litter the body of philosophy. In its modern version, individual consciousness has become the starting point of all knowledge and, as a result, what differs from the self-same has been turned into a cognitive question, into the exploration of the conditions under which the other's existence can be known; this way, the other becomes my knowledge of the other. The Cartesian and Kantian subject constituted the other and the world, according to the subject's own schemata and categories without which, they claimed, the other cannot be reached. Hegel's struggle for recognition assumed that a symmetrical reciprocity exists between the two parties, and posited the end of dialectics as the moment when the same becomes the synthesis of the same and the different.[26] But the unique other cannot be sublated; otherness is not just a moment in the dialectic of the same and the different, but the moment of transcendence of the system. For phenomenology, again, the ego acquires knowledge through the intentionality of consciousness and its adequation with the phenomenal world. Husserl asserted the primacy of self-perception and claimed that the world discloses itself fully to consciousness.[27] As Manfred Frank put it, "[the] Being that stands across from me in the circle of reflection is *my* Being" which has been mistaken for Being as such.[28]

In the universal community of reason, which acts as the horizon for the realisation of the law, the other – the alien, the third and unrepresentable – is turned into the same, the critical distance between self and other is reduced and the experience of value of moral conscience is grounded solely on the representation of the other by the knowing and willing ego. The alternative is the other's exclusion, banning or forgetting. But the other who approaches me is singular and unique; she cannot be reduced to being solely an instance of the universal concept of the ego, nor can she be subsumed as a case or example under a general rule or norm. The law of modernity based on the self's right and the subject's empire is strangely immoral as it tries to assimilate and exclude the other. The other side of the universal legal subject, of equality and autonomy, of law's formalism and its imperative, is the necessary inequality and the lack of autonomy of the alien and the enemy of the nation. The discourse of universality is necessarily a white mythology: the enthronement of free will as the principle of universal legislation is achieved only through the exclusion, disfranchisement and subjection, without free subjectivity, of the other. Communitarianism and cultural relativism, on the other hand, can often become "mythologies of colour," local – and usually much more aggressive – reflections of the exclusions of universalism. The essentialism of individualism, universal rights and the power of "reason" are not far removed from the essentialism of community, the localism of duties and the power of tradition and the past.

And yet it is arguable that a metaphysical residue can be detected in the long history of natural law and can still be traced in popular attitudes to human rights. The continuous flight of meaning, which creates ever-new rights, could perhaps be anchored on an ethics; the groundlessness and world-making power of freedom on a moral foundation. If my right has meaning only in relation to another, whose action or entitlement are presupposed in the recognition or exercise of my right, the right of the other always and already precedes mine. The (right of the) other comes first; before my right and before my identity as organised by rights, comes my obligation, my radical turn towards the claim to respect the dignity of the other. The non-essential essence of human rights, the fleeting universal involved in all particular right-claims, could be the recognition of the priority of the other person whose existence before mine makes me ethically bound and opens to me the domain of language, intersubjectivity and right.[29] This other can be neither the universal "man" of liberalism nor the abstract and formalistic "subject" of law. The other is always a unique, singular person who has place and time, gender and history, needs and desires. If there is something truly "universal" in the discourse of human rights, if a metaphysical trait survives their deconstruction, this could perhaps be the recognition of the absolute uniqueness of the other person and of my moral duty to save and protect her. This unique other, this transcendence in historical immanence, opens the prospect of a postmodern principle of justice.

Notes

1 *Fayed* v. *UK* (1994) 18 EHRR 393; *Saunders* v. *UK* (1997) 23 EHRR 242; *The Former King Constantine of Greece* v. *Greece*, Appl. 25701/94.
2 See generally Francis Fukuyama, *The End of History and the Last Man* (London: Penguin, 1992).
3 Despite the enormous number of books on human rights, the jurisprudence of rights is dominated by neo-Kantian liberals. There are a few notable exceptions: Rolando Gaete, *Human Rights and the Limits of Critical Reason* (Aldershot: Dartmouth,

1993); Michel Villey, *Le Droit et les droits de l'homme* (Paris: PUF, 1983); Bernard Bourgeois, *Philosophie et droits de l'homme: De Kant à Marx* (Paris: PUF, 1990); and Tony Evans (ed.), *Human Rights: Fifty Years On* (Manchester: Manchester UP, 1998). See also Costas Douzinas, *The End of Human Rights* (Oxford: Hart, 2000) and *Human Rights and Empire* (London: Reaktion, 2007).

4 Gabriel Marcel, *Creative Fidelity* (New York: Farrar, 1964) 94.

5 For a background discussion on this point, see generally Costas Douzinas and Ronnie Warrington, *Justice Miscarried* (London: Harvester, 1994) 133–7 and Costas Douzinas and Adam Gearey (Oxford: Hart, 2005) chapters 3 and 4.

6 Leo Strauss, *Natural Law and History* (Chicago: U of Chicago P, 1965) 92.

7 *Declaration of the Rights of Man and Citizen* (1789) [trans. of *Déclaration des droits de l'homme et du citoyen*].

8 Ibid.

9 Jean-François Lyotard, *The Differend*, trans. Georges Van Den Abbeele (Manchester: Manchester UP, 1998) 147 [trans. of *Le Différend*].

10 The USA has declined to become a party to the International Criminal Court and has continued to proclaim its opposition to the new court: see, for example, Marc Grossman, *American Foreign Policy and the International Criminal Court* (2002), US Department of State, available <http://www.state.gov/p/9949pf.htm>, 23 July 2002.

11 That pressure has seen the introduction of the Human Rights Act 1998 (UK) which came into force on 2 October 2000. That Act essentially incorporates into UK law the European Convention for the Protection of Human Rights and Fundamental Freedoms.

12 Hannah Arendt, *The Origins of Totalitarianism* (San Diego: Harvest, 1958) 299.

13 Costas Douzinas and Ronnie Warrington, *Justice Miscarried* 132–85.

14 This includes amongst others the extradition and trial of Slobodan Milosevic, the trials of Saddam Hussein and Charles Taylor and the attempted prosecutions of Augusto Pinochet in Spain and Ariel Sharon in Belgium.

15 The Rome Statute of the International Criminal Court which entered into force on 1 July 2002.

16 "Bush Says No to POW Status for Detainees" (2002), CNN.com, available <http://www.cnn.com/2002/US/01/28/ret.wh.detainees/>, 23 July 2002.

17 Erudition and training in morals and the arts.

18 See Louis Althusser, *For Marx*, trans. Ben Brewster (London: Lane, 1969) 228 [trans. of *Pour Marx*]:

> If the essence of man is to be a universal attribute, it is essential that *concrete subjects* exist as absolute givens; this implies an empiricism of the subject. If these empirical individuals are to be men, it is essential that each carries in himself the whole human essence, if not in fact, at least in principle; this implies an idealism of the *essence*. So empiricism of the subject implies idealism of the essence and vice versa. (Emphasis in original)

19 For a use of the psychoanalytic concept of "overdetermination" in political theory, see Ernesto Laclau and Chantal Mouffe, *Hegemony and Socialist Strategy: Towards a Radical Democratic Politics*, trans. Winston Moore and Paul Cammack (London: Verso, 1985) 97–105.

20 The seminal text is Jacques Lacan, "The Mirror Stage as Formative of the Function of the *I* as Revealed in Psychoanalytic Experience" in Jacques Lacan, *Écrits: A Selection*, trans. Alan Sheridan (London: Routledge, 2001) 1.

21 Jean-Luc Nancy, *The Inoperative Community*, ed. Peter Connor, trans. Peter Connor

et al. (Minneapolis: U of Minnesota P, 1991) xxxvii–xxxviii [trans. of *La Communauté désœuvrée*].

22 Ibid. xxxviii; emphasis in original.

23 See generally Douzinas, *The End of Human Rights* 297–318.

24 Cornelius Castoriadis, "Reflections on Racism," *Thesis Eleven* 32 (1992): 9.

25 William MacNeil, "Law's *Corpus Delicti*: The Fantasmatic Body of Rights Discourse," *Law & Critique* 9 (1998): 45–46. "While freedom of movement and security of the person are treated as crucial civil liberties, no major human rights convention, including the European, creates a general right of residence. Some include no such right at all. Others restrict it to state nationals" (Douzinas, *The End of Human Rights* 322).

26 See generally Douzinas, *The End of Human Rights* 263–96.

27 Douzinas and Warrington, *Justice Miscarried* 161.

28 Manfred Frank, *What is Neostructuralism?*, trans. Sabine Wilke and Richard Gray (Minneapolis: U of Minnesota P, 1989) 297 [trans. of *Was ist Neostrukturalismus?*]; emphasis in original.

29 See generally Emmanuel Levinas, "The Rights of Man and the Rights of the Other" in Emmanuel Levinas, *Outside the Subject*, trans. M. Smith (London: Athlone, 1993) 116; Costas Douzinas, "Human Rights and Postmodern Utopia," *Law & Critique* 11 (2000): 219.

jane flax

SUBJECTIVITY, ETHICS, POLITICS: LEARNING TO LIVE WITHOUT THE SUBJECT

I share the opinion of many that the label "postmodern" is problematic, lumping together often conflicting theorists and practices. Inasmuch as it has any meaning, I still think its sense is best approached by reference to a particular conjuncture of social-historical events and the responses of some Europeans and later some Americans to them. As I argued in *Thinking Fragments* (Flax 1990) these include the Holocaust, the end of colonialism, Hiroshima, the Gulag, and the emergence of new forms of political activity and resistance, especially those of the 1960s, and the Vietnam War. These events undermined the grip of certain Western beliefs including that reason, emancipation, science, truth, progress, and central-ized, legal-constitutional politics are necessarily linked. Instead, a profound skepticism emerged among some Westerners concerning the dominant (pre-Second World War) narrative regarding the meanings of and connec-tions between these terms. Furthermore, the discovery of the Gulag and the death toll of purges in socialist states considerably dimmed the attrac-tion for those on the left of centralized revolutionary communist parties as an instrument of liberation. These events plus the rebellion of women and people of color evoked an identity crisis among some Westerners, that is, some white men. Inasmuch as certain modes of white, heterosexual mascu-linity constituted the dominant normative practices of subjectivity, various legitimacy crises emerged: of subjectivity, politics, and knowledge. Those referred to as postmodernist bear a family resemblance in their attitudes to these events, bearing no nostalgia for the past and seeing the spaces that (briefly) emerged as opportunities to create more playful, interesting, experimental and open-ended practices.

For me, one of the most generative and enduring legacies of this dispa-rate variety of thinking gathered under the rubric of "postmodernism" is a profound shift in the constituting assumptions and limiting conditions of discourses about subjectivity. In my ongoing attempts to think about subjectivity, I find Michel Foucault's work, particularly his last essays, endlessly provocative. (Since it is a violation of his often stated dislike of categorization and this label in particular, I apologize in advance to his spirit for incorporating his work in this way.) His approach is so outside a paradigm prevalent in Western philosophy and psychology that it is difficult to fully appreciate and make use of its radical departures and rich possibilities. Foundational assumptions of this paradigm include that intrinsic to humans is a self and that this self is the locus and cause of our identity. Further, it is assumed that each self possesses and is constituted by an essence or substance and that this essence is best understood in terms of interiority, that is, something that occupies and *is* us deep inside.

On the contrary, Foucault claims that the subject "is not a substance. It is a form, and this form is not primarily or always identical to itself" (Foucault 1997e, 290). Unpacking this statement is neither simple nor easy. In making this claim, Foucault does not offer an alternative account of the self. Rather, as he rejects the idea that it is a substance amenable to more or less adequate accounts, he abandons the entire framework in which the issue is intelligible. He shifts discourse from investigations into the self's true nature to subjectivity. In doing so, he moves outside two positions dominant within existing discourses concerning the self; he is neither an essentialist nor a social constructionist. While his emphasis on socially situated practices might overlap with social constructionist ideas, Foucault pursues a radically different trajectory. He does not assume that a coherent, stable inside is eventually constructed from social relations. Inside/outside is not a relevant binary in his discourse. Rather, for him, no one thing is being constructed; subjectivity is a dynamic process, more a complex network of often conflicting forces, demands and resistance with multiple lines and forms of explanation. For him, no privileged sites of subjective formation can be assumed, and the subject is neither a dependent effect of determinant causes or social relations nor an undetermined autonomous actor.

Furthermore, the locus of his investigations is different; he focuses neither on macro-levels of social structures nor micro-levels of individual subjects. Subjectivities are effects of historically contingent and specific practices; hence, analyzing them requires genealogies of their constituting practices. To grasp his notion of practice, we must sidestep the binaries of thought/action and structure (objective)/experience (subjective). Practices are forms of activity inhabited by thought. Thought is broadly conceived as

> every manner of speaking, doing, or behaving in which the individual appears as a knowing subject, as ethical or juridical subject, as subject conscious of himself

75

and others ... thought is understood as ... action insofar as it implies the play of true and false, the acceptance or refusal of rules, the relation to oneself and others. (Foucault 1997a, 201)

While bounded and historically specific, these practices are not invariant or deterministic structures. As subjects practice the practices that constitute them, both subjects and practices mutate. Only in his last works does this path fully open up. In them, Foucault radically rethinks subjectivity and his previous ideas about power and political action. Central to this rethinking is his elaboration of practices he calls "technologies of the self." Technologies of the self, while related to and potentially shaped by biopower, are not its derivative effects. In exploring them, new possibilities of exercising freedom and creativity emerge. It is puzzling to me that more scholars do not attend to this turn in Foucault's thinking; they often seem fixated on his earlier, less complex writings on power and reiterate criticisms based on these partial readings. I certainly do not mean to suggest that his writings are or ought to be immune from criticism. The absence within them of any sustained consideration of practices of race-ing, gendering and postcoloniality is particularly unacceptable (Stoler 1995). However, so far I have found his later work productive for my own thinking about these practices; their flaws have not yet caused me to abandon them (Flax 1998). Furthermore, despite its many imperfections, in the current conditions of global politics, avoidance or simplistic dismissal of Foucault's work is particularly unfortunate. The intimate and apparently necessary relations between identity politics and violence are viciously evident. The need to resist claims framed in terms of pure identities and teleological destiny is palpable. Contrary to a frequent criticism – that the only politics congruent with postmodernism is "identity politics" or nihilism – these essays are powerful critiques of the foundational assumptions of such practices. Instead, Foucault begins to explore exciting new approaches to politics and ethics congruent with his practice approach to subjectivity and his rethinking of power.

In grappling with his last essays, dissatisfaction with my own various attempts at revisioning subjectivity crystallized. Attempting to enter his universe highlighted some of the inadequacies of my own. In the past, I have developed critiques of deep-inside notions of subjectivity by displacing narratives of innate substance with social constructionist ones. I have also argued for complicating notions of subjectivity by thinking of it as a verb (a set of processes) rather than as a noun (a substance). I have attempted to replace unitary pictures of subjectivity with those characterized by multiplicity, conflict and ambiguity, and treated images of a unitary deep inside as symptoms of various unconscious wishes and political positioning (Flax 1996). However, I now believe that these resistant efforts are insufficient and like any resistance also replicate much of what one seeks to resist.

What remains too undisturbed in my own previous work is the belief that subjectivity *is* a substance, albeit a more complex and transmuting one than the advocates of a deep inside allow. I now think this underlying premise itself – that subjectivity is a substance amenable to more or less adequate accounts – must be refused.

While one can articulate specific objections to particular claims, I do not think it is possible to disprove an entire paradigm. Substantive approaches to subjectivity, like practice ones, operate within and are produced by delimited discursive worlds. I can only give an account of a perhaps idiosyncratic "Foucault effect," recounting some consequences of attempting to reorient my own discourse toward imagining subjectivities as practices. For me a crucial payoff of this approach to subjectivity is that it facilitates a parallel shift I have been attempting in the fields of politics and justice. While some are highly critical (e.g. Nussbaum 2001), other writers, including Wendy Brown (2001), are pursuing a similar trajectory. This shift entails reconceiving the problems and practices of justice through an object-oriented rather than subject-oriented focus. In other words, inquiry and activity center not around questions of identity (who are we and what do we require to be or remain us?) but action (what could be done and what are its consequences?). Arguments for and justification of actions require consideration of their qualities and effects as processes and accounts of their (always imperfectly known and unpredictable) outcomes. Criteria for evaluation might include aesthetic or hedonistic ones or whether actions potentially enlarge or constrain the range of available practices and practitioners, but ontological or teleological claims about fostering development of an individual or collective deep inside would be irrelevant. In what follows, I will provide a sketchy account of some practices constituting contemporary Western subjectivities. I will then outline some paths that open up in regard to rethinking politics and ethics. This rethinking is tentative and needs a lot of work, but for both political and theoretical reasons, I think it is worth pursuing.

I. Practicing subjectivities

A complex political/psychological discourse accompanies substantive approaches to subjectivity. Inherent to its discourse is a distinct truth game (Foucault 1997e, 295–7). Inquiry proceeds along several lines, addressing the universal, the particular and the political. The truth game generates puzzles requiring consideration, including: how do we know what this deep self is in general; what is its substance and do all humans share some (or all) of its constituting elements? What elements of its constitution are variable and what forces cause this variability? Is this general account exhaustive of the field of subjectivity? If not, how can the subject and others recognize what is particular or unique? Normative, political and diagnostic considerations overlap. How can we distinguish between a pathological and an innovative subjective formation? What social practices and institutions are required to support the deep self's unfolding? Under what conditions (and how) are these intersubjective forces accountable for individual subjects' failures to reach full development? Conversely, to what extent can intersubjective formations hold individual subjects responsible for such failures? What is the responsibility of the individual subject to its own constitution and potential and for deploying it in its intersubjective contexts?

A practice approach specifies a different question – "how is it?". "How is it?" requires a genealogy that unpacks at least three kinds of practices: the practices constituting subjects, those that facilitate continuing to practice those practices, and those that sustain their appearance of being. The prior practices constituting subjects, those that presently constitute them, those facilitating practicing their practices and those that sustain their appearance of being are not necessarily the same. Furthermore, all subjective practices interact in wider fields. How and with what they interact is constantly open to change. This may affect the subjective constellation in unpredictable ways. Since subjective time is not linear, old practices may recur.

When we turn our attention to practices, the focus shifts to the generation, enactment, and reformation of subjectivities through networks of narrative, action, embodiment, fantasy, and power. Modern Western narratives about the substantive subject reverse the relations between rationality, autonomy, authority, freedom and power. The supposedly solid agents substance theorists argue subjects require to attain and exercise political efficacy engage in a set of practices, including constructing stories about their subjective formation. Intrinsic to this narrative is that certain subjects possess a stable identity and that the freedom, authority and autonomy of this self generate its actions. History (at least the good parts) is its biography. (The generation of evil or sin belongs elsewhere.) Despite these claims, practices within asymmetric relations of power enable this mode of subjectivity. Such subjects can sustain a certain appearance of being because they practice, invent and re-enact certain subjectivities and relations of power, not because they exercise an innate capacity for agency grounded in an undetermined identity. Agency is an effect of certain practices not a manifestation of the deep self's freedom. Among others, the *appearance* of stability, autonomy and identity is generated and sustained by practices of domination, denial of contingency and will, and projection of determination onto marked subjects. This practice of identity entails control over the normative regulation of subjectivity and the exclusion of aspects that would disrupt its own subjective representation. Its practice of assigning determining substances such as race or gender to marked others allows the autonomous subject to be "free." Practices such as race-ing and gendering are projected outward or denied. Unlike autonomous subjects, the others this generates are embodied, historically situated, raced and gendered (duCille 1994; Mama 1995).

Instead of the immanent unfolding of the subject's autonomy, I prefer thinking about subjectivity through metaphors of travel and diaspora. As Bonnie Honig illuminates, diasporian histories point to the constituting effects on modern subjectivities of exile, relocation, displacement. Paul Gilroy (1993) suggests rethinking modernity via the history of the Black Atlantic, a "webbed network, between the local and the global" (45). Rejecting binaries of Africa/Europe or white/black, Gilroy substitutes incessant travel, the Middle Passage, and practices of movement, mediation, and domination for roots and rootedness. The web is woven via ships and the slave trade between Africa, the Caribbean, Europe and the Americas. The African diaspora into the Western hemisphere is thus an initiating force within Euro-American histories and subjective constellations, and the practice of slavery is one of the constituting elements in all diasporian subjectivities. Various mutually constituting practices generate the subjects of this history: master/slave, normal/deviant, male/female, adult/child, etc. Each dyadic formation and the interactions between dyadic formations shape patterns of freedom, of race and gender, of sexuality, of citizenship and law, and the resulting conventions continue to facilitate contemporary Western and postcolonial practices of subjectivity (Morrison 1992; Mama 1995).

To subscribe to an idealized subjective representation enabled by these practices – the autonomous self – therefore is problematic, especially for subjects who are also committed to practices of justice or equality. It is not a simple matter of "tainted" origins, for there is no necessary relation between the practices that generate a subjective constellation and those required to sustain it. However, in this case, it appears that to sustain its self-representation, the autonomous subject must practice splitting and displacement (Cheng 2001). Perhaps engaging in practices of domination is not necessary to sustain such a subjective representation, although I cannot imagine this. Would subjects with full access to existing practices of freedom willingly remain the exclusive possessors of that which others despise and experience as constraint?

II. The technologies of the self: agency as practice

Thus, autonomy, paradoxically from the substantive point of view, is an effect of particular practices or technologies of the self. Contrary to frequent claims, Foucault does not deny agency but rather relocates its sites of production. He refers to subjects, not persons, of processes of subjectification, not identity. Subject connotes the double sense of actor and acted upon, not as separate aspects of our being but as mutually constituting and contemporaneous processes. These processes simultaneously enable and constrain, empower and subjectify. It is easy to misunderstand what Foucault means by subjectification. Modernist narratives of the autonomous self create a binary: subject/object. If we are not self-generating subjects then we are mere objects, utterly determined by our circumstances. In constructing a different discourse, Foucault rejects this binary and instead tracks its genealogy. In tracking this genealogy, the practices required to generate such a subject become evident. As Foucault puts it:

> I have tried to get out from the philosophy of the subject, through a genealogy of the modern subject as a historical and cultural reality. One can proceed with this general project in two ways. In dealing with modern theoretical constructions, we are concerned with the subject in general. In this way, I have tried to analyze the theories of the subject as a speaking, living, working being in the seventeenth and eighteenth centuries. One can also deal with the more practical understanding found in those institutions where certain subjects became objects of knowledge and of domination, asylums, prisons, and so on. (Foucault 1997c, 177)

In pursuing this project, Foucault "wished to study those forms of understanding which the subject creates about himself" (ibid.). He originally focused on three techniques or kinds of social practices: those of production, signification or communication, and domination. Technologies of production "permit us to produce, transform, or manipulate things" (Foucault 1997d, 225). Technologies of sign systems "permit us to use signs, meaning, symbols, or signification," and technologies of power "determine the conduct of individuals and submit them to certain ends of domination" (ibid.). Although each technology interacts with every other, each also generates its distinctive correlative subject – the working being etc. Thus, the subject's constitution and its relationship to itself change depending on what it is practicing. For example, how I constitute myself in practicing motherhood differs from how I would in teaching. These various forms of subjectivity are themselves historically constituted. Since mothering practices are historically and socially variable, the practicing of mothering has not always constituted the same forms of subjectivity. The historical contingency of subjective constitution has important political consequences; it means that practices of subjectivity are not fixed or immutable. They can be changed, and hence new relations and practices of subjectivity (within and between subjects) are invented and practiced.

As Foucault's work proceeded, he wrote: "I have been obligated to change my mind on several points" (1997c, 177). In pursuing his project, Foucault discovered a fourth type of technique:

> techniques that permit individuals to effect, by their own means, a certain number of operations on their own bodies, their own souls, their own thoughts, their own conduct, and this in a manner so as to transform themselves, modify themselves, and to attain a certain state of perfection, happiness, purity, supernatural power. (Ibid.)

He calls these "technologies of the self." Foucault insists that while technologies of the self interact with those of domination, they are not themselves technologies of domination. On the contrary, technologies of the self can be practices of freedom, creativity, aesthetics and ethics. Such freedom is not absolute or unaffected by its social context. Any self technology does imply "a set of truth obligations: discovering the truth, being enlightened by truth, telling the truth. All these are considered important either for the constitution of, or the transformation of, the self" (ibid. 177–8). Furthermore, the available technologies of the self are "not something invented by the individual himself. They are models that he finds in his culture and are proposed, suggested, imposed upon him by his culture, his society, and his social group" (Foucault 1997e, 291).

Relations of power are intrinsic to technologies of self, as they are to other forms of subjective constitution. However, Foucault does not equate practices of power with those of domination (ibid. 299). Power relations require freedom. For Foucault, power is relational. These relations exist only among practicing subjects. Power relations are "possible only insofar as the subjects are free" (ibid. 292). It is because there is freedom that relations of power exist. Subjects practicing a relation of power may not be equally situated, but each must have some degree of freedom. In power relations, subjects try to control or alter others' behaviors, and they resist others' efforts to control them. Such attempts would be unnecessary or impossible if others in one's social field were mere objects. In engaging in a practice, however, subjects encounter others who are likewise engaged. Since no practice is uniform, differences produce friction and resistance; subjects tend to insist on their own practices. Furthermore, since these relations exist in different forms and at different levels, any subject's situation will vary depending on the relations in which it is located. I might be quite advantaged in one relation and disadvantaged in another. Thus, resistance is intrinsic to power relations (Foucault 1997b, 167); power relations are "strategic games that subject the power relations they are supposed to guarantee to instability and reversal" (Foucault 1997a, 203). Power relations are also mobile and mutating, so positions within them (and the positions available) can shift. In contrast, a state of domination exists when an "individual or social group succeeds in blocking a field of power relations, immobilizing them and preventing any reversibility of movement by economic, political, or military means" (Foucault 1997e, 283). In practices of domination, the strategic options available within a power relation never succeed in reversing the relations among its practitioners. The power relations are fixed and extremely asymmetrical. It is a game whose rules ensure that only one party can win (ibid. 292).

III. Care of the self: practicing freedom

Technologies of the self are vulnerable to colonization by other technologies including those of government or governmentality. Through techniques of governmentality, relations of domination are often established and maintained. Governmentality for Foucault is a variegated set of policing-type practices exercised through both formal technical-rational networks and non-state surveillance activities. A consequence of this colonization is the displacement of other possible self-technologies. Foucault wishes to resist such colonization through juxtaposing resistant practices of subjectivity; he groups these as "care of the self." To articulate such technologies, he investigates texts by classical Greek and Roman writers. In my view what matters about this investigation is not whether it uncovers the truth or deep meaning of the texts. Foucault does not claim to excavate a pristine point where philosophy went astray or forgot something or to rediscover a principle that should have been our foundation all along. Contact with a philosopher does not revive the old, but can produce something new (Foucault 1997e, 295). Rather, what is important is how Foucault imagines other practices of subjectivity via his encounter with the texts (Nehamas 1998, 157–88).

Foucault argues that in the worlds of classical Greece and Rome care of the self was conceived as a task that one must engage in throughout life. It is an activity, not only a form of contemplation. Care of the self is not a preparation for living; it is a form of living (Foucault 1997f, 96). It is a kind of work with its own methods and objectives. In the modern world there has been "an inversion in the two principles of antiquity, 'Take care of yourself' and 'Know yourself.' In Greco-Roman culture, knowledge of oneself appeared as the consequence of the care of the self. In the modern world, knowledge of oneself constitutes the fundamental principle" (Foucault 1997d, 228). Care of the self "was considered both a duty and a technique, a basic obligation and a set of carefully worked out procedures" (Foucault 1997e, 295). It is also a creative and aesthetic practice in which innovation and consideration of beauty and pleasure are central. The point of this technology was to attempt to "develop and transform oneself, and to attain a certain mode of being" (Foucault 1997e, 282).

Furthermore, in the classical world, knowing oneself did not necessarily mean discovering the deep truth lying within. In some practices truth and the subject are not linked through "uncovering a truth in the subject or … making the soul the place where truth resides, through an essential kinship or an original law, the truth; nor is it a matter of making the soul the object of a true discourse" (Foucault 1997f, 101–02). Rather, knowing oneself required internalizing texts concerning how to care for oneself so that the substance of these teachings is literally incorporated and assimilated as one's own practice (ibid.). Philosophy provides "soul service"; it is a therapeutic practice, dedicated to the care of the soul (ibid. 94). It is less concerned with the question of under what conditions the subject can produce reliable truth and more about how subjects should live. Certain kinds of knowledge are necessary for living well, but such knowledge has multiple sources, many of which do not depend for their production or truth upon a purified foundational subject.

Care for the self is not a narcissistic or solitary practice. Relations with others are intrinsic to this mode of being, for care of oneself is understood as necessary for the proper exercise of citizenship and interpersonal relations. One is obligated to care for the self partially out of our duty to others. Extensive work on the self is required if one's practice of freedom is to take place within a way of being that is beautiful, honorable and worthy of praise (Foucault 1997e, 286). If one does not practice the correct power over oneself, one cannot rule others well or be a good friend, relative, parent or spouse. A tyrant is one who is a slave to his desires and forces others to satisfy them. Furthermore, it is understood that carrying out this task requires an assortment of activities and resources, including relations with other persons, especially friends and teachers (Foucault 1997f, 99). Indeed, Foucault argues that practicing care of the self enabled a rich variety of relations (and hence subjective practices), particularly ones between adult males, for which there is no modern equivalent (ibid.).

IV. Politics and ethics

The political correlative of deep subjectivity is the juridical subject. Just as the subject is the foundation of knowledge in Cartesian epistemology, in modern liberal political theory the juridical subject founds and grounds the state. Juridical subjects exist prior to the state; their modes of subjectivization are not effects of governmentality or historically contingent technologies. They temporarily surrender some of their innate powers; the congealing of these powers in institutions of the subject's creation originates the state. Freedom exists as long as the law conforms to their inner being. Conformity to such law is simply obedience to their own reason or will. This genre of political theorizing is thus an identity theory writ large. Modern liberal political theories reflect and depend upon assumptions about their founding subject to account for the state's existence and legitimacy. These assumptions also provide the standards for normatively evaluating the state's laws and policies.

This political discourse logically gives rise to correlative practices: interest group and contemporary identity politics. The logic of the discourse requires its practitioners to define themselves as split subjects; they possess both a universal and a particular will or desire. Their desire takes the form of unitary "interests" (Hirschman 1997). There is a sovereign abstract "I" that can identify and put forth claims based on these bounded interests; for example, as a mother I am interested in child care; as a patient I am interested in health care. A group is an aggregate of sovereign individuals who share an interest. However, the subject cannot be merely an aggregate of its interests, because then it would lack the neutral substance necessary to ground the universal or articulate universally binding principles. Hence it must also possess an undetermined essence, and its capacity for autonomy and the ability to choose freely among its desires without being determined by them are rooted in and enabled by this substance. Thus the capacity for autonomy requires a deep, undetermined subjectivity. As a desiring subject it possesses its "interests," but in its universal being the subject is not possessed by them. No desire or historically contingent practice constitutes the true subjectivity of the chooser. Furthermore, not only are the subject's desires conceived as extrinsic to its true self but the existence of these "interests" is treated as an unproblematic social fact. Neither the conflict and relations of domination that may produce a felt interest nor the fluid and contradictory aspects of subjects and their practices are acknowledged. Subjects are rational individuals who know what is in their interest; these subjects and their interests are not heterogeneous, mutually determined, uncertain in effect or internally contradictory.

Similarly, contemporary identity politics also adopts a logic of a unitary deep inside. This deep inside is not abstract or universal in the sense of constituting every subject. Instead, it is homogeneous and concretely universal. That is, it is a uniform essence constituting a specific class of subjects. This essence grounds a unique subjectivity and generates its difference from all other subjects. Identity politics requires its practitioners to constitute their being through a particular but definitive quality – sexuality, gender, or race, for example. There is a universal and discoverable truth of this being. Individual subjects speak its truth, and this truth warrants the legitimacy of their claims. The truth also serves as the basis for normative evaluation and ethical practices. So, for example, one can be held accountable for not being "black enough," that is, deviating from the prescriptive practices constituting black subjectivity. In discovering this truth and conforming to it, subjects liberate themselves and institute the possibility of freedom.

In my view subject-centered politics – whether of abstract or concrete identities – is deeply flawed, and, as can be seen all too readily in the contemporary world, extremely dangerous. Resisting domination or inventing more just political practices cannot remain contingent on identity, that is, on the subject finding its Truth and seeking to bring itself and the world into conformity with it. This applies equally to subjects in subordinate or dominant positions. The virtue of the subject also cannot depend on its Truth, and its virtue cannot be the basis for stipulating equality of treatment or respect. Subject-centered politics remains within the problematic genre of (auto-)biography; it rests on a nostalgia for a singular "subject of history." It articulates a yearning for a purposive history in which time is the unfolding of this subject's biography. A desire for a guaranteed happy ending motivates it; however variably it may be specified, whether it is to bring freedom into the world, unfold its innate capacities, serve God's will, die a martyr, etc., the subject's redemptive fate is preordained. However, I remain unconvinced that such a subject or fate exists. Although advocates of various possibilities abound, no decisive argument has persuasively identified a single, unitary Truth of our being – reason, victimization, human capacities, religion, etc. – that can unproblematically ground claims to justice or engender ethical practices. I have not been dissuaded from reading these eschatological stories as expressing the fantasies and dreams of situated, complex subjectivities.

Furthermore, identity-based practices lend themselves too readily to practices of irresponsibility, violence, annihilation of the "other," and terrorism. They launch us into investigations of the worth and character of the subject as measured by preordained standards and a search for the commonalities of a subject position that is simultaneously a disciplining of its objects into conformity. Its subjects must be uniform, unworldly, and pure. As the bearer of the redemptive possibilities for humankind, they cannot simultaneously be generators of and invested in relations of domination or even strategic participants in power games. The resistant leakage of intersubjective and intrasubjective heterogeneity and imperfection provokes predictable responses – nihilism, terrorism and totalitarianism. The nihilist develops a protective cynicism and detachment. In contrast to purity all is corrupt, and thus we are responsible for nothing. The terrorist or totalitarian refuses to accept the impossibility of purity and assigns the sources of imperfection to others. For the greater good, vast force is justified to eradicate the polluting ones. Death, even random murder, is justified in the name of the good.

Developing "object-centered" political strategies offers new political possibilities. Objects include modes of pleasure, ways of life, discrete political acts, new power relations, public spaces of all sorts, and ethical commitments as well as material resources. Complex attachments to particular objects and practices replace subject-centered theories and practices. Instead of depending on a unitary or redemptive subject as the agent of change, we can develop practices of politics based on a mutual desire for particular objects or outcomes, for example, reducing or resisting domination in a specific social field. Diversity does not preclude a mutual attachment to particular objects. A powerful motivation for political activity is attachment by highly diverse constellations of subjectivities to a particular object. Their basis of attachment to a common object need not be uniform. However, an attachment to a particular object renders coalitions both possible and necessary. These attachments will unfold and gather force in ways we cannot predict, generating, perhaps, new desires and relations of solidarity and opposition.

Acknowledging that there is no place outside power relations and historical practices need not lead to nihilism or indifferent amorality. Since there is no guaranteed good or neutral outside available, we have to make the best of – or reinvent – the historical practices constituting us. While such politics is not utopian, it is concerned with generating new practices within the worlds constituting subjects in the present time. Its goal is not to reform the given but to unmask its contingency, thereby opening up spaces to imagine new power games or to play existing ones differently. Freedom exists not in a return to or reconciliation with our pure, undetermined essence, but in the capacity to participate in power relations and their accessibility to us. In its focus on action and responsibility, this approach overlaps with Hannah Arendt's (1998) emphasis on action, but it rejects her contempt for "the social" (Pitkin 1998). Since our desires and heterogeneous practices are us, we cannot escape them. Deploying our multiplicity is a requirement for, not an impediment to, acting justly. We cannot articulate any useful principles or practices of justice without or outside the practices that heterogeneous networks generate. Only intense engagement, not a Rawlsian veil of ignorance or a disembodied Arendtian *arete*, can engender reflection upon or resistance to their effects.

How do we foster such politics? Technologies of the self, particularly in the form of care for the self, are an important element. The care of the self can engender an attachment to practicing subjectivity such that ways of life are multiplied and endlessly reinvented. Innovation and creativity requires more than tolerance or a commitment to diversity or inclusivity; for such practices can actually serve to simply validate the ways of life in which the subject is already engaged. For example, following Habermas (1989,

188–299), we could advocate protecting the efficacy of rational discourse and the autonomy of public space and ensuring a broader range of participants within them. However, this approach leaves undisturbed important assumptions including the privilege of reason and speech, rather than a multiplicity of practices including aesthetic ones, as the means of arriving at public goods.

Adherence to mere tolerance can permit subjects a passive attitude toward other ways of life; we can treat them as irrelevantly exotic though valid for others. Instead, no longer able to assume even a purely subjective truth lies accessible within, care of the self requires perpetual tutoring by and engagement with others. We must actively seek them out, imaginatively take up alternatives and consider our own from foreign viewpoints. Others might attain a kind of knowledge of us, engage in a generative self technology or be attached to a good to which we, immersed in our own practices, are blind. Such experimental practices are self-reinforcing, for the more possibilities we actively engage, the more we unsettle the illusion of identity and recognize the consequences of routinely privileging a particular range of commitments.

Thus, contrary to many critics of postmodernism, its necessary ethical correlative is not an "anything goes" relativism. (See Retallack (2003) for a wonderfully elegant illustration of this point.) While we lack recourse to any neutral trump to resolve conflict or a transcendental justification for our actions or chosen ways of life, it does not follow that we are no longer committed to them, obligated to their ethical stipulations or responsible for their consequences. Innocence is ruled out. Part of what each subject realizes in interacting with others is how we are differently affected by determining social relations. We discover that most subjects occupy several places at once – we resist, impose, enjoy and suffer from different kinds of power. While such unevenness is unlikely to disappear, a commitment to multiplying ways of life can also engender investment in playing games of power that minimize domination. Uniformity becomes suspect; it could be a symptom of domination, of a frozen power game that one is obligated to resist whatever one's position might be within it.

To foster a suspicion of uniformity and an appreciation of conflict does require a certain kind of subjective knowledge and a capacity for engaged detachment. However, rational thought is not a sufficient or unproblematic way to attain such knowledge and detachment. We can use our reason to rationalize, to obscure passions motivating a seemingly rational choice. The capacity for detachment rests on the subject's recognition of its own historical contingency, not a presumption of universality. Paradoxically, the more we acknowledge the contingency of our desires, the less we are determined by any one of them. Immersion, not abstraction, allows us to be more objective. We juxtapose one desire against another and realize our own internal instability. In acknowledging contingency, we also recognize that our desires and practices could be otherwise. If they could be otherwise, other practices are equally possible. Recognizing our will, we must take responsibility for such choices while acknowledging that other moves are plausible. While not vitiating our loyalty, our commitments will appear as choices whose continuance depends on our willingness to keep choosing them and their consequences and on our location within networks that generate and render them intelligible.

This engaged detachment is necessary for ethical behavior. Foucault defines ethics as the "considered form that freedom takes when it is informed by reflection" (Foucault 1997e, 284). Reflection, however, is a practice, not an innate capacity. Like any practice, it requires the appropriate technologies and power relations. Like any practice, it must be endlessly renewed and taken up. The capacity for reflection depends upon the continual confrontation among subjects. Instead of a search for consensus, such interaction intentionally seeks disjunctions. Agreement will not necessary result from such interaction, nor is it the governing purpose. When genuine understanding is reached, unresolvable conflict will result as frequently as empathy, reflective equilibrium, or an ideal speech community. Reflection and communication cannot dissolve the diversity of subjective practices and meaning systems. Hence power games are intrinsic to freedom. Ethical politics cannot promise transparent communication or Habermas's universal pragmatics. However, subjects attempting to practice them continually struggle with how "to acquire the rules of law, the management techniques, and also the morality, the ethos, the practice of the self, that will allow us to play these games of power with as little domination as possible" (ibid. 298).

However, practitioners of richer technologies of the self cannot serve as ground or guarantee of emancipatory action; such subjectivities are not simply replacements for unitary ones. Reflexivity cannot perfectly control the other practices of subjectivity and is itself pervaded by them. Subjects may act on hate or narcissistic grandiosity as readily as empathy. Hopes for justice rest in what they might desire or resist desiring, the openness of power games and the practices sustaining them. Contrary to Rousseau, what freedom we might enjoy does not depend on willing the general but on taking responsibility for very particular, context-specific decisions and ensuring the presence of other empowered subjects. We have to accept that practices of freedom require and reflect the willing by unstable subjects in concert with others, equally tenuously situated, of imperfect and uncertain alternatives. This acceptance requires the availability of practices and subjective technologies that Foucault anticipates but we must endlessly reinvent. The willingness to engage in such invention is a logical correlation to that shared absence of nostalgia for grand utopian schemes I mentioned at the beginning of this essay as a characteristic trait of "postmodernist" family resemblance. While the politics arising out of such lack of nostalgia is not utopian, it remains interrogatory, responsible, chastened, and hopeful. Warding off fantasies of unambiguous benevolence, redemption or deliverance does not produce despair or resignation but rather can free the imagination to test the possibilities and limits of its actual powers. In this commitment to imaginatively rework the practices constituting us, the ethics and politics of "postmodernism" are best expressed.

Bibliography

Arendt, Hannah. *The Human Condition*. 2nd ed. Chicago: U of Chicago P, 1998.

Brown, Wendy. *Politics Out of History*. Princeton: Princeton UP, 2001.

Cheng, Anne Anlin. *The Melancholy of Race*. New York: Oxford UP, 2001.

duCille, Ann. "The Occult of True Black Womanhood: Critical Demeanor and Black Feminist Studies." *Signs: Journal of Women in Culture and Society* 9.3 (1994): 591–629.

Flax, Jane. *Thinking Fragments: Psychoanalysis, Feminism and Postmodernism in the Contemporary West*. Berkeley: U of California P, 1990.

Flax, Jane. "Taking Multiplicity Seriously: Some Consequences for Psychoanalytic Theorizing and Practice." *Contemporary Psychoanalysis* 32.4 (1996): 577–94.

Flax, Jane. *The American Dream in Black and White*. Ithaca, NY: Cornell UP, 1998.

Foucault, Michel. "Preface to *The History of Sexuality, Volume Two*." Trans. William Smock. *Michel Foucault: Ethics, Subjectivity and Truth*. Ed. Paul Rabinow. New York: New, 1997a. 199–205.

Foucault, Michel. "Sex, Power and the Politics of Identity." *Michel Foucault: Ethics, Subjectivity and Truth*. Ed. Paul Rabinow. New York: New, 1997b. 163–73.

Foucault, Michel. "Sexuality and Solitude." *Michel Foucault: Ethics, Subjectivity and Truth*. Ed. Paul Rabinow. New York: New, 1997c. 175–84.

Foucault, Michel. "Technologies of the Self." *Michel Foucault: Ethics, Subjectivity and Truth*. Ed. Paul Rabinow. New York: New, 1997d. 223–51.

Foucault, Michel. "The Ethics of the Concern for the Self as a Practice of Freedom." Trans. P. Aranov and D. McGrawth. *Michel Foucault: Ethics, Subjectivity and Truth*. Ed. Paul Rabinow. New York: New, 1997e. 281–301.

Foucault, Michel. "The Hermeneutic of the Subject." Trans. Robert Hurley. *Michel Foucault: Ethics, Subjectivity and Truth*. Ed. Paul Rabinow. New York: New, 1997f. 93–106.

Gilroy, Paul. *The Black Atlantic: Modernity and Double Consciousness*. Cambridge, MA: Harvard UP, 1993.

Habermas, Jürgen. *Jürgen Habermas on Society and Politics: A Reader*. Ed. Steven Seidman. Boston: Beacon, 1989.

Hirschman, Albert O. *The Passions and the Interests: Political Arguments for Capitalism before its Triumph*. Princeton: Princeton UP, 1997.

Honig, Bonnie. *Democracy and the Foreigner*. Princeton: Princeton UP, 2001.

Mama, Amina. *Beyond the Masks: Race, Gender and Subjectivity*. New York: Routledge, 1995.

Morrison, Toni. *Playing in the Dark: Whiteness and the Literary Imagination*. New York: Vintage, 1992.

Nehamas, Alexander. *The Art of Living: Socratic Reflections from Plato to Foucault*. Berkeley: U of California P, 1998.

Nussbaum, Martha. "In Defense of Universal Values." *Controversies in Feminism*. Ed. James P. Sterba. Lanham, MD: Rowman, 2001. 3–23.

Pitkin, Hanna Fenichel. *The Attack of the Blob: Hannah Arendt's Concept of the Social*. Chicago: U of Chicago P, 1998.

Retallack, Joan. *The Poethical Wager*. Berkeley: U of California P, 2003.

Stoler, Ann Laura. *Race and the Education of Desire*. Durham, NC: Duke UP, 1995.

II

MAPPING THE POSTMODERN

john mcgowan

THEY MIGHT HAVE BEEN GIANTS

The postmodernism debate in theory circles can be dated from the publication of Jean-François Lyotard's *The Postmodern Condition* in 1979 to Fredric Jameson's book-length version (finally published in late 1991) of his much-read and much-discussed essays of the mid-1980s.[1] The theoretical debate follows, I will argue, the historical arc from 1968's incoherent but widespread rebellions to 1989's Eastern European revolutions. The term "postmodernism" is still with us as a vague reference to French theory, historical meta-fiction, and eclectic hybrid forms in architecture and art. But the theoretical debate represented by "postmodernism" has, for better and worse, passed from the scene. Yes, the academic discourse around postmodernism had some important and interesting relation to the "culture wars" between traditionalists and progressives that have sullied, if not outright polluted (especially in the USA), public arts policies, efforts at educational reform, and all talk of "values." Unfortunately, the culture wars are all too much still with us since they have proved so useful to America's rightist politicians. But the predictable, pro forma efforts by conservative pundits to blame social ills on academic writers they have never read has little to offer us by way of understanding why "postmodernism" as a concept served to galvanize a group of major thinkers for some ten-plus years fifteen years ago. By confining myself in these remarks solely to the conversation among those thinkers, who were to a very large extent writing about and to each other, I considerably raise my chances of saying something coherent and cogent.

In particular, I am interested in a group of writers who were all born too late to be active participants in the Second World War but were coming of age during that traumatic event – and, especially, in its aftermath of facing up to the death camps and to the atom bomb. Lyotard, Foucault,

Derrida, Jameson, Said, Rorty, and Habermas were all born between 1925 and 1935. The important feminist theorists of the postmodern moment are a bit younger: Cixous was born in 1937, Kristeva in 1941, Spivak in 1942.[2] Crucially, the male writers are not baby-boomers and, consequently, were not students during the 1960s. Their work participates in, as well as reflects, both the rise and the collapse of 1960s radicalism, but the connection is hardly direct and certainly not simple. Their intellectual formation came in the 1950s, not the 1960s, and they were not of the student movement even when they allied themselves with it. All of these writers, the women included, come from complex and very specific intellectual and cultural backgrounds that make generational generalizations pointless. Several – the Palestinian Said, the Algerian and Jewish Derrida, the Indian Spivak, and the Romanian Kristeva – are transplants, living and writing in non-native lands, but others – Foucault and Rorty among them – come from the professional upper middle classes.

All of these writers, with the exception of Rorty, were internationally prominent by the time they were forty. Despite claims that their work was obscure, they earned their precocious academic and international reputations by virtue of playing for very large stakes while making those stakes dramatically clear. Nothing less than the West's soul hung in the balance. The postmodernism debate was about the Western tradition's crimes and accomplishments. All of the participants acknowledged the disasters of the Holocaust, of the economic and political colonization of non-white peoples in the non-West, and the secondary status of female and colored persons in the West. At issue was how fundamental the causes for such evils were. Their abiding question was: what went wrong – and where – and why? Specifically, was Western philosophy – its traditional canons of thought, knowledge production, and rationality – and Western political commitments – to rights, equality, and popular sovereignty under the banner of a universalist humanism – root causes of these crimes or a potential source for protesting against or even remedying them? The Enlightenment, especially, came in for criticism. In retrospect, the European attempt to replace divinely ordained hierarchies with polities grounded on popular sovereignty, the rule of law, and universal rights (all justified and underwritten by reason) seemed a disaster. Specific battles were waged over the terms "reason," "truth," "human" and others. But the main battle was clear: what, if anything, of the tradition could be salvaged, could be justified? How fully and completely had the West gone off the rails?

Admittedly, these dramatic questions were asked in very arcane forms, embedded within technical and exegetical discussions of past writers. Academic protocols sometimes overwhelmed the clear articulation of issues. But the accusations of obscurity were greatly exaggerated. The postmodern theorists' struggles with Kant and Hegel offer a case in point. Kant remains the most important exponent of the Enlightenment and liberalism's humanism, while Hegel represents Western thought's recurrent will to totality, its relentless intellectual imperialism. Yet simple condemnation of these two figures is hardly possible, since Kantian reason (not to mention his explorations of the sublime and of judgment in the Third Critique) and Hegelian historicism remain fundamental constituents of how we think and argue. To tangle with such figures and the complexity of their legacy was to address the meanings of the West in a responsible and thorough way, no matter how opaque the discussion might seem to newcomers.

What I want to consider here is why this debate proved so gripping for a short time – and why it seems so much less gripping today. I will focus specifically on Derrida, Habermas, and Foucault, but this troika is meant to stand in for an entire cadre of writers born between 1925 and 1942. We would, undoubtedly, argue about whom to include in this wider group, but I only need you to grant that some, if not all, of the writers I have already named might plausibly fit the profile. They might have been giants. Their work dwarfs those who come after, continuing to set the intellectual agenda even as they are less and less explicitly discussed or even invoked. The academic world has, as it will, moved on. The postmodernism debate in particular is long over. And the "revolution" that "theory" promised has either occurred or not. The odd thing is how hard it is to tell. Yesterday's controversies become today's received wisdom. Depending on your angle of vision, everything – or nothing – seems to have changed since 1960, a convenient date for marking a time when the academy and the West in general still seemed safely ensconced in their dogmatic slumbers. Standing at the end of 2004, it makes perfect sense to claim that postmodernism as a theoretical shift of epic proportions never happened. But it is equally possible to claim that intellectual work is utterly different today than it was forty years ago. Was postmodernism a passing fad or are we all postmodern now?

Put that way, I can only reply that the question is ill-framed. I don't think an era or a style hangs together in that way, so that a broad label captures some kind of essential features shared by many particulars. No practice (body piercing), art work (architecture), technological innovation (cell phones), or scientific discovery (genetic engineering) is going to hold the key to who we are – fundamentally, truly, and really. And there is the additional problem that people who are differently situated socially are going to live in the same time period, even use the same buildings and institutions, in very different ways. The lines of force and meaning are more dispersed, more conflictual, more partial than a term like postmodernism conveys.

But the term provides a powerful charge of simplicity and clarity. My naïve question is: why did Derrida, Foucault, and Habermas command so much attention, from such widely dispersed quarters? They wrote books that everyone with any kind of intellectual pretensions in the humanities and social sciences had to read. No one has published a book like that in the last ten years. Why not?

I think it is partly an issue of style. Quentin Skinner had it right when he spoke of a "return of grand theory."[3] Charles Taylor wrote: "Foucault's attraction is partly that of a *terrible simplicateur*."[4] Dense as their work is, Foucault, Habermas, and Derrida all work from a grand set of contrasts – between the premodern and modernity in the first two cases, between Western metaphysics and its shadowy other in Derrida's case. Surprisingly, given the fact that the term "postmodernism" came to be affixed to their work, neither Foucault nor Derrida pays much mind to postmodernism per se. Habermas is partly responsible for attaching the label to them in his polemic against the postmodernists, *The Philosophical Discourse of Modernity*. But the modernism/postmodernism contrast does fit the spirit of Derrida's and Foucault's habitual reliance on drawing strong, binary oppositions in their work. And, even more fleetingly although certainly hauntingly, the postmodern makes its appearance as a faintly drawn apocalyptic scene on the far side of our current entanglement in the West's tarnished tradition – famously in Foucault's evocation of the "disappearance of man" at the end of *The Order of Things*.[5]

> If those arrangements were to disappear as they appeared, if some event of which we can at the moment do no more than sense the possibility – without knowing either what its form will be or what it promises – were to cause them to crumble, as the ground of Classical thought did, at the end of the eighteenth century, then one can certainly wager that man would be erased, like a face drawn at the edge of the sea.

This gesture toward a grand-scale historical transformation, one that would usher in a post-human era utterly different from the "modern" liberal era or the "classical" era that preceded it, holds out the promise of the "postmodern" even while refusing to specify what it might look like. Derrida, in his early essays (especially "Structure, Sign and Play in the Discourse of the Human Sciences" and "The Ends of Man"[6]), gingerly takes up this question of a transition from one era to another, ending "Structure" with reference to a "birth" from which some turn their eyes away – "those who, in a society from which I do not exclude myself, turn their eyes away when faced by the as yet unnamable which is proclaiming itself and which can do so, as is necessary whenever a birth is in the offing, under the species of a nonspecies, in the formless, mute, infant, and terrifying form of monstrosity" (*Writing and Difference* 293). In his later work, Derrida will be more direct, albeit no more specific, in his repeated invocations of the "to come" as in his appeal to the "democracy to come" in "The Politics of Friendship."[7]

To some extent, all three writers – Foucault, Derrida, and Habermas – aim to overcome dualisms, to avoid contrastive binaries. They each, in their own way, offer an analysis that denies the existence of an "outside." For the Foucault of *Discipline and Punish*, power encompasses everything and we must jettison our romantic notions of something or some person standing apart from and independent of power; "there is no outside."[8] Similarly, Derrida tells us that we cannot simply step outside of Western metaphysics; deconstruction is a "trembling" of the structure that will not collapse it entirely and must be ever cognizant of "the force and efficiency of the system that regularly change transgressions into 'false exits.'"[9] Habermas is at great pains in the two volumes of *The Theory of Communicative Action* to prove that every utterance is embroiled in the basic contract that underwrites all language use. But a fundamental contrast between freedom and oppression drives all of their work. Foucault turns in his later work to issues of self-mastery in order to develop a model of power that also offers a modicum of freedom; Derrida always held on to the image of an "irreducible alterity" even as he despaired of our ability to locate it or to protect it from the "violence of metaphysics" once we found it.[10] Even as he warns us against delusions of easy escape from "the system" in "The Ends of Man," he also tells us that "a radical trembling can only come from the *outside*" (134). And Habermas's whole project is predicated on distinguishing between the "distorted" speech acts within oppressive societies and the "ideal" speech acts of the truly free.[11] This epic struggle between freedom and its opposite is staged in their work and serves as the grand unifying idea that makes their fine-grained details and sophisticated arguments cohere. The clarity of their work stems from the reader's always being able to map the details back to whether here freedom is being advanced or retarded. The standard of measurement (even if only implicit) can always be wheeled into action.

Even where they cannot see victory – or despairingly predict eternal defeat – Foucault, Derrida, and Habermas are passionate moral advocates for alternatives to the prevailing social order. All three provide readers with a key to the world we live in, "a history of the present," as Foucault put it – one that locates us at the nexus of a series of traceable forces and transformations.[12] In short, they do philosophy of history, as it was practiced in the days when philosophers aspired to reveal the grand patterns that underlay the whole trajectory of the West. And they also do straightforward philosophy, as it was practiced when philosophers aspired to provide the conceptual basis for understanding everything. Neither kind of philosophy had been practiced by someone born in England or America since Hume or Gibbon, with the possible exception of John Dewey. Continental examples were more abundant, with Foucault and Derrida taking up the mantle of Sartre, while Habermas directly follows from Adorno.

The irony, of course, was that Foucault and Derrida, at least, promulgated their grand visions in the name of dismantling what Wittgenstein called "the craving for generality."[13] Wittgenstein identifies this craving with, among others things, "the tendency [which the poststructuralists call essentialism] to look for something common to all the entities which we commonly subsume under a general term" (17); "our preoccupation with the method of science. I mean the method of reducing the explanation of natural phenomena to the smallest possible number of primitive natural laws" (18); and with "the contemptuous attitude toward the particular case" (18). Foucault and Derrida's continual assault against essentialism and their focus on particularity and singularity echoes with Wittgenstein's critique.[14] Habermas is a trickier case, arguing for a less magisterial, "postmetaphysical" philosophy, while still insisting on the necessity for and legitimacy of transcendental claims.[15] Derrida, the most fatalistic of the three, appears to believe that the craving for generality cannot be eradicated, but that it can be controlled by eternal vigilance, by the work of a deconstruction that is never finished.[16] Foucault had greater hopes of finding a new modus vivendi – for intellectual work, for the experience of selfhood, and for living a life.[17] And the price he pays for dismantling coherent identities and sweeping generalizations is that the final volumes of *The History of Sexuality*, endearingly modest, even pedestrian, pale in comparison to the fire of *Discipline and Punish*.[18] Foucault just another scholar working in the salt mines of minutiae? A charming concept, but ...

Yet it is those final volumes that set the tone of scholarship for the past fifteen years. Except for the diehard Deleuzians (god bless their addled pates), the academics have scurried back into their holes. (Negri and Hardt's *Empire*, with its ungainly mixture of Marx and Deleuze and its grand sweep, is to be honored precisely for its ambitions, no matter what reservations we have about its specific arguments.[19]) Our social theory reading group in Chapel Hill, which brought together twenty to twenty-five people each year to read Spivak or Laclau and Mouffe in the old days, has now dwindled to four or five hardy souls. Whether it's post-colonial theory or Spinoza, we can't find a text busy people can agree they need and want to read. The academics I know are not writing books that engage conceptual frameworks directly. They may, in some cases, think their specific historical work or case histories might nudge received ideas or methodologies in one direction or another, but they write as if they think, as one colleague of mine put it, that change in such matters is very slow and comes from careful examination of a quite particular issue.

I am of mixed mind. The "might" in my title reflects my sense that much of the postmodernism debate was awfully silly. Caricatures of the West, of various intellectual traditions and positions, and, especially, of the political consequences of holding certain ideas often prevailed. The exasperation that Foucault expressed in "What Is Enlightenment?" with the tenor of the debate, the simplicities it had introduced, was well justified.

> [W]e must not conclude that everything that has ever been linked with humanism is to be rejected, but that the humanistic theme is in itself too supple, too diverse, too inconsistent to serve as an axis of reflection. ... In any case, I think that, just as we must free ourselves from the intellectual blackmail of "being for or against the Enlightenment," we must escape from the historical and moral confusionism that mixes the theme of humanism with the question of the Enlightenment. An analysis of their complex relations in the course of the last two centuries would be a worthwhile project, an important one if we are to bring some measure of clarity to the consciousness that we have of ourselves and of our past. (44–5)

As it turned out, the West's future did not hinge on the outcome of our theoretical debates. But while the heightened rhetoric and oversimplifications are easy to mock, the passion, ambition, and dramatic clarity of *The Philosophical Discourse of Modernity*, *Discipline and Punish*, and *Of Grammatology* still seem titanic when measured against the best the last ten years have to offer. Furthermore, those books oriented us, giving us the large simplifications and moral stakes that our subsequent work set out to clarify, to nuance. Pluralism has its virtues, both intellectual and political, not the least of which is an egalitarianism that makes giants unnecessary. I have no doubt that detailed work, modest in its scope and careful in its conclusions, is more mature, more attuned to scholarship as a communal enterprise. But when I see the ambition that animated the work of my troika only displayed these days by the likes of Steven Pinker and Niall Ferguson, I think the company of a few clumsy, even megalomaniac, giants in the Marx–Nietzsche–Sartre line would be a fine thing.[20]

Currently, only conservatives who want to reaffirm a basic, unalterable human nature (like Pinker) or urge America to adopt wholeheartedly an imperial role (like Ferguson) are thinking big. The left is in retreat in the West – and that makes me think that postmodernism might best be "periodized" as lasting from 1968 to 1989, with the inevitable academic time lag explaining why it took a while to burst into print and some time after historical events rendered it moot to stop occupying academic imaginations. That year of failed revolutions – 1968 – precipitated the desire for overarching interpretations of the West and for radical, total solutions. Paradoxically, even Lyotard's famous turn away from "grand narratives" in *The Postmodern Condition* was presented as a radical – and pervasive – break from previous practices. The very notion of postmodernity works against the assertion of historical continuities; it posits a change that alters the very conditions of life and thought. That this revolutionary change was more desired than actual always made the label "postmodern" problematic. Foucault, Derrida, and even Habermas were all gesturing toward desired, and perhaps impossible because ideal, transformations. Hence all three shied away from proclaiming that some radical break had already been accomplished. Even Lyotard retreated from the notion that we were already postmodern, tying himself into knots over the question of whether "postmodernism" named a precise historical period or instead stood for an attitude that was present, if submerged, in all eras.[21] Only the dystopian Jameson actually claimed that postmodernism had arrived, was our current reality. In short, the postmodernism debate partook of the revolutionary hopes of 1968 insofar as it was organized around the notion of a complete transformation of a West that was understood as being all of one piece. It was a revolution that had not happened, that was "to come."

The year 1989 put an end to all that. Interpreted as the triumph of the West, the fall of communism not only deprived the left of its favorite alternative to Western liberalism but also undermined the thesis that the West was rotten to the core, everywhere and in every time. That the oppressed peoples of Eastern Europe associated the West with freedom made the more extreme denunciations of the West by privileged Western intellectuals look like political naïveté or, worse, bad faith. Between the end of communism and the onset of globalization, the left was put on the defensive, working piecemeal and frantically to protect as many of the threatened components of social democracy as possible. Freed from the implied contrast with socialism and the real presence of a second "superpower" in the Soviet Union, capitalism embarked on a new round of ruthless exploitation of labor while the USA turned into a swaggering bully. Now it was the right that promulgated – and actually achieved – wide-scale change (although hardly total transformation as envisioned in the most radical dreams and theories of revolution). The change in tone and approach is manifested in one of the last things Derrida wrote before his death. He looks to "Europe, as a proud descendant of the Enlightenment past and a harbinger of the new Enlightenment to come" to stand as a counterweight to globalization and American imperialism. But he also cautions: "That doesn't mean that any grand revolution is about to remove the power centres that emerged victorious from the cold war." The best hope he offers is that "constant pressure from the counter-globalisation movement and ordinary people the world over" will "weaken" the triumphant and "force them to reform."[22]

As I have indicated, I am of two minds about the loss of the grand clarity and flourishes of theory's style at the height of the postmodernism debates. A sensible and sober Derrida is, like a cautious Foucault, a letdown. But surely such sobriety does indicate both the way forward for those who wish to change the West's ways and the slow, complex work any successful reform movement will have to do. There is no magic wand that will make it all disappear, no theoretical analysis or rhetorical bravado that will unlock the door to freedom. Postmodern theory failed if its aim was to deliver a better world. But the passion and wide-reaching vision with which it pursued that goal of a better world was – and remains – exemplary. I am only willing to applaud the current return to "careful" scholarship that attends to the small continuities and disruptions within a complex, non-unified, and contested Western tradition if such scholars are driven by the grand and passionate desire of the postmodern giants for a freedom that the West still continues to deny to most people, Westerners and non-Westerners alike.

Notes

1 Jean-François Lyotard, *The Postmodern Condition*, trans. Geoff Bennington and Brian Massumi (Minneapolis: U of Minnesota P, 1984); Fredric Jameson, *Postmodernism or, The Cultural Logic of Late Capitalism* (Durham, NC: Duke UP, 1991). The key interventions by Jameson in the mid-1980s were his "Introduction" to the Lyotard text cited above; and essays in *New Left Review* 146 (1984): 53–92; *Social Text* 15 (1986): 65–88; and in Hal Foster (ed.), *The Anti-Aesthetic* (Port Townshend, WA: Bay, 1983): 111–25. All of these essays, albeit expanded and somewhat revised, are included in the 1991 book.

2 Besides the works by Lyotard and Jameson cited in the previous note, representative works particularly relevant to postmodernism by each of these writers are: Jacques Derrida, *Of Grammatology*, trans. Gayatri Chakravorty Spivak (Baltimore: Johns Hopkins UP, 1976); Michel Foucault, *Discipline and Punish*, trans. Alan Sheridan (New York: Vintage, 1979); Jürgen Habermas, *The Philosophical Discourse of Modernity*, trans. Frederick Lawrence (Cambridge, MA: MIT P, 1987); Richard Rorty, *Contingency, Irony, and Solidarity* (Cambridge: Cambridge UP, 1989); Edward Said, *Orientalism* (New York: Pantheon, 1978); Hélène Cixous, *"Coming to Writing" and Other Essays*, trans. Sarah Cornell et al. (Cambridge, MA: Harvard UP, 1991); Julia Kristeva, *Powers of Horror*, trans. Leon S. Roudiez (New York: Columbia UP, 1982); Gayatri Chakravorty Spivak, *In Other Worlds: Essays in Cultural Politics* (New York: Routledge, 1988).

3 See Skinner, *The Return of Grand Theory* (Cambridge: Cambridge UP, 1985).

4 Charles Taylor, "Foucault on Freedom and Truth" in *Foucault: A Critical Reader*, ed. David Couzens Hoy (New York: Blackwell, 1986) 82.

5 Michel Foucault, *The Order of Things* (New York: Vintage, 1973) 387.

6 "Structure, Sign and Play in the Discourse of the Human Sciences" in *Writing and Difference*, trans. Alan Bass (Chicago: U of Chicago P, 1978) 278–93; and "The Ends

of Man" in *Margins of Philosophy*, trans. Alan Bass (Chicago: U of Chicago P, 1982) 111–36. The original dates of the essays are 1967 and 1968, respectively.

7 Jacques Derrida "The Politics of Friendship," trans. George Collins, *Journal of Philosophy* 85 (1988): 632–44.

8 *Discipline and Punish* 301.

9 See "The Ends of Man," esp. 134–36.

10 See the early (1963) essay "Violence and Metaphysics: An Essay on the Thought of Emmanuel Levinas" in *Discipline and Punish* 79–153. The phrases "absolute alterity" and "the absolutely irreducible exteriority of the other" recur throughout the essay. For two instances, see 91 and 93.

11 For a succinct account of Habermas's views, see "A Philosophico-Political Profile," trans. Peter Dews, in *Habermas, Autonomy and Solidarity: Interviews with Jürgen Habermas*, ed. Peter Dews (London: Verso, 1986) 149–90, esp. 157–66.

12 *Discipline and Punish* 31.

13 Ludwig Wittgenstein, *The Blue and Brown Books* (New York: Harper, 1960) 17–18.

14 See, for example, Foucault's discussion of method in "What Is Enlightenment?" where he writes: "it seems to me that the critical question today has to be turned back into a positive one: in what is given to us as universal, necessary, obligatory, what place is occupied by whatever is singular, contingent, and the product of arbitrary constraint?" (45). "What Is Enlightenment?," trans. Catherine Porter, in *The Foucault Reader*, ed. Paul Rabinow (New York: Pantheon, 1984).

15 For Habermas's attempt to articulate a "modest" contemporary philosophy that still retains some ability to offer "general" and "transcendent" perspectives, see his essay "Philosophy as Stand-In and Interpreter," trans. Christian Lenhardt, in *After Philosophy: End or Transformation?*, eds Kenneth Baynes, James Bohman and Thomas McCarthy (Cambridge, MA: MIT P, 1987) 296–315.

16 I have discussed at length Derrida's "tragic" view that Western metaphysics and its violence cannot be overcome in *Postmodernism and its Critics* (Ithaca, NY: Cornell UP, 1991) 89–121.

17 The essay "What Is Enlightenment?" is crucial here, but see also "The Ethic of Care for the Self as a Practice of Freedom," trans. J.D. Gauthier, SJ, *Philosophy and Social Criticism* 12 (1987): 112–31.

18 Do we witness a similar retreat from "grand" theorizing in the careers of Derrida and Habermas? Yes and no. Habermas has become less transcendental if we interpret (as I am inclined to do) his later work on norms and law as acknowledging that these societal forms are not universal but tied to specific polities or international agreements/institutions. But it is not clear that he is willing to go that far toward relativism. And I don't quite know what to make of the later Derrida, with his simultaneous *rapprochement* (discussed below) with the European legacy he once scorned and his gestures toward a transcendent and religious "call" as the basis of his work.

19 Antonio Negri and Michael Hardt, *Empire* (Durham, NC: Duke UP, 2000).

20 Steven Pinker, *Blank Slate: The Modern Denial of Human Nature* (New York: Viking Penguin, 2002); and Niall Ferguson, *Empire: The Rise and Demise of the British World Order and the Lessons of Global Power* (New York: Basic, 2004).

21 See *The Postmodern Condition*, esp. 71–82.

22 Quoted from Derrida, "Enlightenment Past and to Come," trans. John McGowan, *Le Monde Diplomatique* 6 Nov. 2004, available <http://mondediplo.com/2004/11/06derrida>.

douglas kellner

REAPPRAISING THE POSTMODERN: NOVELTIES, MAPPING AND HISTORICAL NARRATIVES

From the early 1980s into the 1990s, debates over the modern and the postmodern were the hottest theoretical game in town. Passionate controversies raged over the differences between modern and postmodern theory and the relative merits and defects of each; over whether we lived in a modern or postmodern epoch, or a hybrid transition period; and over the differences between modernism and postmodernism in the arts and over which was more appropriate to the contemporary moment. Fiercely one-sided postmodern polemics excoriated modernity and the Enlightenment as repressive, exclusionary, legitimating reductive positivism and scientism in theory, bureaucratic, rationalizing, and normalizing of social domination, while also celebrating postmodern difference, novelty, and ludic hedonism. Modernists retorted with attacks on alleged postmodern irrationalism, relativism, and the nihilism or superficial irony that characterized some versions. Players in the theory game were forced to take sides with the Pomos or Mos, or sit on the sidelines and miss out on the fun (and conference invitations, publications, and academic capital).

By the end of the 1990s something of a truce emerged between advocates of the modern and the postmodern. In the realm of theory, it was recognized that classical modern theory and the Enlightenment had its progressive and regressive features, as did postmodern discourses, and many contemporary theorists began drawing on both traditions, although rabid partisans remained on each side. In social theory, the distinction between the modern and postmodern was normalized as a legitimate form of conceptualization, although differences remained over its usefulness in general and whether specific phenomena were or were not postmodern. Likewise, debates continued over whether we were or were not living in a postmodern era, and while serious differences remained one could discuss the issue without the partisan overtones and passions of the previous period and mediate between the one-sided positions. Likewise, in cultural theory, debates over modernism and postmodernism in the arts continued, although some found the contestations confusing and not particularly useful.

In this paper, based on my own two decades plus involvement in the controversies and work on a trilogy of interrogations of the postmodern with Steven Best (Best and Kellner 1991, 2001), a book and a reader on Jean Baudrillard (Kellner 1989b, 1994), two Fredric Jameson readers (Kellner 1988; Kellner and Homer 2004), and countless articles on the topic, I sort out appropriate uses of the discourse of the postmodern, and the usefulness of the postmodern turn in contemporary theory, as well as some abuses of the discourse.[1] I first suggest that distinctions between the modern and the postmodern in a wide range of issues can highlight novelties in the contemporary moment and discontinuities with the past, but that the distinction in question between the modern and the postmodern must be clearly explicated and the differences articulated (although in some cases there may be an overlap between continuities and discontinuities that blurs the issue). Next, I'll argue that postmodern discourses help provide theoretical mappings and social narratives of the major novelties and developments in contemporary society, culture, and theory and can articulate continuities and discontinuities with the past in the present moment. Finally, I'll argue that a multiplicity of modern and postmodern discourses helps illuminate and articulate the complexity of the present moment and that the more strong theories we have at our disposal, the better work we can do as theorists and critics.

I. Use and abuse of the postmodern

Since my first article on the postmodern in 1988, "Postmodernism as Social Theory: Some Problems and Challenges," and through my work with Steven Best, we insisted that if the discourse of the postmodern were to be analytically responsible, there should be distinctions between modernity and postmodernity as historical epochs; modernism and postmodernism in the arts; and modern and postmodern theory. For a distinction between the modern and postmodern to have force in any domain, there must be a clear distinction between what is modern in a specific case and what is postmodern. The latter has often been used, however, as a cover concept for a variety of novelties of the past decades, but without adequate analysis and articulation.

There is little doubt that the contemporary moment has been one of great transformations and novelties, with the past several decades exhibiting vertiginous change, turmoil, and upheaval. Dramatic metamorphosis and surprising novelties are characteristic features of the present age. This "great transformation" (see Polanyi 1957), comparable in scope to the shifts produced by the industrial revolution, is moving toward a postindustrial, infotainment, and biotech mode of global capitalism, organized around new information, communications, and genetic technologies. As we enter the third millennium, scientific and technological revolution are key elements of the global restructuring of capitalism which includes: the growth of far-reaching transnational corporations; intensified competition on a planetary scale; the moving of industry and manufacturing to the developing world, while investment flows into the overdeveloped world; trade laws which protect transnational corporations at the expense of human life, biodiversity, and the environment; computerization of all facets of production and distribution, along with expanding automation; heightened exploitation of labor; corporate downsizing; greater levels of unemployment, inequality, and insecurity; and the advent of a digitized and networked economy and society. The scientific–technological–economic revolutions of the era provide new financial opportunities, openings for political amelioration, and a wealth of ingenious products and technologies that might improve the human condition – and they are producing at the same time explosive conflict, crisis, and catastrophe. Hence, the turbulent transmutations of the current condition are highly contradictory and ambiguous, with both promising and threatening features.

After the terror attacks on the USA on 11 September 2001 and the resultant Terror War launched by the Bush administration, striking first at Afghanistan and then Iraq, the contemporary situation is a highly perilous one, rendered more uncertain and frightening after George W. Bush's 2005 Inaugural Address which threatened to strike anywhere and anytime in the name of "freedom." Globalization has met its Other in Islamicist radicalism and with Bush's unilateral militarism the global world is increasingly Hobbesian with life ever more nasty, brutal, and, for many, short. Globalization itself simultaneously creates friends and enemies, wealth and poverty, and growing divisions between the "haves" and "have nots" (Kellner 2002, 2003). Yet the downturn of the global economy, intensification of local and global political conflicts, repression of human rights and civil liberties, and general increase in fear and anxiety have certainly undermined the naïve optimism of globophiles who perceived globalization as a purely positive instrument of progress and well-being.

The novel permutations and mutations of globalization and the contemporary era are sometimes subsumed under the label of the "postmodern," although few discussions link the condition to the constellations of the wide-ranging scientific and technological revolutions, the global restructuring of capitalism, and a turbulent world of political conflict.[2] From this perspective, the concept of the "postmodern" serves as a marker to highlight the new, to call attention to discontinuities and ruptures, and to signal that an extensive range of novelties are appearing which require fresh analyses, theories, and practices. But for the postmodern to have theoretical and political weight, it must be articulated with the profound alterations of the day in order to be given concrete substance and force. If the term is to be used responsibly and to illuminate the novelties of the present moment and discontinuities between the present and past, clear distinctions must be made between the modern and the postmodern in specific fields.

The concept of the postmodern is most constructive when it calls attention to something new, to a distinctive difference from modern phenomena, and thus illuminates what is unique and characteristic in the present age. For example, in *The Postmodern Adventure*, Steven Best and I argue that the emergence of a new technoculture is a genuinely novel and arguably postmodern phenomenon. Emergent technoculture involves original spaces such as the hyperreality of television or computer cyberspace. It involves new global modes of communication and culture like the Internet and e-mail, and innovative forms of business like e-commerce. It encompasses new modes of work and capital valorization, as well as a global dispersion of labor in outsourcing. Technoculture has produced original forms of research and education, and novel modes of commercially and technologically mediated communities.

Life online thus constitutes one important emergent form and space of the technoculture, providing the matrix for novel identities and communities. This sphere has been explored in ongoing studies by Sherry Turkle (1984, 1995), who, in the mode of ethnographic social science, describes the emergence of personal computer technologies and the novel forms of interaction, identities, and experiences that they are producing. She interprets the shift from big computers to personal computers as symptomatic of a postmodern shift to an innovative type of computer technology and novel forms of subjectivity and culture. For Turkle, big IBM mainframe computers are bound up with centralization, massification, hierarchy, big government or corporations, and are thus a figure for modernity itself. Further, modern computers are connected with mechanistic science that is universalist, rationalist (there is one way to do it), and top-down, with a cult of experts and hierarchy; it is also, for Turkle, rooted in hard masculine science which is logical and abstract.

By contrast, Turkle claims that personal computers are bound up with a postmodern logic and aesthetics. On her account, postmodern computer technologies are "soft" and "feminine" (e.g. more concrete and ductile), subject to tinkering, more graphic, and more expressive, merging art and technology. Whereas modern mainframe computers required highly specialized knowledge and were accessible only to a techno-elite, postmodern personal computers are "user-friendly," lend themselves to experimental activity in a wide range of multimedia and promote creative and multifaceted selves. PCs thus nourish a postmodern culture of the iconic surface, for while old modern computers required depth-oriented thinking and in-depth technological know-how to get behind the screen, current computers operate on the surface, requiring only that one point and click to navigate cyberspace.

Furthermore, personal computers, on Turkle's analysis, enable a more decentralized, individualist, and variegated culture which can generate postmodern selves – multiple, fragmented, constructed and provisional, subject to experiment and change. "Windows," for Turkle, is the privileged metaphor for postmodern subjectivity – dispersed, decentered, and constructed. Computer software windows open the subject not only to the workworld of texts and word-processing but also to the emerging realms of simulation, cyberspace, and interactive multimedia culture. The result is awareness of the variety of roles we play and dimensions to our subjectivity. So, for example, in one window Jeannot does word-processing and is a professional or academic self. In another, he does e-mail and is a private person, although one can go back and forth from personal to professional or mix them together. In Internet chat rooms, Jeannot can assume whatever identity he wants and can take on multiple identities: a young black lesbian in the morning, a liberal male politico in the afternoon, and a transgendered literary critic at night. Switching to a multimedia window, Sherry can be a more ludic and aesthetic self, playing music, and downloading tunes from Kaasa or Gnutilla, looking at film or video clips, accessing aesthetic images from art galleries and museums, or engaging new computer art forms. In surfing the web she can be a *flâneur* or slacker self, cruising, browsing, and navigating – interesting metaphors themselves worthy of scrutiny. Or, in her Internet web window, she might be doing serious research, enhancing her professional and scholarly subjectivity and cultural capital, blogging her personal life, or producing digital art.

From this perspective, what those in the cyberculture call RL ("real life") is just one more window, one more perspective or domain of interaction, one more mode of subjectivity and identity. For Turkle and Mark Poster (1990), computer technologies create novel identities, subjectivities, and realms of experience and interaction such as cyberspace, as well as original forms of communication and social relations within the emergent technoculture. Such theories, however, exaggerate the rupture with the past, failing to note continuities, and the ways in which such novelties are rooted in the structures of modernity (e.g. that the new technoculture is a part of a new stage of capitalism and integrally connected with globaliza-tion).[3]

Distinctions between the modern and the postmodern can also be illustrated in terms of analyses of contemporary war, although, as in all the domains of debates over the modern and postmodern, there are quite different analyses of what constitutes postmodern war and what actual historical events would encompass and illustrate postmodern war. The Vietnam War has frequently been described as "postmodern," signifying its qualitative difference from previous "modern" wars, but one could argue that such characterizations are often unwarranted. Fredric Jameson, for example, has claimed that Michael Herr in his Vietnam book *Dispatches* (1978) evoked "the space of postmodern warfare."[4] Jameson argues that:

> The extraordinary linguistic innovations of this work may still be considered postmodern, in the eclectic way in which its language impersonally fuses a whole range of contemporary collective idiolects, most notably rock language and black language: but the fusion is dictated by problems of content. This first terrible postmodernist war cannot be told in any of the traditional paradigms of the war novel or movie – indeed, that breakdown of all previous narrative paradigms is, along with the breakdown of any shared language through which a veteran might convey such experience, among the principal subjects of the book and may be said to open up the place of a whole new reflexivity. (Jameson 1991, 45)

Jameson is alluding here to the postmodern critique of representation and the insight that concepts, narratives, and theories do not merely reflect "the real" but construct their own reality. He claims that Herr's *Dispatches* suggests that the Vietnam War unfolded in an entirely original and unrep-resentable postmodern space, which transcended all the older habits of bodily perception, representing a "virtually unimaginable quantum leap in technological alienation" (Jameson 1991, 45). Jameson takes Herr's book on Vietnam as evidence of the impossibility of mapping the "postmodern" space of Vietnam and as itself part of the cultural logic of the postmodern. One could argue, however, that Vietnam was in some ways a modern war with a national liberation movement colliding with a colonial puppet regime and neo-imperialist superpower. Yet with Jameson one could also indicate how Vietnam points to more fully postmodern war and see it as a transitional event between modern and postmodern war.

For the term "postmodern war" to have analytical substance it must be distinguished from modern war, and its defining features need to be clearly delineated. Fully postmodern war would be high-tech war in an electroni-cally mediated battlefield that radically fuses humans and technology, while increasingly replacing people with machines. A postmodern military would be reorganized to fight new types of war with new technologies. Yet the term "postmodern war" can be easily misused and abused. In general, utilizing the term "postmodern" in a meaningful way requires that one develop a systematic contrast with the "modern." In this way, postmodern wars would be conceptualized as a rupture with previous forms of modern war, although continuities should also be emphasized. This requirement has not been met in many texts which have presented the Vietnam and Gulf Wars as "postmodern."

Bruce Cumings, for example, describes the 1991 Persian Gulf events as "our first postmodern" war (1992, 127). Although he mentions a "postmodern optic" through which the war was perceived (103), and "postmodern facsimile" of the war with its media constructions and iconography (127), he does not provide a systematic analysis of what makes the war "postmodern." Indeed, claiming that the "victory celebration in New York was distinctly postmodern," with its theme music from *Star Wars*, sky battle between Scuds and Patriots, and colossal fireworks display, overlooks the media hype of all victory celebrations (which simply didn't happen in Vietnam) in modern societies and wars. This sort of media spectacle was congruent with the contrived political extravaganzas of the Reagan years that manipulated good old modern advertising and PR techniques that have been around for a long time. Unless the concept of "postmodern" is rigorously theorized, it is just an empty slogan with no real cognitive content, and obscures more than it clarifies.[5]

In general, the discourse of the postmodern often intimates that something needs to be theorized, that it is novel and does not fit conventional theories, that it is a perplexing and troubling new phenomenon that requires further analysis. Yet just using the term "postmodern" as a buzzword short-circuits such analysis. It is a way of avoiding theorizing and is a sign of lazy thinking, or a facile attempt to be faddish and *au courant*. Thus, although the concept of a postmodern war can be provided with empirical content, one might resist making a totalizing claim for the Vietnam War and the 1991 Gulf War as "postmodern" in the sense that they embody an absolutely new type of warfare. Consequently, while the 1991 war against Iraq anticipates a form of postmodern war in its successful construction of a media spectacle and in the further advancement of the implosion of humans and machines and movement toward more high-tech forms of combat, the continuities with modern wars are sufficient to characterize it as between the modern and postmodern rather than as an entirely new stage of warfare or history (see Kellner 1992; Best and Kellner 2001).

Hence, the discourse of the postmodern is valuable in forcing critical theorists to question previous theories and accounts and to attempt to describe and analyze the novel phenomena of the computer, media, and technological society, and/or continuities with the past. If the concept of postmodern war illuminates what is new and original about military technology and practice in the contemporary moment, the discourse effectively calls attention to important transformations.

In the realm of theory, the postmodern turn consists of a movement away from the mechanistic and positivistic conception of modern science, along with a repudiation of Enlightenment optimism, faith in reason, and emphasis on transcultural values and human nature. Postmodernists typically reject foundationalism and transcendental subjectivities within theory, the modernist emphases on innovation and originality in art, and a universal and totalizing modern politics. With the belief that modern theories and politics have become reductive, illusory, and arrogant, diverse postmodern theorists, artists, and activists emphasize counter-values of multiplicity and difference, anti-realism, aesthetic irony and appropriation, ecological perspectives, and a proliferation of competing forms of struggle.

From the 1980s, I have been sympathetic to many of these postmodern critiques of modern theory, and will indicate in the course of this text what I think is most valuable, but also advocate the advancement and reconstruction of the best elements of modern theory, culture, society, and politics, rather than their negation, as in some extreme versions of postmodern theory. Thus I would reject one-sidedly affirmative or negative stances toward assorted postmodern theories and have attempted to extract and develop what I and my collaborators consider to be valuable postmodern positions, while criticizing problematic ones. Rather than pursuing the modern logic of the either/or (e.g. either the modern or the postmodern), one can pursue a postmodern logic of both/and, drawing on both modern and postmodern traditions and situating the present era between the modern and the postmodern – a position I'll explicate in the following analyses.

II. The politics of mapping

An aesthetic of cognitive mapping – a pedagogical political culture which seeks to endow the individual subject with some new heightened sense of its place in the global system – will necessarily have to respect this now enormously complex representational dialectic and invent radically new forms in order to do it justice … The political form of postmodernism, if there ever is any, will have as its vocation the invention and projection of a global cognitive mapping, on a social as well as a spatial scale.

Fredric Jameson[6]

To some extent, while the concepts of the modern and modernity are primarily Western discourses, they had analogues and anticipations throughout the world. And while there is a shadow side to modernity, hidden by its legitimating ideologies, there is also a heroic aspect, as modern explorers roamed the unknown world in search of fame and fortune. Voyagers needed reliable maps of the heavens, seas, and land, and themselves sketched the parameters of the unmapped worlds they sought and surveyed. A world market was appearing with the dawn of modernity, cities were proliferating which required mappings and orientation, and desacrilized modes of science were investigating nature and the cosmos. Once fully developed by the eighteenth century, modern discourse sought to eradicate premodern religious ideologies and to replace mystical qualitative modes of thought with alternative quantitative scientific models that emphasized mathematics and the experimental method.[7] Modern science gravitated toward a mechanistic outlook that eradicated all traces of life and purpose from the universe, seeing nature as mere matter in motion and resources for human colonization. The modern scientific method was ruthlessly deterministic and reductionistic, describing a simple and static world of regularities, constants, and fixed laws of nature.

Thus, the commercial bourgeoisie were not the only adventurers of the modern world, for the other principal pioneers were the discoverers who charted the heavens, the seas, the land, and the hidden laws of nature. From Copernicus to Newton, from Columbus to Magellan, and from Mason and Dixon to Lewis and Clark, the architects of the modern world uncovered and mapped previously unknown spaces, and made it possible to generate and reproduce modernity, for others to follow in their footsteps, and for new worlds and experiences to be constantly opened, investigated, and sketched.

The quantitative mania of modern science quickly spilled over into the nascent "social sciences" as, by the eighteenth century, there were attempts to construct a "social physics" or "social mathematics," to locate the "laws" of human behavior so that culture could have the same order and regularity as nature. As Foucault (1975, 1980) revealed in his genealogies of modern types of power in the form of discipline and normalization of subjects' bodies and minds, mapping is a capturing and mastering of the recalcitrant and unpredictable, an attempt to impose constructed order on heterogeneous phenomena, reducing multiplicity to identity, and otherness to unity.

Modern mapping was not neutral or innocent by any means; rather, the cartographical projects of modernity were attempts to gain domination over nature and society and were intimately implicated with the "primitive accumulation of capital" (Marx).[8] Science was driven not only by a "desire for truth" but also by the pragmatics of the political and economic objectives of colonialism. Foucault's (1977) emphasis on the dialectic of power/knowledge is evident during the early colonial period of modernity. Numerous kinds of scientific and technological knowledge – relating to navigation, astronomy, agriculture, and so on – were necessary for the colonial "adventures" to be possible in the first place. They were stimulated by the need, for example, to improve the ability to travel by land and sea, to mine minerals, and to identify useful plants. Imperialist conquests also provided a laboratory for the fledgling efforts of modern science and technology, generating vast amounts of wealth and resources for the accumulation of knowledge.

The European colonialists are not known for their honesty and generosity. In the case of modern science, once conquerors like the Spaniards plundered the knowledge of the "old world" cultures, they slaughtered or enslaved their people and stigmatized them as backwards and inferior. Today, many cultural theorists and activists are calling for a "multicultural science" (see Best and Kellner 2001, chapter 3), yet the irony, as Sandra Harding (1999) observes, is that modern "European" science has been multicultural since its inception, and, however "original" Western culture may be, the distinction between Western/non-Western is now highly contested and a key part of the culture wars. The alleged universality of European culture is in fact a disguised locality, the product of distinct ideologies and institutions belonging to modern European nations. For the sake of accuracy, it might be preferable to say that "Western science" is a *bricolage* of stolen knowledges, from Egypt to Islam to China, along with its own local contributions and its mechanistic and quantitative mappings.

Maps are often seen as translucent windows to the world, but this realist conception misses the limited perspective of every such "window" and the interests of the architect who designs it. As Denis Wood writes, "'Mirror,' 'window,' 'objective,' 'accurate,' 'transparent,' 'neutral': all conspire to disguise the map as a ... *reproduction* ... of the world, disabling us from recognizing it for a social construction" (1992, 22). But perhaps a window is not an inappropriate metaphor since, while the glass may not be translucent, windows are, after all, small and selective openings to the world. By opening one portal, maps close others; even a massive world map attains its impressive scope by obscuring regional details. The central irony of cartography is that for a map to be accurate and useful, it inevitably misleads. As Wood states, "Not only is it easy to lie with maps, it's essential. To portray meaningful relationships for a complex, three-dimensional world on a flat sheet of paper or a video screen, a map must distort reality" (1992, 76).

Indeed, a map is made to scale, and thus is a simulation of the territory it visualizes. The paradigm shift in postmodern cartography involves a move from seeing maps as objective representations of the world to understanding them as rhetorical and political devices, portraying not only physical relationships but also social relationships. That maps are made from an interested standpoint, that they are political, is clear if one considers the construction of modern nation-states that arbitrarily drew borderlines through contested terrains, often driving off original inhabitants who were forced to emigrate because of their ethnicities or religions. A more local US example would be the demarcation of geographical boundaries through gerrymandering, whereby politicians outline their districts in a way that determines who votes and which votes count, altering social space to match selective criteria of class, race, or ideology. Certainly one of the most blatant instances of the politicization of maps involved those of seventeenth-century North America, as drawn up by Spanish, French, and English colonialists, who somehow forgot to designate the territory as already belonging to a myriad of Native American Indian cultures.

In general, maps have both cognitive and political functions. To draw a map is to make sense of the world, to enable individuals to visualize and control their environment. But it also establishes relations of power, delimiting territoriality and constructing artificial boundaries, instructing people where they are safe and at home and where it may be risky and forbidden to dwell. Maps comprise attempts by observers to discern the contours and nature of the world in relation to the individual and specific social groups. They are optics and ways of seeing that enable people to perceive their world from a perspective useful to the viewer, but they are often constructed by ruling social and political forces. All maps, therefore, have both objective and subjective dimensions. To avoid an overly literal notion of mapping as mere picture making, it is crucial to emphasize that mapping is essentially a cognitive and political process and that there are numerous modes of mapping, not only geographical and scientific, quantitative and qualitative but also religious, philosophical, literary, and political forms. Each mapping constitutes a distinctive attempt through which individuals and groups try to situate themselves within society and nature, or even the cosmos at large.

Quantitative maps are produced by scientists, geographers, archaeologists, and explorers, relying on mathematical methods and technologies such as the compass, telescope, and computer. Scientific maps include astronomical maps of the heavens, navigational maps of the oceans and seas, geographical maps of the land, neurological maps of the brain, medical maps of the body, genetic maps of chromosomes, such as have been assembled by the Human Genome Project and Celera Corporation, and even representations of the prodigious World Wide Web by cybergeographers in search of more efficient ways to transmit information. The "end of science" debate, in effect, is an argument over whether or not the modern mapping adventure basically has drawn to a close, and whether there is agreement over which are the best and most reliable forms of mapping (see Best and Kellner 2001, chapter 3).

Qualitative maps range from religion and philosophy, to normative social and political theory, to fiction and other types of aesthetic mapping. Religion, for example, is a cosmological mapping that seeks to locate the ontological and spiritual place of the subject in the world, rather than its spatial location, and it requires wonder rather than mathematics or technologies, faith rather than proof and evidence. Religion asks: "What is this world in which I live? Who created it and for what reason? What purpose, if any, do I have here?" Of course, spatial coordinates can figure importantly in religious mappings. Christian maps – constructed by Ptolemy, Dante, and others – were geocentric charts that ensconced human beings at an illusory center of the cosmos, and thereby provided existential comfort for those who adhered to them. Modern scientific mappings sought to demolish biblically based geocentric maps in favor of new cosmic creation stories like the Big Bang. A cosmology need not be religious, of course, but it does entail situating human beings within the universe as a whole, as do new postmodern scientific cosmologies which typically combine science and narrative, description and interpretation.

Theories, too, are a form of mapping, a way of enabling individuals to see and navigate the world. The Greek word *theoria* derives from vision, and theories help one to see what exists in the natural and social worlds, they grasp the fundamental aspects of experience, the underlying connections and relations, and the vast structures and processes that constitute shared sociohistorical reality. Modern philosophy and social theory arose with modernity, mapping the novelties of modern society, conceptualizing its basic ideas, ways of seeing, methods of investigating reality, and discourses of truth and objectivity. Theories are optics or perspectives on the world that illuminate phenomena and features on which they focus intently, though each has its blind spots, thereby requiring multiperspectivist vision for an adequate grasp of the world. Competing philosophies, social theories, and other analytical discourses thus offer distinct ways of mapping, ordering, analyzing, and in some cases criticizing and reconstructing the world.

Utopian maps depart from the distinction between what is and what can be, between actuality and potentiality, as they envision the realization of possibilities for human freedom, charting the "not-yet." As Ernst Bloch (1986) noted, there are utopian longings in all the great philosophical, religious, and aesthetic mappings, desires that yearn for a better world and sketch visions of a good life. Judaic conceptions of law and justice, Christian notions of community and redemption, Enlightenment visions of equality, freedom, and democracy, and Marxian conceptions of communism, all project images of a superior world and yearnings for increased freedom, happiness, and community. Likewise, Bloch suggests that popular culture, too, contains its utopian strivings, as, for example, advertising both evinces and conditions desires for existential reformation. Indeed, following Bloch, Jameson (1991) argues that all media culture must present some utopian content, some fantasies of a preferable life, to attract mass audiences.

Modern literature and art constitute another key mode of qualitative mapping. Artists, whether consciously or not, often offer vivid portrayals of the social relations and ideologies of their time, as well as concrete descriptions of everyday life and human experience. For many, aesthetic maps are as valuable as scientific or sociological maps, because they render social processes and experiences in artistic form, concretely illuminating the subjective structures of experience. The novel, for instance, attempted to chart the escapades of the newly liberated modern individual seeking adventure and fortune in the exciting world of modernity, adapting to fresh experiences and fashioning a distinctive self. In the era of modernist aesthetic experimentation, starting with Baudelaire and the avant-gardes of the nineteenth century, constructing original styles of art and making one's own life a work of art provoked aesthetic adventures that constantly sought the new, the innovative, the modern, the monumental, and the revolutionary.

The result was an explosion of modernist art forms that uncovered singular universes and dimensions of experience, from the spontaneous unconscious to the carefully constructed, from the realist to the abstract, from the typical to the bizarre and extreme, often contesting traditional representational means of mapping reality. Modern art crossed previous frontiers of form and subject matter, concocting ever new figures, styles, and engagements with the full range of contemporary experience. Moreover, aesthetic maps not only concretize and dramatize the experiences of everyday life in a way that theoretical maps cannot, often they are also sources of utopian longing and normative critique. Some outstanding examples of critical aesthetic maps would be George Grosz's scathing satires of bourgeois life; John Heartfield's photomontages attacking capitalism and Nazism; and Bertolt Brecht's plays which relied on a theatrical technique – the "alienation effect" – that sought to promote critical reflection in the audience.

Thus, mapping can be conceptualized in a broad, multidimensional sense that includes various quantitative and qualitative representations, charting not only geographical, navigational, and astronomical spaces but also human experience of space, time, everyday life, and sociopolitical transformation. Maps are spatial, temporal, and experiential; they portray existing configurations and transmutations, while tracing evolving processes in nature, society, and history. Modes of representation are therefore transitory and need to change as the conditions they seek to depict themselves unfold. Consequently, we should continually update our theoretical and practical perspectives, and if mutations are significant enough it is necessary to invent markedly innovative modes of representation. Indeed, the tumultuous transformations of the contemporary moment themselves require fresh postmodern visions, theories, and politics.

III. Crises of mapping and theorizing the contemporary moment

Investigations of various topics and levels of abstraction that are collected here are united in the intention of developing a theory of the present society.

Max Horkheimer

What's going on just now? What's happening to us? What is this world, this period, this precise moment in which we are living?

Michel Foucault

Postmodern theory seeks novel mappings to represent emergent social conditions, economic shifts, sciences, technologies, experiences, and identities in the contemporary moment. In his classic essay "Postmodernism, or The Cultural Logic of Late Capitalism" (1984, revised 1991), Fredric Jameson vividly describes the disorientation of contemporary life, which includes the loss of social spatial coordinates, the confusing "hyperspace" of postmodern architecture and culture, the decline of historical consciousness, the waning of affect leading to emotional numbness and detachment, and the cooptation of resistance and abolition of critical distance. The thrust of this original historical situation entails a *crisis in mapping*, involving both the obsolescence of the guides to the modern epoch and the inability of subjects to maneuver their way through space and time in traversing the buildings, cities, cultural spaces, and transnational global environment which envelop them. The postmodern condition for Jameson also involves a proliferation of forms of simulation and hyperreality in a situation stranded between a buried historical past and an unimaginably different future. Realizing that diverse types of spatial, temporal, and existential vision are crucial for individuals to regain critical awareness and sociopolitical agency, Jameson concludes his essay on postmodernism with a call for new modes of "cognitive mapping." For Jameson, these cartographies comprise both theory and fresh creations of pedagogical art: "The political form of postmodernism, if there is any, will have as its vocation the invention and projection of a global cognitive mapping, on a social as well as a spatial scale" (1991, 54).

In the contemporary moment, the boundaries of the modern world are breaking down and we need to discover and produce theoretical and practical guides that will help us understand and navigate the tempests and turmoil of the day. Postmodern *metacartography* responds to this situation by reflecting on the various processes of mapping and the contributions and limitations of the classical theories of modernity and the fledgling charting of the postmodern. Different people use distinctive maps to make sense of the world, deploying divergent ideas, models, and theories to organize their experience, to orient themselves in their environment, and to reduce multiplicity and disorder to structure and order. Mappings also help construct personal identities, pointing to ways of being in the world, existential options, and sense-making activities, as when social groups emulate "heroes of production" or "heroes of consumption" (Lowenthal 1961), or individuals follow the fashions and style of celebrities.

Indeed, the postmodern turn involves the dissolution of older traditional and modern identities and the construction of new ones. Whereas traditional identity maintained stable roles and social functions, modernity problematized social identity, providing new possibilities to construct varied and richer subjectivities (Kellner 1995). The ability to switch identities intensified problems of alienation and authenticity, as individuals felt that they were being severed from their true selves while passionately seeking their genuine or higher nature. The postmodernization of identity in turn has engendered disparate searches for the authentic and real, as ersatz identities proliferate, resulting in the growth of oppositional identity subcultures and politics. An always-proliferating image and media culture, supplemented by the psychological games of the Internet where one can experiment with self-construction in ludic performative modes, generates a further expansion of identity (see Turkle 1995; Best and Kellner 2001, chapter 4).

A theory of the contemporary moment that mediates between the modern and postmodern can deploy a diversity of theories to attempt to capture the complexity and conflicts of the contemporary era. While there are clearly important continuities with the modern era (Robins and Webster 1999), the changes wrought by scientific–technological revolution and the proliferation of a new global economy affect all aspects of politics, culture, and everyday life. In this conjuncture, one encounters startling metamorphoses that some are theorizing as the advent of a new postmodernity, qualitatively distinct from the modern era. These developments are highly ambiguous. On the positive side, there are exciting possibilities for fresh experiences in cyberspace, unparalleled potential for medical advances, and increased opportunities for labor and leisure. One also finds promising political openings and movements such as the protests against the Seattle WTO meetings in December 1999, the anti-IMF and World Bank demonstrations in Washington, Prague, and Sydney in 2000, and the global movements against the Bush administration war in Iraq from 2003 to the present which signal innovative coalitions and activism against capitalist globalization.

But there are worrisome dangers that plague the scientific, techno-logical, economic, and other shifts and mutations of our time. In some ways, the postmodern adventure may confront us with the dystopias that have haunted the modern mind, from Mary Shelley's *Frankenstein*, which anticipated genetic engineering and marketable body parts, to the futur-istic visions of H.G. Wells whose *Island of Doctor Moreau* and *Food of the Gods* appear prescient concerning the biological mutations and technolog-ically created species engendered with unforeseen consequences. Orwell's *Nineteen Eighty-Four* anticipated the panoptic society of the present, with surveillance techniques becoming ever more sophisticated and privacy increasingly diminished. Similarly, Huxley's *Brave New World* prefigured the prevailing situation, as eugenics looms on the horizon, cloning has arrived, and sundry brands of "soma" (e.g. Prozac, Ecstasy, and metham-phetamine) and pleasure machines and multisensory spectacles are readily available in a high-tech, consumerist, pharmacopian society of the spectacle (see Best and Kellner 2001, chapters 3–5).

The "dialectics of the present" thus involves living through a highly chaotic and conflictual situation. Resisting both attempts to deny any fundamental ruptures or novelties of the existing sociohistorical situa-tion, as well as hyperbolic claims for a postmodern rupture, it is best to envisage the prevailing condition in a zone between the modern and the postmodern. Here one finds continuities and discontinuities with the past, striking changes and enduring structures, peppered with perpetual conflicts between the old and the new. From this perspective, the present situation is a contradictory amalgam of progressive and regressive, positive and negative, and thus highly ambivalent phenomena, all difficult to chart and evaluate.

In the contemporary moment, society, culture and identity are all under-going a tremendous rethinking. They are currently all in a state of crisis and confusion, largely through the impact of always-proliferating communica-tion and genetic technologies and scientific theories and cosmologies. We are in a condition somewhat analogous to the remapping of the cosmos in the era of Copernicus, Brahe, Kepler, and Galileo. Because of intense social and technological developments not only are numerous human beings reshaping their ethnic, gender, and political identities, but humanity as a species is starting to seriously rethink its status in response to ecology and environmental ethics, evolutionary theory, and "smart machines." With supercomputers like IBM's Deep Blue outwitting chess masters, and genetic engineering and cloning technologies transcending species bound-aries and portending the fabrication of individuals in a Brave New World of designer bodies and babies, the very fate and future of the human being itself is at stake.

The postmodern moment, if nothing else, is indeed risky, and not just for a few entrepreneurs or finance capitalists; rather, the future of humanity and other complex life-forms is being mortgaged to a rampaging capitalism and profit-driven science and technological development. Nuclear waste and weapons proliferation, biowarfare, the growth of the global arms market, terrorism, DNA splicing, xenotransplantation (inserting animal blood and organs into humans), loss of cultural diversity and biodiversity, the greenhouse effect, and global capitalist reorganization, to name just a few things, are leading the human race into dangerous ground and a possible endgame of social and ecological devolution. The postmodern voyage beyond the observable into the very stuff of life, past the limits of the human into novel configurations of humans and technology, provides new powers and capacities for the human species. Technoscience not only enables humans to better manipulate the natural world but also to produce new natures and beings with highly volatile results.

Yet as contemporary societies continue to transgress ethical and ecological limits, begetting proliferating problems and intensifying crises, there is growing recognition of the need to impose limits on the excesses of capitalist modernity and its sciences and technologies, while constructing more humane and ecological values, institutions, and practices to sustain life on earth. Without this latter aspect of the postmodern adventure, the mutating dynamics of capitalist overdevelopment might bring the adventure of evolution to a tragic close, at least here on this planet. The evolution of the universe itself is the greatest adventure story of all, a twelve to fifteen billion-year odyssey, involving the maturation of organic matter from inorganic matter, life from non-life, and its subsequent earthly unfolding over 4.6 billion years, advancing from carbon and hydrogen atoms to DNA and the first proteins, to plants, animals, and human beings. Evolution has generated boundless diversity and ever new and more complex forms of life.

Hence, critical reflection on the pathologies and illusions of modernity and their continuation in the present is an important part of the postmodern condition. A shift in mindset consequently should be informed by an enhanced awareness of limits, contingency, and unpredictability, along with non-hierarchical thinking. This new Gestalt also requires repudiation of the modern will to power over society and nature, revulsion toward arrogant Western-centric humanism, disenchantment with a solely disenchanting worldview, and renunciation of the fantasy of control and belief in the technofix for critical social and ecological problems. Where modernity was predicated on the values of control, endless growth, mastery of nature, and a cornucopian world of limitless resources, a key aspect of a critical theory of the contemporary moment is the systematic dismantling of this discourse and the reconstruction of the best aspects of modernity

– humanism, individuality, enlightened reason, democracy, rights, and solidarities – to be tempered by reverence for nature, respect for all life, sustainability, and ecological balance.

Thus, it could be argued that we are now between the modern and the postmodern, in an interim period between epochs, where we are undergoing spectacular changes in all realms of life. Just as the Renaissance was a long period between the premodern and the modern without easily datable beginnings and endings, so too is humanity entering a period of protracted transformation between the modern era and a new era for which the term "postmodern" serves to call attention to novelties and discontinuities. Some contemporary ideologues, despite the catastrophes of the post-9/11 period, continue to project a salvationist and linear historical narrative, believing that science, technology, and capitalism will solve all human problems and create a new world of wealth, democracy, and well-being. The postmodern assault against grand historical narratives has been used to undercut the metanarrative of historical progress, but there have also been postmodern claims that we are at the "end of history" in a perfected state of capitalism and democracy (Fukuyama 1992).

Far from breaking with religious values and narratives, in many ways science and technology have only deepened them. For their advocates are claiming that genetics and eugenics will perfect us and bring us grace without the need for divine intervention. On the other hand, the juggernaut of capital, technology, and science undercuts religious cosmologies and provides a highly secular and materialist ethos, focusing people on surviving and succeeding in a rapidly fluxating present. As we proceed into the third millennium, the postmodern moment is extremely ambiguous and contradictory. There are trends within the postmodern that celebrate a return to tradition, and there has been an upsurge of religious faith and millennial thinking. But there are also new forms of postmodern identity politics, possessive individualism, and a willingness to embrace the destruction of the past and tradition for the glories of the present moment (see Best and Kellner 1997, 2001).

IV. Transdisciplinary and multiperspectivist mapping

There is *only* a perspective seeing, *only* a perspective "knowing"; and the *more* affects we allow to speak about one thing, the more complete will our "concept" of this thing, our "objectivity," be.

Friedrich Nietzsche

Dialectical thought has meant the most advanced state of knowledge, and it is only from this, in the last analysis, that decisive action can come.

Max Horkheimer

Current developments exhibit so many twists and turns, and are so highly complex, that they elude simple historical sketches, reductive theoretical explications, and facile generalizations. What is required is a multidimensional optic on the trajectory of the present age that combines historical narrative and critical social theory. Mapping the contours of the contemporary moment accordingly involves an enterprise that crosses theoretical borders into a novel transdisciplinary and multiperspectivist space.

The social maps called classical social theories are to some extent torn, tattered, and fragmented, and in many cases outdated and even obsolete. Fresh theories need to be constructed constantly, using both the resources of past theories and salient sketches of the contemporary era to make sense of our current historical condition. Maps and theories provide orientation, overviews, and contexts. They show how parts relate to each other and to a larger whole. If something new appears on the horizon, a good map will chart and contextualize it, including sketches of future configurations of potential promises and perils. But while numerous older theories and authorities decay and are discredited, others continue to provide important guideposts for thought and action today.

Given my concerns for mapping, I would oppose the self-refuting postmodern attacks on theory that are sometimes advanced by writers such as Lyotard, Foucault, and Rorty. Lyotard's prescriptions against grand narratives and big theories are performatively contradicted by his own concept of a "postmodern condition" which surely requires a grand narrative to make and justify such a claim. Although Foucault has been presented as a critic of modern theory and advocate of micro theory and politics, surely much of his major work is a sweeping genealogical mapping, diagnosis and critique of modernity that combines micro and macro theory and politics. And while Rorty often polemicizes "against theory" *tout court*, much of his best work, such as *Philosophy and the Mirror of Nature* (1979), is highly theoretical, often providing sweeping historical vistas and critique.

I would also reject extreme postmodern assaults on a "hermeneutics of suspicion" that strives to overcome social illusions, mythologies, and fetishized appearances by locating underlying forces and causes of domination and destruction.[9] Without theory, interpretation, and critique we are as lost and hapless as Columbus on his first voyage. Theory and interpretation are necessary to the extent that the world is not completely and immediately transparent to consciousness. Since our social and cultural situation is difficult to grasp, especially in a hypercapitalist culture of spectacles, simulacra, and disinformation, we need to comprehend how our lives are being shaped and controlled. Postmodern claims that "theory" necessarily commits the sin of illicitly totalizing irreducibly heterogeneous phenomena are themselves reductive and homogenizing. Ludic postmodern calls for formalistic analysis oriented toward surfaces and the aesthetic pleasures of the text disarm a cultural studies and political hermeneutics that reads culture in terms of social and ideological conflicts and contradictions. To refuse interpretative depth is to extend reification to "critique" itself by reducing analysis to description of surface and form detached from radical theory and politics (see Best and Kellner 1987). The postmodern argument for the renunciation of critique and transformative politics thus becomes a self-fulfilling prophecy.

Theory at its best can provide *social maps* and inform *historical narratives* that supply spatial and temporal contextualizations for the present age. These critical theories should study society holistically, moving from specific phenomena and modes of human experience into an ever-expanding analysis. Such inquiry may extend from the individual self, to its network of everyday social relations, to its more encompassing regional environment, to its national setting, and finally to the international arena of global capitalism. Within this dialectical framework, social maps shift from one level to another, articulating complex connections between economics, politics, the state, science and technology, media culture, everyday life, and their contending discourses and practices. I still find the most powerful methodology for social analysis to be a historically informed, dialectical method that sees human reality as evolving and conflict-ridden. This outlook grasps societies and history in general as coherent wholes, while analyzing society as a differentiated structure comprised of multiple levels – economics, politics, science, technology, culture, and so on – each of which has its own history, autonomy, and conflicts.

Together, social maps and historical narratives study the points of intersection between individuals and their cultures, between power and knowledge. To the fullest degree possible, they seek to lift the veils of ideology and expose the given as contingent and the present as social constructs, while providing visions of alternative futures. Theories and narratives, then, are meant to overcome quietism and fatalism, to sharpen political vision, and to encourage translation of concepts into practice in order to advance personal freedom, social justice, and ecological preservation and reclamation. Theories and narratives should not be confused with the territories and times they analyze; they are approximations of a densely constituted human world that requires theories and imagination to conceive and depict. Nor should social mappings be seen as final or complete, since they must be constantly rethought and revised in light of new information and rapidly changing situations. Mappings and narratives can thus only be provisional, reports from diverse explorations that require further investigation, testing, and revision.

On the whole, border crossing, a transgressing of boundaries between fields carefully delineated and segregated under the regime of the modern, is a productive aspect of the postmodern turn in both theory and the arts. Theoretical crossings of disciplinary borders that subvert the modern academic division of labor have given rise to a vast array of studies that have provoked novel insight and activity. Earlier attempts at both modern and postmodern transdisciplinary work tended to be carried out within the realms of cultural and social theory. Yet the revolutions in science and technology require broadening our theoretical perspectives and optics. Previously, calls for transdisciplinary work concerned integration of the perspectives and the methods of the social and cultural sciences, often without regard for significant components of the natural sciences or the new philosophies of science and technology. One might affirm, however, inclusion of both the natural and the social sciences to overcome the gap between the "two cultures" (Snow 1964), along with analysis of the impact of technological innovations, in order to provide more integrated and comprehensive frameworks for theory and critique today (Best and Kellner 2001).

Formerly, major philosophers from Diderot to Dewey and many in the humanities and social sciences stayed in touch with cutting-edge developments in science, looked to scientific method as the source of knowledge, and critically engaged the latest creations of scientific theory. Indeed, the major social theorists of the eighteenth and nineteenth centuries saw science and technology as the driving motors of change and progress that would lift humanity from the dungeons of premodernity. They regarded science and technology as major civilizing forces that would bring a rational society in their wake. Karl Marx championed science and technology as liberating forces and went so far as to equate human emancipation with advancement of the "productive forces" of society. Likewise, John Dewey directly linked science and democracy (1995), claiming that the scientific method of experimentation was the best pedagogy for education and the form of a democratic society and culture.

However, with a variety of critiques of modern science developing in the twentieth century, ranging from phenomenological and feminist assaults on scientific objectivity to critical theory attacks on positivism, many leading theorists and schools distanced themselves from science, ignored its developments, and did not engage its results. This was and is, however, arguably a crucial mistake. Instead, science should once again become part of a transdisciplinary optic and should be returned to its status as a valuable theoretical resource. While one should avoid the uncritical modern embrace of science and technology, such as was advanced by classical liberalism, Marxism, and pragmatism, one should also eschew totalizing critiques that reduce science and technology to one-dimensional reason and a force of social domination. Like it or not, science and technology have been major constituent forces of modernity, and similarly are key catalysts of change for postmodernity. As such, they need to be engaged in light of their momentous importance and carefully theorized so that their positive potentialities can be realized and dangers confronted through theoretical critique and political struggle.

Accordingly, critical theories of science and technology appreciate their emancipatory potential, but also critique their limitations, risks, and possible destructive effects. A critical theory of science and technology strives to overcome one-sided affirmations or rejections, produces dialectical perspectives that distinguish between positive and negative features and consequences, and grasps contradictions and ambiguities in these highly complex and significant phenomena. Critical theories of science and technology are also transdisciplinary and historical. Transdisciplinary interpretation is necessary because science and technology have shaped our society and identities to such a profound degree that they are part and parcel of our culture, the stuff of everyday life, and are interfacing with our very bodies and subjectivities in unpredictable ways. A critical theory, for example, that synthesizes philosophy, sociology, and anthropology, but ignores the impact of science and technology on culture, clearly is limited in its ability to grasp the fundamental dynamics of the current conjuncture.

Thus, a postmodern transdisciplinary theory should include reflections on science, technology, and ecology in a multiperspectivist project that integrates critical social theory, cultural studies, science and technology studies, race theory, postcolonial analysis, feminism, and environmental concerns. Such an enterprise draws on the most useful resources of both modern and postmodern theory, as well as on theoretical and fictional mappings. Consequently, a critical theory of the contemporary moment must be transdisciplinary and multiperspectivist. One of the major contributions of the postmodern turn is that in light of the complexities, contradictions, and dangers of the present moment there is a need for multiple interdisciplinary theories to capture the novelties of the present, the continuities and discontinuities with modernity, and the problems this situation generates. Thus engaging novel conditions requires new theories, and the drama of the postmodern forces us to look at new things in new ways, a condition that will no doubt continue as we enter the already approaching future.

Notes

1 This is my first set of reflections on the topic of the postmodern since publishing *The Postmodern Adventure* with Steven Best in 2001, and my comments here draw on the work done with him. We decided that the concept of the postmodern was too polarizing for the work we've wanted separately and collaboratively to do in the past

few years, although I at least, as these comments will indicate, find the discourse of the postmodern useful if appropriately elaborated and contextualized.

2 Many discourses of the postmodern largely make shifts in technology responsible for the rupture with modernity, as in Baudrillard (1983, 1993) who neglects the significance of the restructuring of the global capitalist economy. While Jameson (1984, 1991), Harvey (1989), and others relate postmodern culture to transformations of capitalism, their initial engagements with the postmodern in the texts just referenced do not adequately engage the roles of scientific and technological revolution. Others, like Lyotard (1984), interpret the "postmodern condition" largely through mutations of discourse and culture. See Best and Kellner (1997, 2001), who argue that if notions of postmodernity, or a postmodern condition, are to have any force, they must receive a sociohistorical grounding in analysis of the conjuncture of scientific and technological revolution, the global restructuring of capitalism, the political struggles, and new forms of culture, subjectivity, and everyday life of the contemporary moment.

3 Poster argues in *Mode of Information* (1990) that the mode of production is now transcended in importance by the mode of information as a fundamental principle of organizing society. I would argue, however, that the modes of production and information are intertwined as a new stage of capitalism. In "Postmodern Virtualities" (1996), Poster highlights the importance of perceiving the connection of postmodernity with new media and new subjectivity, but does not link these phenomena with the restructuring of capital and globalization.

4 Numerous critics have followed Jameson in interpreting the Vietnam War as "postmodern"; see the studies in Bibby (2000). Likewise, many books, articles, and dissertations read Herr's *Dispatches* (1978) as a postmodernist text. So far the concept of "postmodern war" is only beginning to be adequately developed; see Chris Hables Gray's book on *Postmodern War* (1997) for serious attempts at conceptualization with much interesting material, and Best and Kellner (2001).

5 To give further examples, Miriam Cooke published an article, "Postmodern Wars," that opened with some rather general remarks concerning their "cluster of defining characteristics" (1991, 27). But although she offers a six-page analysis of the war against Iraq, she presents no sustained argumentation concerning why the war should be seen as "postmodern." Instead, the term "postmodern" is often deployed simply to describe novel phenomena that have not yet been theorized. Similarly, Rob Wilson (1992, 67f.) refers to the "postmodern reconfiguration in which the Gulf War took place," its "postmodern register of cyborgian grandeur," the "postmodern night" of our current situation, the "postmodern nation-state in which these weapons were designed and constructed," "postmodern production," "a postmodern economy of instantaneous sign-flow and modular bricolage," the "postmodern transnational scene," the "postmodernity of the international market," Bush senior as a "postmodern American Adam," "postmodern ratification in the oil deserts of Kuwait and Saudi Arabia," and the Patriot missile as a "postmodern hero of the technological sublime," ad nauseam, without theorizing what was "postmodern" about any of this.

6 The following sections on mapping are influenced by Jameson (1988, 1991), and draw upon work with Steven Best.

7 See Crosby (1997) for illuminating discussion of the turn to quantitative modes of representation in Western Europe during the early modern age and the contrasts with earlier premodern modes of mapping the world.

8 In *Violent Cartographies* (1997) Michael J. Shapiro argues that maps are functions of power in which borders and terrain are artificially constructed and legitimated in ideological discourses and narratives. Part of the challenges of the contemporary

moment involves undoing the violent cartographies of modernity (nation-state, national borders, scientific and academic disciplines, forms of culture, identities, and so on) in the contemporary era, and the construction of alternative mappings and border-crossing.

9 Ironically, at the very time in which the epochal transformations that generated the postmodern debates were becoming evident, a mode of postmodern theory, promoted by followers of Lyotard and a misunderstood Foucault, argued for the suspension of "grand narratives," "totalizing theory," and the more global and macro theories of classical theory in favor of local narratives, micro theory and politics, and more modest theoretical perspectives (see Lyotard 1984; Best and Kellner 1991). Against this version of postmodern theory, I and my collaborators have long argued for a reconstructed type of the global and critical perspectives of classical social theory that is necessary to theorize contemporary social and theoretical developments. Yet one could also combine global and local projects, micro and macro theory and politics, thus mediating modern and postmodern perspectives (see Best and Kellner 1991, chapter 8; Cvetkovich and Kellner 1997, Introduction).

Bibliography

Baudrillard, Jean. *Simulations*. Trans. Paul Foss, Paul Patton and Philip Beitchman. New York: Semiotext(e), 1983.

Baudrillard, Jean. *Symbolic Exchange and Death*. Trans. Iain Hamilton Grant. London: Sage, 1993.

Best, Steven and Douglas Kellner. "(Re)Watching Television: Notes Toward a Political Criticism." *Diacritics* 17.2 (1987): 97–113.

Best, Steven and Douglas Kellner. *Postmodern Theory: Critical Interrogations*. London and New York: Macmillan and Guilford, 1991.

Best, Steven and Douglas Kellner. *The Postmodern Turn*. New York and London: Guilford and Routledge, 1997.

Best, Steven and Douglas Kellner. *The Postmodern Adventure*. New York and London: Guilford and Routledge, 2001.

Bibby, Michael (ed.). *The Viet Nam War and Postmodernity*. Amherst: U of Massachusetts P, 2000.

Bloch, Ernst. *The Principle of Hope*. Trans. Neville Plaice, Stephen Plaice and Paul Knight. Cambridge, MA: MIT P, 1986.

Cooke, Miriam. "Postmodern Wars." *Journal of Urban and Cultural Studies* 2.1 (1991): 27–40.

Crosby, Alfred W. *The Measure of Reality: Quantification and Western Society, 1250–1600*. Cambridge: Cambridge UP, 1997.

Cumings, Bruce. *War and Television*. London: Verso, 1992.

Cvetkovich, Ann and Douglas Kellner (eds). *Articulating the Global and the Local. Globalization and Cultural Studies*. Boulder, CO: Westview, 1997.

Dewey, John. *Democracy and Education*. New York: Free, 1995.

Foucault, Michel. *Discipline and Punish*. Trans. Alan Sheridan. New York: Pantheon, 1975.

Foucault, Michel. *Language, Counter-Memory, Practice*. Trans. Donald F. Bouchard and Sherry Simon. New York: Cornell UP, 1977.

Foucault, Michel. *The History of Sexuality, Volume 1*. Trans. Robert Hurley. New York: Vintage, 1980.

Fukuyama, Francis. *The End of History and the Last Man*. New York: Free, 1992.

Gray, Chris Hables. *Postmodern War*. New York: Guilford, 1997.

Harding, Sandra. *Is Science Multicultural? Postcolonialism, Feminism, and Epistemologies*. Bloomington: Indiana UP, 1999.

Harvey, David. *The Condition of Postmodernity*. Oxford: Blackwell, 1989.

Herr, Michael. *Dispatches*. New York: Avon, 1978.

Jameson, Fredric. "Postmodernism, or The Cultural Logic of Late Capitalism." *New Left Review* 146 (1984): 53–92.

Jameson, Fredric. "Cognitive Mapping." *Marxism and the Interpretation of Culture*. Ed. Larry Grossberg and Cary Nelson. Urbana: U of Illinois P, 1988. 347–58.

Jameson, Fredric. *Postmodernism, or, The Cultural Logic of Late Capitalism*. Durham, NC and London: Duke UP, 1991.

Kellner, Douglas. "Postmodernism as Social Theory: Some Problems and Challenges." *Theory, Culture & Society* 5.2–3 (1988): 240–69.

Kellner, Douglas (ed.). *Postmodernism/Jameson/Critique*. Washington, DC: Maisonneuve, 1989a.

Kellner, Douglas. *Jean Baudrillard: From Marxism to Postmodernism and Beyond*. Cambridge and Palo Alto: Polity and Stanford UP, 1989b.

Kellner, Douglas. *The Persian Gulf TV War*. Boulder, CO: Westview, 1992.

Kellner, Douglas. *Baudrillard. A Critical Reader*. Edited with Introduction. Malden, MA and Oxford: Blackwell, 1994.

Kellner, Douglas. *Media Culture*. London and New York: Routledge, 1995.

Kellner, Douglas. "Theorizing Globalization." *Sociological Theory* 20.3 (2002): 285–305.

Kellner, Douglas. *From September 11 to Terror War: The Dangers of the Bush Legacy*. Lanham, MD: Rowman, 2003.

Kellner, Douglas and Sean Homer. *Fredric Jameson: A Critical Reader*. London and New York: Palgrave Macmillan, 2004.

Lowenthal, Leo. *Literature, Popular Culture, and Society*. Englewood Cliffs, NJ: Prentice Hall, 1961.

Lyotard, Jean François. *The Postmodern Condition*. Trans. Geoff Bennington and Brian Massumi. Minneapolis: U of Minnesota P, 1984.

Polanyi, Karl. *The Great Transformation: The Political and Economic Origins of Our Time*. Boston: Beacon, 1957.

Poster, Mark. *The Mode of Information*. Cambridge and Chicago: Polity and U of Chicago P, 1990.

Poster, Mark. "Postmodern Virtualities." *Cyberspace/Cyberbodies/Cyberpunk*. Ed. Mike Featherstone and Roger Burrows. London and Thousand Oaks, CA: Sage, 1996.

Robins, Kevin and Frank Webster. *Times of the Technoculture*. New York: Routledge, 1999.

Rorty, Richard. *Philosophy and the Mirror of Nature*. Princeton: Princeton UP, 1979.

Shapiro, Michael. *Violent Cartographies: Mapping Cultures of War*. Minneapolis: U of Minnesota P, 1997.

Snow, C.P. *The Two Cultures: And a Second Look*. Cambridge: Cambridge UP, 1964.

Turkle, Sherry. *The Second Self. Computers and the Human Spirit*. New York: Simon, 1984.

Turkle, Sherry. *Life on the Screen. Identity in the Age of the Internet*. New York: Simon, 1995.

Wilson, Rob. "'Sublime Patriot.'" *Polygraph* 5 (1992): 67–77.

Wood, Denis. *The Power of Maps*. New York: Guilford, 1992.

mike gane and nicholas gane

THE POSTMODERN: AFTER THE (NON-)EVENT

The postmodern – at least in the social sciences – has somehow disappeared from view. Could this be because it was so successful in clearing away modern concepts and theories that it "worked itself out of a job" (Bauman in Gane 2004, 17)? Or did the postmodern disappear because it *failed* in this task? Alternatively, and more banally, did the postmodern disappear because it simply slipped out of fashion?

I

Each of these explanations seems equally plausible, but is there not a danger in posing the question in this way: to talk categorically of what the postmodern is or is not, and to talk of its successes and failures, of its origins, causes and effects? Could the search for the truth of *the* postmodern be nothing more than a modern strategy of conceptual and theoretical closure? This seems to be the case for thinkers who dismiss the term postmodern on the grounds that it lacks any conceptual precision, or any empirical grip on so-called "reality." Gellner, for example, despite having been read as a postmodern "Crocodile Dundee" thinker (Agassi in Hall and Jarvie 1992, 213), falls into this camp when he says that postmodernism is "strong and fashionable" but it is "not altogether clear what the devil it is" for "clarity is not conspicuous amongst its marked attributes" (Gellner 1992, 22). Already in such a reading, modern values of clarity, consensus and convergence are privileged over heterogeneous ways of thinking that accept and work with ambiguities, uncertainties and complexity. The very idea that the postmodern has to *mean* something, that this meaning is to be *clear*, and that any movement that is postmodern in orientation is to be necessarily one and *unified* in aim is already to work from modernist value presuppositions, and to promote these over any alternative perspective. The postmodern, if it stands for anything at all, embraces the reverse of each of these ideals: plurality, dissensus, or, more generally, anything dis- (that which is apart or away from, that which is removed or expelled from, that which is the reversal of action). Thus, on looking back on the 1980s, the postmodern has meant many things, none of which are "correct" in the modern sense: an experimental or *paralogical* mode of thinking (Lyotard 1984a), a new mode of production and consumption (Jameson 1991), a new petty bourgeois ideology (Lash 1990), a new realm of neo-tribal sociality (Maffesoli 1996), a fiction best explained as a product of late modernity (Giddens 1991), a new configuration of time-space (Harvey 1989), a kind of urban space (Soja 1989), a form of posthumanism (Hayles 1999), and no doubt more.

The postmodern, then, has no unambiguous, fundamental and agreed essence to speak of, even though most social science textbooks have sought to find one. Even the idea that like the modern (Foucault 1997) the postmodern is an *ethos* – a mode of thinking that cannot easily be captured – is only *one* sophisticated attempt to give it a definitive content. Such an ethos, if it has any basis, it said to play out through the celebration and play of heterogeneity. This version of the postmodern has proved the most difficult for the social sciences to accept, for it has no predefined rules, no established methods, no unified viewpoint, and works towards complication rather than clarity. For many, the postmodern this stands for is the worst of all, for it is seen to lead to the abandonment of academic rigour. But for others it signifies the emergence of a vital new freedom as opportunities for creative work open up in a world without pre-given value-standards. In this reading, postmodernism is about *the pleasure of death* (the death of the author, of universality, of meta-narratives, of absolute truth, of progress, and so on). It is about working into the unknown in the absence of all foundations. In its Nietzschean form it is about the revaluation of all values: overcoming rather than critique. In its post-Nietzschean form, meanwhile, critical theory gives way to *fatal* theory, or to what Baudrillard (1990) calls *fatal strategies*.

II

There are complex dependencies at stake here. The postmodern, for example, might be said to come before the modern (Lyotard 1984a), for it is that which exists outside the rules of all existing games. In this reading, the postmodern is a new game that becomes modern the moment that rules are no longer formed after the event but known in advance. The connection between the modern and postmodern is comparable here to the interplay between normal and revolutionary science (Kuhn 1996), with oscillations between the modern (knowledge ordered by existing rules) and postmodern (the pursuit of knowledge through rules that have yet to be formulated) taking place continuously throughout culture. This reversible relation shatters modern narratives that map the passage from the "premodern" to the modern through to the postmodern in a linear way. History is seen instead to be made up of a multiplicity of competing narratives, none of which are "true" in the traditional sense. What emerges instead is a series of power/knowledge (Nietzsche/Foucault (Nietzsche 1968; Foucault 1980)) or power/force (Nietzsche/Deleuze (Deleuze 1986)) relations in which the intrinsic value of knowledge or culture is secondary to the capacity for domination (contrary to Enlightenment belief): the best move in a game does not always win, for it depends who has control over the rules.

The idea, however, of cyclic connections between modern and postmodern phases, and hence the paradox that modern may come after postmodern episodes, has precursors, notably the theory of organic and critical episodes identified by writers at the beginning of the nineteenth century (Gane 2003, 37–42), and again at the end of the 1930s with the work of Bataille (Hollier 1988). The specific character of the recent postmodern episode was one of joyous abandonment and relief from the burdens of the reductive rationalism of socialist and humanitarian grand moral narratives. Was this movement, like other such episodes, linked to political setback and even defeat – for example the historic defeat of the socialist and communist projects? Did it then mark a decisive passage into a new epoch, or has a counter-movement been able to close this particular space? Far from being too radical, did the recent postmodern episode fail to extend its analyses sufficiently deeply?

III

Perhaps the most radical challenge of the postmodern is the thesis that there can no longer be a stable and secure hierarchy of different genres of knowledge or culture or politics. It is often argued that the idea that the grand narratives established by modernity are at an end is itself contradictory since this itself is a grand narrative. But things are more complex, since it is not clear at all that the new thesis is of the same type: it could take the form of an ironic or agonistic perspective rather than a "grand" narrative. This radicalism is not simply the assertion of a negation but a change of terrain towards a more nominalistic epistemological position. This idea that universal ideas are mere names shifts analysis to the question of language. "There is no such thing as society," for example, is a characteristic expression of the moment of *letting go* of a naïve sociological realism in favour of a much more cynical style of thinking. This radicalism can be extended to the deconstruction of all the major categories, even the "individual." In the history of social thought such radical nominalistic moments are often followed by the "return of the repressed" or the "release of elements" formally held in place by a dominant discursive formation. At this moment of "gentle apocalypse" (Barthes cited by Culler 2002, 109) the pleasure in the postmodern is most evident. But this pleasure always emerges in relation to what has been repressed – and how – within modernity itself. The problem of anti-postmodern positions is that they make the mistake of reading this pleasure as an indulgence, as beyond the scope of rigorous analysis. It is often the case, however, that at this moment new forms of rigour are precisely the site of the most interesting and significant new contributions that reveal modernist orthodoxies as insensitive to particular, crucial "details." This can give rise, surprisingly, to a postmodern Marx, or Durkheim, or Simmel, or Parsons, or feminism.

In spite of this, the idea of *letting go* of grand narratives has been unpalatable for many, as it has been associated with a lapse in intellectual standards and has even been seen as a path towards nihilism, as critics of so-called relativism such as Leo Strauss (1953) have long insisted. But attacking grand narratives need not lead to nihilism, just as pleasure need not be self-indulgent. Pleasure could, for example, indulge the "other." The postmodern, as Nietzsche foresaw (1990), might involve a series of revaluations rather than the rejection of all values. Through the course of such work, new values might be born, or older values that lie repressed within existing bodies of knowledge be released into the fray (what Foucault, following Nietzsche, called the project of *genealogy*). Modern readings of the postmodern here tend to confuse the refusal to construct universals or grand narratives with an act of ethical and political indifference. But the postmodern places the presuppositions and forms of modern politics under attack, so that the exclusionary structures underpinning the social, the political, or so-called "democracy" are brought into view. The game for postmodern thinkers is not to invent new hegemonic political forms but to affirm alternatives, and to embrace rather than resolve difference (Lyotard's (1988) *differend* is an example). The charge that "anything goes" in such an exercise is merely a projection of a modern desire to regulate what counts as knowledge according to established rules or norms. In the postmodern it is not that there are no intrinsic truths for the author (either of events or texts) but rather that the author can exercise little control over the destination of meaning. In the face of this, history and texts are opened up to different readings, voices and perspectives so that all aspects of knowledge become sites of contestation (Bakhtin 1981). What emerges from this new agonistic culture is not a space in which anything goes, but rather the promise of a new, invigorated sphere of politics. An example: in modernity, racism and sexism underpinned institutional structures and even the basic structures of philosophical knowledge (from the "Rights of Man" to the gendering of Descartes's "I think therefore I am"). In the postmodern *this no longer goes*. The presuppositions of knowledge are no longer seen to be transcendental but located, and therefore connected intimately to a range of different power structures that can be *contested*. "Knowledge is power" becomes "power is knowledge," but not in any absolute sense since knowledges create their own genealogies (Borges 1999, 363–65), and the categories used to organize the "official" histories of disciplines can change rapidly (what was modern becomes postmodern). Knowledge becomes knowledge*s*, and power power*s*.

IV

Perhaps, then, as many commentators have pointed out (again in an attempt to clarify and systematize), the postmodern itself can be broken down into elements. First, there is a radical disenchantment with the modern project itself (in some fields, modernism within modernity is defined much more clearly than in others). Second, and in part depending on the way in which this critical disenchantment has played itself out, there is the moment of the "return of the repressed," borne out, most famously, in Foucault's (1980, 81–82) concern for the repressed otherness of subjugated knowledge. Third, there may then be a moment when indicative new values or forms may emerge. Certainly in the early nineteenth century, with first the Saint-Simonian religion (around 1828–31 (Durkheim 1962)) and then the religion of humanity founded and organized on the model of the Catholic hierarchy by Comte (Comte 1968), there were radical attempts to inject traditional forms with new content that can clearly be seen as a specific kind of postmodernist project (Wernick 2001). Ridiculed at the time, it seems clear today that these new religious movements, with the missionary zeal associated with new cults, were early attempts to complete modernity's project.

Against this background it might be possible to make an assessment of the recent postmodern episode. It has been suggested that what is characteristic of recent times is that no new values have been forged, and instead of the "return of the repressed" what has happened is more of a release of elements into a moral vacuum (Gane 2003, 163–64). This position is tied closely to the basic idea that Western values are becoming increasingly alike and interchangeable. This argument is found commonly in recent debates over the structure of "global culture," and is anticipated by Max Weber in his so-called "rationalization thesis" (Gane 2002, 15–44).

Baudrillard (1993, 113–23) calls this new transversalism the "hell of the same": a hell in which more and more values are being produced, but with nothing essentially new entering the system – only the eternal repetition of what is already present. This situation whereby culture endlessly duplicates itself is underpinned by a condition of *hypertelia*, in which the ends of consumption multiply beyond all bounds. While this condition is new, it is defined by the accelerated production and circulation of equivalence. Hence Baudrillard sees not "a resigned abandonment of old values but rather a mad overdetermination, an exacerbation of these values of reference, function, finality and causality" – in these terms, what fills the moral vacuum are recycled values (perhaps what might be called, following Beck (2000), "zombie" values) that refuse death: "something redundant always establishes itself where there is nothing left" (Baudrillard 1990, 11).

In this perspective it is possible to *contrast* the recent postmodern episode with previous ones and to suggest one of two things. Perhaps it – *this* postmodern – has been an event that in its very nature cannot be defined or conceived because no coalescence within its field of vital elements has taken place. Or perhaps the postmodern failed because it did little to disturb modern culture, and any new values it did produce were quickly assimilated into the system (this is the line of the later Lyotard (1997, 3–15), who argued that postmodern culture soon became commodified). There are two ways of assessing this. One is that the opportunity was simply missed and the moment for such creativity passed with only a symptomatic "negative theology" as its witness. The other concludes that no such creative activity is now possible because the recent postmodern episode, despite appearances, is not the equivalent of an earlier moment for the creation of values, and hence offers neither the prospect of a completion of social change nor the moment of inauguration of a radically new epoch. This position inverts the positive, Nietzschean confidence in the revaluation of all values into a deeply pessimistic, and ultimately nihilistic, vision of the failure of the new. Either the new is not really new at all (a common critique of "new" political values such as Giddens'/Blair's Third Way (Giddens 1998)), or alternatively, or perhaps at the same time, all that is possible is a project of critique that remains caught within the basic structures of whatever is being opposed.

What should be called the "non-event" of postmodernism is, in this latter view, merely part of the failure of untimely transcendent emancipatory political projects. *This* postmodernism could not therefore figure as a moment of transmodernism between stages of the uneven progression of modernity itself. Perhaps the profound opposition that manifested itself from staunch socialists and intellectuals on the left (from Eagleton (1996) to Kellner (1989)) is somehow explicable in this light: all that is left for socialists is a conservation project in a world where the initiative has passed to the right (social democratic through to the various religious fundamentalisms and then to Le Pen). Perhaps the most important loss is that even the basic left–right division of political forces is no longer clearly identifiable. Hence Giddens (1994) talks of a political culture that is "beyond Left and Right," while Baudrillard (1993) calls this a *transpolitical* situation. It is scarcely surprising that the "emancipatory" project is now a commitment to the old values and rhetoric, for it does not have the confidence to attempt to create new values either within or against postmodernism. Neither does it attempt to give birth to any new organizational forms, or any new kinds of discipline. It appears that there is tangible relief in this camp with the ending of the postmodern episode. Perhaps what we see today is a new fundamentalist retrenchment and regrouping of the left (e.g. Žižek 2002) determined to end the anti-foundationalism of postmodern radicalism, following its failure to live up to the project of attempting to "unthink" itself (Wallerstein 1991).

V

Not much comfort is to be gained, however, from standing on the old foundations, even if they have been subjected to realignment along new fault lines. This is because the binary oppositions (such as left and right) that gave modern thought its apparently secure foundations have everywhere been crossed, leading to a world characterized by *transversalisms*. No longer, for example, is it possible unambiguously to demarcate what is human from what is an object or a technology (hence the debates over the inhuman (Lyotard 1991), the posthuman (Hayles 1991; Fukuyama 2003) and cyborg culture (Haraway 1991; Gray 2002)), what is material from what is "ideal" (the question of intellectual property), or what is real as opposed to hyperreal or virtual (Baudrillard 1993). Even key concepts, such as the social (and its separation from the cultural or political), are now notoriously difficult to define. Postmodern thinking (inspired by the writings of Nietzsche, Bataille and Foucault) initially addressed these new uncertainties in the terms of a philosophy of the limit: what are the limits of different concepts or genres of knowledge and how might they be transgressed? But with the emergence of transversal culture, today there is little talk of limits, transgression or what Nietzsche earlier called "overcoming." Rather, the focus of so-called critical philosophy has shifted. The Nietzsche–Bataille–Foucault concern with the limit has given way to Deleuzian analysis of rhizomatics: those connections across genres or limits that mark out the transversality of contemporary cultural and social forms from those of previous periods. At a surface level, this means the mapping of new network relations: of flows rather than structures. At a deeper level, questions are asked of what happens when the binary categories or cultures that had previously been separated cross over into each other: when, for example, the borders between human and machine, masculine and feminine, "East" and "West," and so on can be crossed in new ways and hence start to disappear. At this point, what appears to emerge is not a stable new order of things but rather a series of multiple connections characterized by chaos and confusion.

The certainty of the modern order (with its linear narratives and its ideology of progress) disappears here. One thing to have emerged in its wake is a new vitalism in which there is a regression into that which has yet to be either captured by cultural capitalism or scarred by the ongoing vitiation of all basic categories. This new focus on "life" (see, for example, Lash 2002) seeks fundamental and vital sources of energy that have yet to be captured and tamed by any system. The problem with this, however, is that every instance of life has its (genetic) code, and can only exist as life and be understood as such within a given, and more often than not closed, system. Power and life are thus not mutually exclusive categories but, as Foucault (1990) showed in his writings on *bio-power*, are interwoven into and through each other. In this reading, vitalism only offers a path into a series of primordial elements that cease to be either primordial or radical as soon as they are treated as such. For this reason, vitalism offers no way out. Similar paths of enchantment have been sought before through the appeal to the unconscious (in, for example, Lyotard's early *Driftworks* (1984b)) or to the childhood of thought (Lyotard 1992), which, while disruptive and agonistic as ways of thinking, achieved few lasting effects.

VI

Postmodernism has come and gone as a new kind of intellectual aftershock. The massive failures of the projects of the radical left to transcend liberal democratic capitalism, the collapse of the communist camp, the ascendancy of affluent consumerism and information technologies, together with the restructuring of the states in the West by neo-conservatism from 1980 in the context of the defeat and decomposition of the "proletariat" are the seismic events to which postmodernisms correspond. What emerges in this situation is a spirit of postmodernism that welcomes a loser's tolerance. A new situation arises in which the radical left tries both to welcome diversity as multiculturalism and radical institutional pluralism. But this, in turn, provokes traditional conservative forces (on issues such as the family, religion, the body, etc.). The result is a new virulence of right-wing fundamentalism and extremism that subsequently takes the initiative. In response, the left – now itself divorced from its own past failed hegemonic projects – has only one space in which to move: the centre in support of liberal democracy against what is perceived as neo-fascism (particularly in France).

In the radical move to disassociate itself from the oppressive aspects of modernism and progressivism, the postmodern became defenceless against such a virulent reaction. What has been clearly absent (for the most part) is any equivalent radical move within the spirit of postmodernism to define a practice of intolerance. There are at least two general problems here. First, at the level of the social, there is the question of justice. On the one hand, there is a notion of liberal tolerance as "repressive tolerance" – a thesis developed in the 1960s by Marcuse and Barrington Moore (Wolff, Moore and Marcuse 1969), but more recently extended greatly by Baudrillard and others. On the other hand, there is Lyotard's (1988) thesis that with a multiplicity of differends there will only be a kind of terrorist injustice as long as it attempts to establish one dominant totalizing regime of truth. Second, at the individual level, it could be suggested that the "end of the social" results in the "society of individuals," and that far from liberating individuals as free subjects out of a restraining power network it is within the individual that all the problems of "correctness" are finally deposited. This is achieved not in the mode of "other-directedness," or through a new governance of the self, but through a new managerialism of the self appropriate to the ethos of lifestyle consumerism.

VII

This could well be where all the theoretical problems with postmodernism are most evident. This conclusion reduces the cultural aftershock effects visible in the "non"-event itself (the diffraction, fragmentation, dispersal effects across so many intellectual domains) to the posited seismic events of social transformation themselves. Mapping of the features of the new conjuncture might in theory help if only, of course, an unambiguous technique were available. A modernist sociology of postmodernism has been advocated and developed (incidentally by Bauman 1992), but the most radical mapping has been that associated with methods that combine "postmodern" science and literature, which theorizes the "modern" itself as artifice in a perspective which takes reflexivity to a new level (Hayles 1991). This said, however, the opening up of spaces for new postmodern styles of analysis has, for the most part, been wasted in the social sciences and in politics. Such spaces continue to be occupied today by the "anti-modernists" of previous contestations (ethnomethodology, rhetoric and discourse methods, deconstruction, poststructuralism, etc.). The "postmodern" episode was therefore a "non"-event *of a new type*. For a moment the links, bonds, grounds, networks, systems, were weakened. There was a moment of relaxation (not rupture): those who had "never been modern" had always read their horoscopes, but those who had passed through modernity could in this moment take a new interest in theirs. The question thus arose: if we do not live our lives – and cannot live them – in the main as enlightened rational beings, how do we live?

"We," however, has always been a troublesome word for postmodernists, who tend to call the very idea of a shared basis to (social) life, i.e., that there is a thing called humanity, into question. Postmodern lives are treated, for the most part, in radical disjunction from each other, with little concern for how they are tied together or arranged collectively through the play of institutions. Postmodern thinking, as a consequence, showed little concern for (social) structure, and focused instead on questions of identity (which was often seen to be decentred) and movement (in the form of "flows"). Recently, however, the question of structure or bonding has returned (in a loose way) in a renewed concern for modernity: reflexive (Beck, Giddens and Lash 1994), liquid (Bauman 2000), or risk (Beck 1992). This return of the modern, albeit in a refigured form, waves goodbye to the resources and energies of the postmodern. Gone, for example, is the call for political/ aesthetic/theoretical experimentation. Gone is the attack on the universal and its related meta-narratives. In its place is a new meta-narrative of uncertainty centred upon causes and, more than before, (*side-*)*effects*. Alongside this, a new hierarchy is said to have emerged in which *everyone* has their place: a hierarchy of risk (which neither the poor nor the rich can escape (Beck 1992)), or movement (Bauman 1998). This is tied to the vision of a global society (marked out by fluid or mobile structures or *networks*). In this new world (the world of the second modernity), global risks – including those of terrorism or environmental catastrophe – are said to tie us together in new ways. Meanwhile, the question of what these ties actually look like falls once again into the (extended) province of modernist theory (which can be traced back to Hobbes).

VIII

The return of the modern (reflexive, risk or liquid) hence brings a reversal of the postmodern: whereas uncertainty was something to be valued and embraced, it is now treated as an unavoidable burden. The dictum of paralogy – "into the unknown" – is today seen less as a promise of emancipation and more as an expression of some kind of common plight. Whereas the postmodern opened theory to new forms of invention and boundary crossing, the "reflexive" (Beck 1992) or "liquid" turn (Bauman 2000) in response seeks to close down these avenues by seeking new foundations and securities. As an aftershock, the postmodern simply fades away. Panic over? Or is it just beginning?

Bibliography

Bakhtin, M. *The Dialogic Imagination*. Trans. Caryle Emerson and Michael Holquist. Austin: U of Texas P, 1981.

Baudrillard, J. *Fatal Strategies*. Trans. Philip Beitchman. New York: Semiotext(e), 1990.

Baudrillard, J. *The Transparency of Evil*. Trans. James Benedict. London: Verso, 1993.

Bauman, Z. *Intimations of Postmodernity*. London: Routledge, 1992.

Bauman, Z. *Globalization*. Cambridge: Polity, 1998.

Bauman, Z. *Liquid Modernity*. Cambridge: Polity, 2000.

Beck, U. *Risk Society*. London: Sage, 1992.

Beck, U. "The Cosmopolitan Perspective." *British Journal of Sociology* 51.1 (2000): 79–105.

Beck, U., A. Giddens and S. Lash. *Reflexive Modernization*. Cambridge: Polity, 1994.

Borges, J.L. *The Total Library*. Trans. Eliot Weinberger et al. London: Lane, 1999.

Bourdieu, P. *Distinction: A Social Critique of the Judgement of Taste*. Trans. Richard Nice. London: Routledge, 1984.

Comte, A. *A System of Positive Polity*. Trans. J.H. Bridges et al. New York: Franklin, 1968.

Culler, J. *Barthes: A Very Short Introduction*. Oxford: Oxford UP, 2002.

Deleuze, G. *Nietzsche and Philosophy*. Trans. Hugh Tomlinson. London: Continuum, 1986.

Durkheim, E. *Socialism and Saint-Simon*. Trans. Charlotte Sattler. New York: Collier, 1962.

Eagleton, T. *The Illusions of Postmodernism*. Oxford: Blackwell, 1996.

Foucault, M. *Power/Knowledge*. Trans. Colin Gordon et al. New York: Random, 1980.

Foucault, M. *The History of Sexuality Volume One*. Trans. Robert Hurley. Harmondsworth: Penguin, 1990.

Foucault, M. "What is Enlightenment?" Trans. Catherine Porter. *Michel Foucault: Ethics, Subjectivity, Truth*. Ed. P. Rabinow. Harmondsworth: Penguin, 1997.

Fukuyama, F. *Our Posthuman Future*. London: Profile, 2003.

Gane, M. *French Social Theory*. London: Sage, 2003.

Gane, N. *Max Weber and Postmodern Theory*. Basingstoke: Palgrave, 2002.

Gane, N. *The Future of Social Theory*. London: Continuum, 2004.

Gellner, E. *Postmodernism, Reason and Religion*. London: Routledge, 1992.

Giddens, A. *The Consequences of Modernity*. Cambridge: Polity, 1991.

Giddens, A. *Beyond Left and Right*. Cambridge: Polity, 1994.

Giddens, A. *The Third Way*. Cambridge: Polity, 1998.

Gray, C.H. *Cyborg Citizen*. London: Routledge, 2002.

Hall, J. and I. Jarvie (eds) *Transition to Modernity*. Cambridge: Cambridge UP, 1992.

Haraway, D. *Simians, Cyborgs and Women*. London: Routledge, 1991.

Harvey, D. *The Condition of Postmodernity*. Oxford: Blackwell, 1989.

Hayles, N.K. (ed.). *Chaos and Order: Complex Dynamics in Literature and Science*. Chicago: U of Chicago P, 1991.

Hayles, N.K. *How We Became Posthuman*. Chicago: U of Chicago P, 1999.

Hollier, D. (ed.). *The College of Sociology*. Minneapolis: U of Minnesota P, 1988.

Jameson, F. *Postmodernism, or the Cultural Logic of Late Capitalism.* Durham, NC: Duke UP, 1991.

Kellner, D. *Jean Baudrillard: From Marxism to Postmodernity and Beyond.* Oxford: Blackwell, 1989.

Kuhn, T. *The Structure of Scientific Revolutions.* Chicago: U of Chicago P, 1996.

Lash, S. *Sociology of Postmodernism.* London: Routledge, 1990.

Lash, S. *Critique of Information.* London: Sage, 2002.

Lyotard, J.-F. *The Postmodern Condition.* Trans. Geoffrey Bennington and Brian Massumi. Manchester: Manchester UP, 1984a.

Lyotard, J.-F. *Driftworks.* Trans. Roger McKeon et al. New York: Semiotext(e), 1984b.

Lyotard, J.-F. *The Differend.* Trans. Georges Van Den Abbeele. Manchester: Manchester UP, 1988.

Lyotard, J.-F. *The Inhuman.* Trans. Geoffrey Bennington and Rachel Bowlby. Cambridge: Polity, 1991.

Lyotard, J.-F. *The Postmodern Explained to Children.* Trans. Don Barry. Sydney: Power Institute of Fine Arts, 1992.

Lyotard, J.-F. *Postmodern Fables.* Trans. Georges Van Den Abbeele. Minneapolis: U of Minnesota P, 1997.

Maffesoli, M. *The Time of the Tribes.* Trans. Don Smith. London: Sage, 1996.

Nietzsche, F. *The Will to Power.* Trans. Walter Kaufmann. New York: Random, 1968.

Nietzsche, F. *The Twilight of the Idols.* Trans. R.J. Hollingdale. Harmondsworth: Penguin, 1990.

Soja, E. *Postmodern Geographies.* London: Verso, 1989.

Strauss, L. *Natural Right and History.* Chicago: U of Chicago P, 1953.

Wallerstein, E. *Unthinking Social Science.* Cambridge: Cambridge UP, 1991.

Wernick, A. *Auguste Comte and the Religion of Humanity.* Cambridge: Cambridge UP, 2001.

Wolff, R., B. Moore and H. Marcuse. *A Critique of Pure Tolerance.* London: Cape, 1969.

Žižek, S. (ed.). *Revolution at the Gates.* Trans. M.S. Levin et al. London: Verso, 2002.

III

THE POSTMODERN AND THE TWENTY-FIRST CENTURY

akbar s. ahmed

POSTMODERNISM AND ISLAM: WHERE TO AFTER SEPTEMBER 11?[1]

Ideas and practice of multicultural harmony, eclecticism and juxtapositions, which were at the heart of what commentators called postmodernism, were halted in their tracks on 11 September 2001. While exact definitions of postmodernism were contested – was it merely the epoch that followed "modernity" or something radically different? Was it nothing more than a European intellectual movement? – there was general recognition of its main features: the mingling of diverse sources, a juxtaposition of the high and the low, the use of irony and humor and an ambiguity toward, if not outright rejection of, any monolithic ideology with a one-size-fits-all and one-style-suits-all worldview, which was called a Grand Narrative. Leading thinkers of postmodernism such as Jean-François Lyotard and Jean Baudrillard reminded us that even Marxism, which was once seen as the Grand Narrative par excellence, was now just one of a thousand brands of ideology on sale in the supermarket of ideas. The analogy with the shopping mall, itself seen as a temple to postmodernism, became part of the definition of postmodernism.

On September 11 no one could miss the symbolism of the attack on the heart of the financial center of the Western world. Nor could one miss the symbolism of the strike on the Pentagon, the heart of the military might of America. But something else had also been struck: postmodernism lay buried in the rubble on that fateful day.

In many important ways September 11 was the day the new century began. For most of the twentieth century the USA had led a coalition of nations against the Soviet Union and its allies in what was called the Cold War. Both sides propagated their own Grand Narratives: the former was characterized by capitalism, multinational corporations and democracy; the latter by central planning, state ownership and dictatorship. With the fall of the Berlin Wall in 1989 it appeared as if Grand Narratives would simply fade away and the ideas and style of postmodernism would triumph.

After September 11, the Grand Narrative, which was assumed dead if not buried, was back with a vengeance especially in the USA. God, Christianity and talk of the crusades were back at center stage and supported by the power of the mightiest military on earth. The challenge to postmodernism thus did not come from the expected quarters – neither French philosophers nor American architects. It came from George W. Bush at the White House and Osama bin Laden in the caves of Tora Bora in Afghanistan, who jointly struck a mighty blow to the concept and practice of postmodernism. Both advocated and came to embody their own versions of a Grand Narrative which saw opposed ideas as false and evil.

In his unilateralist approach to foreign policy, treatment of foreign prisoners at Guantanamo Bay and turning a deaf ear to international organizations such as the World Trade Organization, Bush embodied the new Grand Narrative, which he vigorously advocated in his speeches. Bush's shibboleth "You are with us or against us" summed up his personal philosophy and foreign policy. Bush's "war on terrorism" itself became an expression of the Grand Narrative. At one stroke, local and different histories, cultures and traditions were brushed aside to find a place for the reinvigorated Grand Narrative.

The Grand Narrative instantly found its philosophers. Samuel Huntington had already published "The Clash of Civilizations?" in 1993 (*Foreign Affairs* 72.3 (summer 1993)), an idea and title inspired from an earlier article by Bernard Lewis, "The Roots of Muslim Rage" (*Atlantic Monthly* (Sept. 1990)). The discourse of conflict dominated intellectual discussion and further marginalized postmodernist thinking.

The post-September world has confirmed for us that the Grand Narrative is back. Its chief architect is, of course, George W. Bush, but he has a team around him who implement the new vision with the zeal of the crusaders – men like Richard Cheney, Donald Rumsfeld and John Ashcroft. Muslims were not only being bombed at will in Afghanistan and Iraq but picked up and interrogated or deported on flimsy grounds in the USA. Muslim males were asked to register with the authorities in a program that to them appeared sinister because it singled them out. Arrests were made on flimsy grounds and stories of bungling and brutality were reported. Thousands of Muslims escaped to Canada or were deported to their homes of origin with shattered lives. Their hopes of being part of the American dream lay in tatters.

Well-known religious figures rallied round Bush by emphasizing the Christian nature of the USA and attacking Islam. The Reverend Franklin Graham, who offered the invocation at Bush's inauguration, called Islam "a very wicked and evil religion." The Reverends Jerry Vines and Jerry Falwell attacked the Prophet of Islam using inflammatory language. These attacks, widely disseminated in the media, helped feed into and reinforce already existing stereotypes of Muslims. To many Americans the religion of Islam simply meant terrorism or extremism. Muslims felt they were under siege, with their religion, culture and honor under attack.[2]

Bush's insistence that it was a "war on terrorism" and not against Islam, his visits to the Islamic Center in Washington, DC and his meetings with Muslim leaders were lost in the roar of Islamophobia coming from those who supported him. The contradiction was lost in the Grand Narrative that dominated the political and even much of the intellectual landscape after September 11. To challenge or oppose this monolith was to risk being labeled a traitor or simply un-American.

Those Muslim leaders who could have played the role of mediators arguing for more nuances in the interpretation of the Grand Narrative and more sympathy in understanding buckled under the pressure from Washington and became mere camp followers and yes men. President Pervez Musharraf of Pakistan, whose country became a frontline ally in Bush's "war on terrorism," fell into line without any serious attempts to act as a political or cultural interlocutor. So enthusiastic was his acceptance of Bush's philosophy that his countrymen began to call him "Busharraf" in contempt. Like other Muslim dictators in alliance with Washington, Musharraf used Bush's "war on terrorism" as an excuse to suppress legitimate opposition to his rule.

Why then, if postmodernism is indeed fatally struck, is there any relevance to a discussion about postmodernism and Islam?

The answer is reflected in a discussion I had a decade ago at the house of Charles Jencks, one of the leading figures of postmodernism, when he convened a meeting in London. I suspect I was there because of my book *Postmodernism and Islam: Predicament and Promise* (1992), which had recently been published. Amidst the splendor of a decidedly postmodernist décor, some leading intellectuals were asked to define where they stood in the different phases of the postmodernist movement. There was a quiet air of triumphalism about the participants. An ideological movement they represented had won the day.

When my turn came, I pointed out that it was difficult for me to place myself in a postmodernist category as not only was the definition of postmodernism itself ambiguous but the discussion had not reached the main body of the Muslim world. Muslim societies, still mainly rural and tribal, were struggling to come to terms with the nation-states in which they found themselves after the Second World War. Indeed, the struggle in the Muslim world was still very much with the main issues of modernity

– the relationship between a strong central state asserting its own version of the Grand Narrative and tribal groups; the question of national identity; the debate about the limits of economic development as a marker of progress, etc.

Besides, I pointed out, there was a rejection of Western modernity in many parts of the Muslim world. People pointed to the injustices faced by Muslims in Palestine, Kashmir, Chechnya and the Balkans. Countries like Afghanistan were in turmoil and millions of Afghans had been forced to flee their homes. An anger and hatred festered in the Muslim world and people blamed the West, especially the USA, for their plight.

Muslim societies were still grappling with issues of modernity and still had a long way to go before they made the transition to postmodernism. The distinguished postmodernists present looked distinctly uncomfortable at my frankness. Their assumptions were ethnocentric and rested on the belief that all world civilizations would passively follow the path to postmodernism. As I had made clear, this was not the case. It seemed to them that my Muslim culture was clearly a notch or two below theirs in the evolutionary ladder of human societies. I felt I was at a club whose members might not invite me again.

However, I did point out that postmodernism created a predicament and tension for those with traditional ideas of religious belief in the disturbing skepticism, juxtapositions and contradictions. At the same time it also offered the promise of cultural, sociological and political under-standing between and within different societies as its premise was inclu-sivist. I observed that in some respects I saw a certain commonality in postmodernism and Islam: the universal humanism and acceptance of others which lay at the heart of both, for example. I cited the verses in the Quran which emphasize that there is no compulsion in religion and that God has created different nations and peoples to encourage mutual toler-ance and understanding. Indeed, I had emphasized the predicament and promise of postmodernism in its relationship to Islam by making this the subtitle to my book.

Reading the book again, I note that the arguments remain relevant for the post-September world in which we find ourselves. The ideas and actions of men like Osama bin Laden, al-Qaeda and the Taliban would be influenced by the mood of anger in the Muslim world and in turn feed it. They too were creating a Grand Narrative. They portrayed Jews, Christians and the nations of America and Israel as evils that had to be fought. The attacks on New York and Washington were a tragic but logical progression of this line of thinking. There was cause and effect here.

While some things have changed dramatically – the re-emergence of the Grand Narrative, for example – others have not. Take the discussion of the media. I noted the sense of frustration that Muslims felt in seeing themselves portrayed negatively. This problem has become even more acute after September 11 and continues to cause misunderstandings on both sides.

In attempting to define postmodernism, Roland Barthes wrote of "a moment of gentle apocalypse."[3] Others base their definition on what they called "panic theory."[4] We lived in a world of panic sex, panic art, and panic culture. More recent works remained alarmist.[5] The sense of the world being out of control and of imminent apocalypse has magnified after September 11.

The understanding of Islam is more important than ever: its 1.3 billion people continue to grow; it has fifty-seven states, at least one of which is nuclear; it has a presence in the West (estimated at about seven million Muslims in the USA and two million in the UK); and the fact that the nineteen hijackers of September 11, Osama bin Laden and Saddam Hussein – possibly the most hated individuals in Western societies in the first years of the twenty-first century – are Muslim.

The relationship of the West with Islam and its understanding of that religion will be troubling, challenging and stimulating. That is why any discussion that helps to bring mutual understanding becomes relevant. For the time being everything is colored by talk of "terrorism" and the intellectual discourse framed in the context of the "war on terrorism." The very temples of postmodernism – the mall, the airport and the tourist sites – are now high-security zones. It is too early to predict in what directions either postmodernist or Islamic thinking will move. Neither the scholars nor the commentators have recovered sufficiently from the impact of September 11 to begin the process of objective analysis.

But postmodernism is, if nothing else, resilient. Ideas of universal acceptance, compassion and understanding are difficult to erase. While Islam is being demonized by many in America as a religion of terrorists and extremists, books on Islam are doing brisk business at the bookstores. Maulana Rumi, a Muslim mystic born centuries ago in what is now Afghanistan, is one of America's favorite poets. Rumi's example in itself is evidence that the spirit of postmodernism still survives the Grand Narrative. Indeed, it is desperately needed in the violent and anarchic world that September 11 has engendered. The predicament of living in the early part of the twenty-first century will be assuaged by the promise and practice of universal compassion and understanding that lie at the heart of both postmodernism and Islam.

Notes

1 The discussion in this article derives from my book *Postmodernism and Islam: Predicament and Promise* [1992], new ed. (London: Routledge, 2004).
2 See my *Islam under Siege: Living Dangerously in a Post-Honor World* (Cambridge: Polity, 2003).
3 Roland Barthes quoted by Susan Sontag in "Writing Itself: On Roland Barthes," Introduction to *A Roland Barthes Reader*, ed. Susan Sontag (London: Vintage, 1993) xxii.
4 Arthur Kroker and David Cook, *The Postmodern Scene: Excremental Culture and Hyper-Aesthetics* (London: Macmillan, 1988) i.
5 Anthony Giddens, *Runaway World: How Globalization is Reshaping our Lives* (New York: Routledge, 2003).

mckenzie wark

GOODBYE TO ALL THAT

1. It's all a question of how one thinks of time. Valéry: "We later civilizations ... we too now know we are mortal. We had long heard tell of whole worlds that had vanished, of empires sunk without a trace, gone down with all their men and all their machines into the unexplorable depths of the centuries ..."[1] The modern is not so much a period in aesthetics as an aesthetic of the period. To invoke the modern is to invoke a temporality of the passage by which things vanish from an inchoate present, to trace the line of the past.

2. The modern was, after all, just a figure, an inescapable image of time. Jameson: "one cannot not periodize." The modern was a very particular kind of sign, a tempo, a time signature.[2] Likewise, the postmodern – it was just the necessary other, the adjacent signifier. It was what the modern was not. And yet it had this one significance: the modern no longer attained its meaning in relation to a predecessor – the ancient – but a successor – the postmodern. It's a shift in timekeeping. The drummer moves the accent from the preceding to the anteceding beat.

3. The desperate attempts to ascribe a positive content to categories defined by a mere temporal negation is the sure sign of ideology at work. Lukács: "Modern critical philosophy springs from the reified structure of consciousness."[3] In thinking itself modern, and in thinking itself as modern, the modern temperament turns time itself into a thing, bounded by what precedes it. Postmodern critical philosophy does not escape this reifying gravity, it merely updates it.

4. The modern was the great temptation for artists and intellectuals. It creates a positive identity by purely negative force. The modernist is the one who determines what is not modern. What is not modern calci-

fies out of the flow of culture as a thing of the past. Hope is invested in the empty place marked for that which has not yet been beaten into temporal shape as an artifact of the old order.

5. Eventually, this negative process of marking time consumes itself. The beat catches up with itself, and finds within itself a meta-beat, a move of such consummate elegance that intellectuals will make a good living for quite a time by merely repeating it. The postmodern opens as a new negative horizon, as the modern itself ossifies into a thing of the past.

6. Time and again, intellectuals will try to assign meaning to the modern and the postmodern. Whatever one is, the other isn't. Lists proliferate. A small industry emerges. Compare and contrast. Myriads of things emerge as potential candidates under the respective headings of modern and postmodern, each defined by what it is not, as each props the other up. A slew of forgettable books ensues.

7. The quarrel between ancients and moderns gives way to the quarrel between moderns and postmoderns, but without solving the inherent limits of this mere temporalizing practice. Not much meaning ever stabilizes around the act of temporal cleaving. This very indeterminacy is – for a time – the very thing that makes the postmodern look like it says something of some interest.

8. The unanswered question – ironically enough given the temporal fetish of the modern gesture – is "why now?" Why the shift in accent from what precedes to what antecedes the modern? Maybe it's something to do with consumer culture, with simulation, with the breaching of the bounds between high and low culture. The answers are tentative, and never very satisfactory, and in any case can always be somebody else's problem. The specialists in culture deflect the question off to political economy, while the specialists in the latter return the favor.

9. The postmodern is a symptom, but of what? The answer might be clearer if we were clearer as to what the symptom was in the first place. The postmodern symptom is not this or that feature of the cultural landscape designated as such. This, after all, is just the reified consequence of a critical practice that takes culture to be a domain of things that it can parse with the relentless beat of "now" and "then." The symptom is the critical practice itself, or rather its practitioners. The question is not to identify the thing intellectuals determined was postmodern. The question is to determine the altered provenance of these intellectuals themselves.

10. In talking about culture as if it could be nominated as a domain of objects, some from the now, some from the then, intellectuals are really only describing their own mirror image. The question of "why now?" is best approached not from the point of view of the cultural object, but

of the cultural subject. What passage took place that shifted the accent from something (or rather someone) to come to someone who came – and went? The periodizing, temporalizing machine, always moving on, always open toward a future yet to come, consumed its own agents, closing the space within which they felt free to nominate a past as past.

11. In brief, the intellectual's relation to that great engine of temporalization, the commodity economy, passes from something peripheral to something quite central. The status of partial exemption from the cycle of production and consumption is erased, although not quite in the way that the intellectual often imagines it.

12. Capitalism, ironically enough, might be an infernal engine of transformation – "all that is solid melts into air" and all that – but it has itself been reified as if it were merely a trans-historical thing. It always is and always was and always will be. This is not just the mantra of its apologists; it is wanly accepted even by its supposed critics. The best they can manage now is a simulated form of "resistance." Critchley: "Is resistance itself the most felicitous response to late capitalism? Is it not too reactive in the Nietzschean sense? Should we not, rather than opposing late capitalism reactively, seek to think through some kind of active affirmation of its enormous creative and destructive energy?"[4] But perhaps that very move requires a thinking beyond this mode of periodizing, beyond late capitalism, toward something altogether different and still rather "early."

13. What if the commodity economy had already had two quite distinct historical phases, of which "capitalism" was only one? Might this not clarify the terms in which we could see the current moment as a passage to a third? This might be a quite different way of reimagining the temporalizing gesture. Rather than merely qualify an ahistorical fiction of capital eternal as "late capitalism" or "information capitalism" or whatever, perhaps there's a way of thinking the commodity economy as historical in the strong sense. It has stages, and these succeed one another, logically if not strictly temporally. And it could in some sense come to an end.

14. Here is a story about the commodity economy. First comes the transformation of land into private property. All the local, negotiated rights are extinguished. A peasantry still in command of the immediate means of production is transformed into a class of tenant farmers. A feudal ruling class holding traditional privileges is transformed into a pastoralist class with outright ownership of land, which extracts rents from its tenant farmers. This is the first "modern" class relation.

15. This transformation of land dispossesses a great mass of peasants, who find themselves in the towns and cities. There they are transformed

into workers by a rising capitalist class, which claims the tools and resources of manufacturing as its private property. The worker is now obliged to sell labor power to this capitalist class, who profits from the difference between the cost of this labor and the price it receives for the finished articles of the manufacturing process. This is the second "modern" class relation.

16. The "intellectual" (or the "artist") occupies a strangely liminal position in both these transformations. To be an intellectual is neither here nor there. One is neither farmer nor pastoralist; neither worker nor capitalist. One may advocate in the name of town or country, but that is really just to prefer one scene of class conflict to another. But generally, to the extent that an intellectual is modern, is an agent of modernity, speaks in its name, invokes its ideological trappings, all this means is naming as past all that belongs to the feudal world preceding both these transformative struggles.

17. The modern artist and the modern artist's interpreter, the modern intellectual, sits uneasily not only between capitalist and worker but between the industrial economy of capitalist and worker and the agricultural economy of pastoralist and farmer. This precarious position is only maintained by the insistent nominating as other of something outside of both great historical struggles – the archaic, the traditional, the premodern. Granted, the objects that crystallize out in this domain may be recruited as critical weapons against this or that aspect of the modern experience. The modern intellectual may embrace the modern or react against it. Either way the structural relation is much the same. It's a question of retaining a precarious position outside of two parallel class struggles, of keeping open the domain of the aesthetic, for example, or the "public sphere."

18. This liminal, inessential position of the artist and intellectual is the key reason for the proliferation of big commitments – to communism, to fascism; to anti-communism, to anti-fascism. Or – it amounts to much the same thing – to art for art's sake, or to the subordination of art to constructivist ideas of aestheticized production. If there was an overriding commitment it was to modernity itself, perhaps not least out of a nagging sense that the categories of the intellectual and the artist where themselves the biggest anachronisms.

19. What if capitalism was not the last word in the progressive abstraction of the commodity form? What if there was a stage beyond? The commodity economy begins with the transformation of land into private property, sundering the motley feudal ties, and producing two antagonistic classes, farmer and pastoralist, with the latter extracting a surplus out of the former in the form of rent. The second phase produces even

more abstract private property forms that can encompass complex means of production, but which yet again produce two antagonistic classes, worker and capitalist, with the latter extracting a surplus from the former in the form of profit. The third phase produces a still more abstract private property form, which turns the old negotiated rights of copyright, patent and trademark into "intellectual property." This privatization of information produces a new class struggle, between what one might call the hacker class, producers of information, and a vectoralist class, who own the vectors along which information moves and the means of realizing its value. This is the new "postmodern" class relation.

20. With the emergence of so-called intellectual property as a private property right, intellectuals of all kinds lose their liminal status and are incorporated into the central productive processes of the commodity economy. They are no longer the servants or self-appointed leaders of other classes, but a class in their own right – the hacker class. While the intellectual division of labor accelerates, producing arcane distinctions among kinds of intellectual labor, this labor is nevertheless for the first time rendered equivalent by the abstraction of intellectual property. Marx could write of money, the general equivalent, that it makes X number of coats worth Y amount of wheat, but with the extension of the private property form to information, X number of my copyrights are worth Y number of your patents. It's all the same to the market, no matter what arcane distinctions scientists may hold between themselves and musicians, or writers, or programmers. The hardening of patent and copyright into absolute private property rights "modernizes" the relation of the intellectual to the commodity economy.

21. One attempt to provide modernity with a positive content was the ideology of the information society or the postindustrial society. These quintessentially modernizing discourses attempt to abolish antagonism from the social terrain by simply declaring it obsolete. But it is quite another thing to argue that the class relation, far from disappearing, mutates into a new form. Moreover, the emergence of a new terrain of class struggle between hackers and vectoralists does not render obsolete those previous forms of class relation. On the contrary, at the start of the twenty-first century, the great struggles remain those of the transformation of peasants into farmers through the expropriation of their land, and the transformation of the landless surplus peasantry into industrial workers. It is just that these intense class struggles are happening elsewhere, far from what Viénet called the "overdeveloped" world.[5] The form of these struggles is marked, however, by the imposition of new antagonisms. The struggle over land is also the struggle

over the ownership of the genetic material of the seed stock. The great workhouses of the underdeveloped world labor to make goods stamped with trademarks and copyrights owned by others, using industrial processes patented elsewhere.

22. If one cannot not periodize, one might at least periodize in a way that reveals the present as a site of struggle, in both continuity and difference from the struggles of the past. As a periodizing gesture, the postmodern consigned to the dustbin of history class struggle, the totality of the commodity economy, the historical evolution of the forces of production – and much else that returns with a vengeance early in the twenty-first century. The postmodern was critical theory's way of leaving the twentieth century by becoming merely hypocritical theory. From now on, it declared, power is elsewhere, or everywhere, or just too complicated.

23. Postmodern talk betrays a constant anxiety about its own timeliness. The irony is that this very timeliness defeats the critical irritant of the asynchronous that is critical theory's weapon of last resort. Debord: "When 'to be absolutely modern' has become a special law decreed by some tyrant, what the honest slave fears more than anything is that he might be suspected of being behind the times."[6]

24. Perhaps it is time to revive a distinction that Gramsci made between the organic intellectual, connected to the emerging points of conflict, and the traditional intellectual, who sinks like sediment to the backwaters of the social order, cast off by the temporal energies of the commodity economy. Seen in this light, it is not an accident that artists and intellectuals working in the traditional mode could only declare what was dead in the modern. They were merely revealing, in this gesture, their own obsolescence. The new appeared elsewhere, under other names, nominated by organic intellectuals who emerged spontaneously at the new sites of struggle.

25. Those intellectual labor processes most thoroughly touched by the coming of the digital are the ones which threw up the new contradictions, and generated the new intellectual movement which filled the vacuum left in the wake of the postmodern turn. The digital terrain, at one and the same time, opens toward a brave new world in which scarcity is a thing of the past, and yet which is under relentless pressure from a new "business model" in which the commodity economy would perpetuate itself through control over information rather than land or capital. ADILKNO: "On leaving the twentieth century, the world has acquired a sixth continent that encompasses and dwarfs the previous five."[7]

26. With the coming of the digital, information escapes from scarcity. It is finally possible to imagine a realm of the free play of production

beyond the realm of work. This possibility is glimpsed early on by programmers – those leading organic intellectuals of the new stage of the commodity economy. Stallman: "Hacking means exploring the limits of what is possible, in a spirit of playful cleverness."[8] But hacking quickly finds its limit when it comes up against the rise of the vectoralist class, which seizes upon the abstraction of information as the basis of a new kind of private property – intellectual property – built on but distinct from traditional forms of patent and copyright. Information becomes the new zone of conflict. Kroker and Weinstein: "politics is about absolute control over intellectual property by means of war-like strategies of communication, control, and command."[9]

27. The formerly liminal character of intellectual labor dissolves on contact with the privatization of information. All forms of intellectual labor are rendered equivalent, and a new class emerges – the hacker class. Whether it is programming language or the English language, whether one works with the diatonic scale or the periodic table, one is a hacker. What makes one a hacker is the equivalence thrust upon one and all by the necessity to sell one's hacker-power to a class that owns the means of realizing its value – the vectoralist class.

28. The ideology of "intellectual property" is nothing but the blurring of the line between producers of new information – the hacker class – and those who come, in the long run, to be its owners – the vectoralist class. As Courtney Love says, it's the media industries who are the pirates.[10] To which one might add the drug companies, agribusiness, indeed all of the corporate world, to the extent that it is shedding manufacturing capacity, outsourcing and off-shoring supply, and attempting to control the whole production cycle through the management and policing of its portfolios of brands, patents and copyrights.

29. The postmodern was merely the symptom of the decay of traditional intellectual formations, not least the decline from critical theory to hypocritical theory, as theory was swallowed by the academy just as the academy was swallowed by that even bigger fish – the commodity economy, as "imagineered" for the twenty-first century by the vectoralist class. And while this might just repeat the modernizing gesture, it might do so in a new way: the postmodern can now be assigned the status of a thing of the past, along with all the other ancient relics. The new terrain that opens up, however, has the tantalizing prospect of offering a renewal not only of the great categories of class, history, production, dare I say even totality, but also of the utopian promise of a world beyond scarcity, after the commodity form.

30. The promise of a realm beyond scarcity might be restricted to the one thing that escapes necessity – information – the peculiar ontological

properties of which are as yet poorly understood. Understanding information is now a practical rather than theoretical matter. The mission of the hacker class as a class might be to hack into existence practices by which information can be extracted from the commodity form and returned to the realm of the gift. The realm of the gift might no longer be a realm of particulars, where each gift relation imposes a particular and limited obligation. Rather, the gift may in the era of file sharing and peer-to-peer networks become as abstract as the commodity form. The obligation it imposes may be borne more lightly, but might extend beyond the immediate other toward the infinite.

31. If the commodity economy is a philosophy made concrete, the emergent forms of an abstract gift economy, in which information may be freely hacked, in which difference escapes from scarcity, might point to a wholly new concretizing of a quite other philosophy. Far from being consigned to the dustbin by the postmodern gesture, the double project of the critical and the utopian – the negative and the positive beat respectively – might only now be finding its conditions of renewal. "In this tiresome age, when even the air melts into airwaves, where all that is profane is packaged as if it were profundity, the possibility yet emerges to hack into mere appearances and make off with them. There are other words and they are this one."[11]

Notes

1 Paul Valéry, *The Outlook for Intelligence*, trans. Denise Folliot and Jackson Mathews (Princeton: Princeton UP, 1989) 23.

2 Fredric Jameson, *A Singular Modernity* (London: Verso, 2002) 29.

3 Georg Lukács, *History and Class Consciousness*, trans. Rodney Livingstone (London: Merlin, 1971) 110.

4 Simon Critchley, *Ethics, Politics, Subjectivity* (London: Verso, 1999) 139.

5 René Viénet, *Enragés and Situationists in the Occupation Movement* (New York: Autonomedia, 1992) 14.

6 Guy Debord, *Panegyric*, vols. 1 and 2, trans. James Brook and John McHale (London: Verso, 2004) 66.

7 ADILKNO, *Media Archive* (New York: Autonomedia, 1998) 48.

8 Richard Stallman, *Free Software, Free Society* (Boston: GNU, 2002) 15.

9 Arthur Kroker and Michael A. Weinstein, *Data Trash: The Theory of the Virtual Class* (New York: St. Martin's, 1994) 6.

10 Courtney Love, "Countney Does the Math," *Salon* 14 June 2000.

11 McKenzie Wark, *A Hacker Manifesto* (Cambridge, MA: Harvard UP, 2004) 389.

arthur kroker and marilouise kroker

SUSPICION OF THOUGHT

To the question: "what is the meaning of postmodernism today?" we respond with three counter-questions: *aesthetically*, why is postmodern performance art so dangerous in contemporary politics under the sign of terrorism? In terms of *body and power*, what is the meaning of the postmodern body in the new biometric state? And finally, in the arena of *dark futurism*, what is the relationship of (unrepresentable) postmodern intimations and (hyperreal) post-humanism? What, that is, do the Rings of Saturn have to tell us about the necessary tension between past and future – identity and difference – that is the essence of the postmodern condition?

I. Why is postmodern performance art so dangerous?

Consider these three incidents: in Buffalo, New York, Steve Kurtz, a member of the Critical Art Ensemble, is indicted for bio-terrorism, later "reduced" to mail fraud. In Toronto, Steve Mann, inventor of the wearable computer and Professor of Computer Engineering, had his EyeTap wearable computer physically removed by airport security. In Nacogdochez, Texas, two young artists – Robert Ladislas Derr and Lynn Foglesong-Derr – who only wanted to publicly mourn the deaths of the Columbia astronauts by circling their prostrate bodies with chalk while reading passages from Jean-Paul Sartre were ordered by US Marshals to immediately cease and desist. As one Marshal said: "In Texas, the only form of mourning permitted is flowers, flags and ribbons."

Art may not be terrorism, but it is dangerous. In a state of univocal power, art is fully indeterminate. It can be interpreted on many different levels. The performance art you see is not necessarily what I see, and certainly not what is seen by the FBI. Postmodern performance art is ironic, parodic, singular. Always an art of the impossible and the ineffable, postmodern performance raises unsettling questions of absence: are there colors not seen before? Are there feelings not felt before? Are there actions not taken before? Are there possibilities not thought before?

Consequently, what does it mean when postmodern performance art becomes politically dangerous? What implications follow from the fierce and persistent persecution of postmodern artists and theorists? What is it about postmodern art and theory which is so deeply threatening to the state, and which so quickly triggers an official response revealing the facialization of power as hyper-paranoia? When art is under suspicion, when theory is under suspicion, is it possible that we are actually in the presence of a critical fracture in the otherwise smooth surface of power? Is it possible that today postmodern artists and theorists can be persecuted precisely because the state recognizes in their language of bodily performance a fundamental challenge not only to the state's monopoly over symbolic exchange but even more critically a counter-theory of the body which the high-security state has done everything in its considerable powers to eliminate from view? In the contemporary political condition of security and terrorism, bodily presence is at stake once again, with the state actively engaged in harvesting the body within the framework of the resurrected binaries of the war on terrorism. It is now forbidden to destabilize this framework of understanding. It is now criminal to create unlikely juxtapositions. It is seen as hostile in an artificial environment of high-security realism to speak on behalf of the hyperreality of parody, irony and indeterminacy. Everything must remain within its categories. Everyone must stay within the frame. Artists cannot be scientists. Engineers cannot be artists. Photographers cannot go beyond the optics of the lens to publicly grieve a catastrophic accident of space technology. The Critical Art Ensemble cannot parody biogenetic food. Steve Mann cannot have enhanced vision in the context of airport surveillance. Robert and Lynn are physically forced to erase the chalk marks of their accidented bodies.

II. Body invaders dub/remix

The postmodern body is a war machine.

Interpellated by ideology, networked by data flows, inscribed by political rhetoric, colonized by the image matrix, its boundaries blurred, its identity increasingly prosthetic, the postmodern body today is a violent and seductive scene of invasion and coding. Data tracked and data mined, the postmodern body remains a hyperbolic sign of postmodern times.

Not a radical break, the opening decade of the twenty-first century with its virtual scrubbing and despotic cleansing of the social scene from the alien threat of terrorism from within and without is in reality the flipside of the neo-conservative political agenda of the 1980s. Postmodernism returns now as both the ruling political code of the militarization of global culture and an epochal moment of insurrectionary rebellion against the simulated totality of the war on terrorism.

Thesis 1: body aesthetics

If, today, there can be such an intense fascination with the fate of the body, might this not be because the body no longer exists? For we live under the dark sign of Foucault's prophecy that the bourgeois body is a descent into the empty site of a dissociated ego, a "volume in disintegration," traced by language, lacerated by ideology, and invaded by the relational circuitry of the field of postmodern power. And if there is now such an insistent demand for the recovery of "subjectivity," this would indicate that hyper-subjectivity has become the condition of possibility for the operation of power at the fin de millennium. An ultra-subjectivity for an entire society in ruins living on the excess energies of (its own) "borrowed power" becomes interesting only because it is so deeply parasitical of a culture, whose key techno-logical feature is that the mind is on its way to being exteriorized again. The struggle for the happy return of subjectivity would then be complicit with the deepest grammar of power in the postmodern condition and, for a culture living under the sign of Bataille's general economy of excess, the body to excess would be its perfect analogue.[1]

Or just the reverse? Not so much a fascination with the disappearance of the body but culture shock at its appearance in the terminal terms of mortality. Breaking through the sound-barrier of an ideology which would claim that the body is a "volume in disintegration," and through the light-barrier of simulation, the real, material body surfaces now as a triumphal sign of the sovereignty of time over virtuality. Certainly not the body to excess, but the return of the body in the minimal form of the language of persistence: on one side the persistence of time and duration; on the other, the persistence of the body's demand to be recognized for its singularity in a culture of surveillance and tracking. Definitely no longer an era of hyper-subjectivity, the body is now the site of mini-subjectivity: the subjugation of the body to low horizon personalities with no definite political ideas, ideal subjects for the occupation of the bodily territory of subjectivity by scanner culture. In this case, the bodily correlate of the primary code of the war on terrorism – "You are either with us or against us" – is the emergence of a new body type coded to be "with us." Accommodationist, fused with the objectifying lens of state power, its skin surface literally swollen by the aleatory signs of consumerism, its perception cut to the acceptable dogmas of official political rhetoric: these are the dominant traits of the appearance of the body in the twenty-first century. Schooled in the language of an earlier form of postmodernism with its emphasis equally on the tattooing of flesh by the signs of culture and its interpellation by ideology, the postmodern body redux territorializes its flesh by tattoos, scarification, and piercing, just as much as its self-perception is marked by the language of disintegration, dissociation, and laceration. The postmodern body today is the multimedia body.

While the aesthetics of the disappearance of the postmodern body of the 1980s was defined by the critical sensibility of poststructuralism, the aesthetics of the postmodern body redux of the early twenty-first century adopts a positive poststructural attitude as its way of being in an increasingly terrorized world. Stripped of its moment of critique, positive poststructuralism indicates a new body type that rapidly adapts to its new condition as a volume in disintegration, lacerated by ideology, traced by language, a node on the circuit of relational power. To the nihilism of its prevailing political culture, the postmodern body redux replies with the language of hyper-nihilism. To the immanent critique of poststructuralism, the postmodern body redux responds with a double gesture: both testing the limits of the meaning of a body as a "volume in disintegration" and challenging power with the remix possibilities of dissociation, laceration, and interpellation. To the original aesthetics of postmodernism, the postmodern body of the new century responds with the language of remix. It makes of its own topology of political despair the cultural material for a body that would be remix: a sign of danger and possibility.

Thesis 2: the multimedia body

Everywhere today the aestheticization of the body and its dissolution into a semiurgy of floating body parts reveals that we are being processed through a media scene consisting of our own (exteriorized) body organs in the form of second-order simulacra. And subordinations of the body to the apparatus of (dead) power are multiple. Ideologically, the body is inscribed by the mutating signs of the fashion industry as skin itself is transformed into a last, decadent and desperate, search for desire after desire. Epistemologically, the body is at the center of a grisly and false sense of subjectivity as knowledge of the body (what Californians like to call "heightened body consciousness") is made a basic condition of possibility for the operation of postmodern power: the "cynical body" for a culture of cynical power. Semiotically, the body is tattooed, a floating sign, processed through the double imperatives of the cultural politics of advanced capitalism: the exteriorization of all the bodily organs as the key telemetry of a system that depends on the outering of the body functions (computers as the externalization of memory; in vitro fertilization as the alienation of the womb; Sony Walkmans as ablated ears; computer-generated imagery as virtual perspective of the hyper-modern kind; body scanners as the intensive care unit of the exteriorization of the central nervous system); and the interiorization of ersatz subjectivity as a prepackaged ideological receptor for the pulsations of the desiring-machine of the fashion scene.[2]

This description of the postmodern body is only an indefinite prolegomenon to the creation of the multimedia body. What really disappeared in what might be called the first-order postmodern condition was the modernist conception of the body with its artificial belief in the inviolability of the body's territorial sovereignty. Consequently, if postmodern theory of the 1980s could reflect so deeply and so persistently on the loss of the body's immunity from the power of the virtual it was due to an almost nostalgic belief that something autochthonous and primal to the bodily experience was lost forever with the processing of its "(exteriorized) body organs in the form of second-order simulacra" through the media scene. The rebellion of nostalgia was the hallmark of first-order postmodernism. Stripped of its illusions and certainly liberated from its primary desire to reclaim the imaginary terrain of the modernist body as antidote to virtual power, second-order postmodernism has always only known screened culture as its primal. *Ideologically*, the multimedia body is a complex mix of often incommensurable signs: constantly scanned by the surveillance-machines of screened culture; yet just as constantly mixing and remixing its gestures, attitudes, preferences, movements, sounds and images as ways of being singular in a world that would be totalizing. *Epistemologically*, the multimedia body might well have always known itself as a cynical object – recoded by recombinant technology, edited by the image-machines of simulation, processed by scanners, its every organ a site of the power of dispossession – but for all of that, cynicism always has its fatal double – the will to be remix, to recombine the codes, to remix the sounds, to play back to the waiting ear of cynical power the material gestures of an emergent body that would be individuated. *Semiotically*, the remix body tattoos the media world with the floating signs of its own insurrectionary appearance. To the technological exteriorization of bodily organs as the nervous system of advanced capitalism, the remix body learns to dub/remix the sounds and images of the body externalized. The remix body invents imaginary tracks for prosthetic memory, prosthetic bodies, prosthetic wombs, prosthetic ears. It does this not for purposes of nostalgic critique but as active, creative explorations of what the externalized nervous system of the modernist body has to tell us about the mind/machine interface, about the fate of the electronic body which now, having successfully harvested human flesh, rides the beam of light to a future unknown and uncertain. Pointers on the way to a new (electronic) habitation, artists of the remix body shape-shift the future, recode the codes, turntable the sounds, facialize the power of streamed capitalism. In response to the "interiorization of ersatz subjectivity as a prepackaged ideological receptor for the pulsations of the desiring-machine of the fashion scene" the remix body works to exteriorize in the multiple languages of music, art, video, dance the sounds of its own "ersatz subjectivity." Taken as a beginning-point more than a definite ending, the "interiorization of ersatz subjectivity" presents a seductive challenge to the art of the remix. How to recover the rhythms of interiority in a postmodern culture that privileges the spectacle of the surface? How to discover the forgotten terrain of the "ersatz" in a political culture which, under the pressure of the apprehended threat of political terrorism, seeks to recuperate the policed language of a stultifying normality? How to speak anew of "subjectivity" in a society where the objectifying language of political sameness strives to make of the sign of subjectivity itself an alien threat? With *floating body parts* as its content, *remix* as its artistic attitude, and the reality of *vacated subjectivity* as its aesthetic challenge, the multimedia body is precisely that point where the lament of first-order postmodernism of the 1980s implodes into the creative resistance of the remix culture of twenty-first-century second-order postmodernism.

Thesis 3: mind invasion and soft reality
Virtual heads: the US Air Force has uncovered a virtual flaw – the inadequacies of the body reflexes of pilots – in the creation of ultrasonic jet fighters. According to aircraft designers, the human body is no longer capable of absorbing, let alone responding to, the "information environment" of jet fighters at hyper-speeds. From the perspective of aerial technology, the human body *is* obsolete and, as Stelarc predicts, what is needed is a new body fit for the age of ultra-technologies. In fact, this is just what designers have created, at least beginning with the *heads* of fighter pilots. To compensate for the inability of human vision to match the speed and intensity of the information environment of jet fighters, designers are equipping pilots with virtual heads: special helmets which block out normal ocular vision and, by means of a video screen projected on the inside of the mask, feed the pilot at a slowed-down and selective pace, strategic information about his aerial environment: altitude, presence of other aircraft, speed, target range. A system of perspectival vision, therefore, for the advanced outriders of teleonomic society.[3]

Today, jet fighter pilots are not the teleonomic outriders they once were. Their perception is now *our* perception of soft reality – a slowed down, selective reality. In a quick reversal of the laws of postmodern media, the virtual heads of fighter pilots have now come inside the human brain.

Literally, we navigate contemporary media culture in the form of an almost organic virtual helmet which allows us to ride out the storm of information overload by way of the selected "reality" of Reality TV, 24/7 news, computer games, digitized laugh tracks, virtual sports. Like fighter pilots cocooned in their virtual helmets, *our* perception is also screened. Streamed by the media apparatus, we participate every day in a truly virtual war where civilians have disappeared, and only soldiers are real and visible. Definitely having nothing to do with the imaginary of virtual reality, the new reality is hyper-digital. It is tightly coded, prepackaged, always "late breaking news," always the terrorism of simulated panic. Riding the electronic currents of streamed media means that the virtual helmets of fighter pilots have come inside us and that it is *our* perception which is radically reworked by media: blocking out "normal ocular vision"; entertaining the bored eye with aerial information about its threatening external environment; feeding perspectival-vision-coded ideological signs for identifying potential scapegoats, political terrorists, viral contagions, boundary breaches in the bunkers of the postmodern self, society and culture. Living inside the virtual helmet of digital media is the essence of soft reality.

Soft reality? That's what happens when the brain is invaded by too much information, when digital reality allows us to move from "diaries and pocket cameras" to "sound and digital image recording supplemented with such data as temperature, heart rate, location, web pages visited, compute/ device usage logs" (Mission Statement for the Association for Computing Machinery Conference, "Archival Retrieval and Personal Experience," New York, 10–16 Oct. 2004). Presented as a way of "augmenting biological memory," this perspective seeks to pack the biological brain with the excessive content of its media archive. Identifying multimedia memory as personal memory, soft reality holds that *we* are the sum of our electronic prosthetics. Here, the virtual helmet comes alive in the form of a media archive that is deeply autobiographical.

Augmented human memory is actually the autobiography of mind invasion in a media culture of soft reality. The mind is invaded with junk memory, factual memory. *Junk memory?* That's when information overload looks for the delete button and crashes instead. *Factual memory?* That's the mind augmented with information flows with such overwhelming density and speed that the mind implodes into its own absence – an (electronic) culture of recall memory, where memory extensions interface the brain with informatics.

Thesis 4: the new biometric state

Body McCarthyism: why the hysteria over clean bodily fluids? Is it a new temperance movement driven by the prevailing climate of reactionary

politics which, by targeting the body as a new surveillance zone, legiti-
mizes the widening spread of a panoptic power apparatus and heightens
distrust of our own circulatory systems? Or is it a panic symptom of a more
general anxiety about the silent infiltration of viral agents into the circulatory systems of the dead scene of the social: an invasion which succeeds
in displacing fear about the threatening external situation into the inner
subjective terrain of bodily fluids?

A *urinal politics* would be one that privileges the body anew as the target
of the power of the panoptic, sublimates anxieties about the catastrophe
without onto the body as a text for an immunological discourse, and speaks
the discourse of clean bodily fluids with such evangelical zeal because, like
the radiating light waves from a long-past explosion of a gigantic super-
nova, it has only now reached the telematic sensors of Planet One. The
rhetoric of clean bodily fluids is really about the disappearance of the body
into the detritus of *toxic bodies, fractal subjectivity, cultural dyslexia, and
the pharmakon* as the terror of simulacra in the postmodern condition.
The intense fascination with sanitizing bodily fluids, with clean urination
for the nation, is also a *trompe l'oeil* deflecting the gaze from the actual
existence of the contaminated body (as the sine qua non of the technifica-
tion of culture and economy in the high-intensity market setting) and the
obsolescence of bodily fluids as surplus matter in telematic society (*Body
Invaders: Panic Sex in America* 10–11).

In the new biometric state, your history is embedded in a card; your
future is scanned; and your life is imprinted. Biology is security. Framed
by a dialectic of security and terrorism, set in motion by a technological
alliance between biology (biometric identifiers) and digitality (database
surveillance), and circulating through the body in the form of bio-power,
the new biometric state is the decisive product of the war on terrorism.
Sweeping aside traditional protections of privacy and civil rights in the name
of combating terrorism, the new biometric state takes full advantage of the
specter of terrorism to install a fundamental regime change in the future
of political culture. Populated by biometric subjects, tracked by electronic
scanning, and invaded by the sign of biogen, from food to surveillance, the
new biometric state represents that epochal moment when the language of
biology, fleeing its previous association with the history of epistemological
struggles, allies itself with a form of power which speaks in the name of
absolute security in a dangerous world.

Strategies of bodily purification

What postmodern theory first analyzed as an upsurge of Body McCarthyism across the bodily landscape of panic sex in America has now been
generalized into the disciplinary essence of contemporary politics. Today,

different regimes of bodily purification are at work: the *"trusted traveler"* program at American airports with its prescanning of frequent business travelers in the telematic form of iris identification and fingerprinting; the immunization of the body politic from the threat of domestic and foreign *terrorism*, with state-orchestrated campaigns of mass hysteria directed at the scapegoating of any signs of difference, Muslims and political dissidents and civil libertarians and artists; the protection of the "American homeland" from the threat of *viral contagion*, with the bunkering down of America from anything from the always threatening "outsider"; the proliferation of "biometric identifiers," as *the* newly emergent form of surveillance in the culture of preventive security. In each instance, the libidinal politics of panic security attempts to immunize two orders of bodies: the national-symbolic body of the "American Homeland" which now finds itself beleaguered and threatened by transparently politically orchestrated fantasies of "alien" attacks: from radioactivity, chemicals, atomic bombs in suitcases, airplanes as missiles; and the apparently threatening body of the individual citizen which is viewed as requiring preventive certification in advance as to its safe security status.

The biometric subject

Slipping beyond its theoretical origins in structuralism, the sign of the perfectly immunized body becomes the operating code of political culture. Although it will be costumed appropriately for the political theatre of the new biometric state, it still remains a sign-system, and thus subject to the overriding rules of signification. Nothing can ever finally escape the cycle of mythology; not only ancient gods and satyrs with their temptations to hubris inevitably washed up – exhausted, disillusioned – on the shores of contingent reality, or the triumphant rise and slow decline of ideas, powers, and sexes, but also now the inevitable cycle of all the signs of panic security which, trapped in a mythic cycle of excess and ruins, still cannot resist the temptation of a more ancient rebellion. Call it what you will – the demand for absolute security, the hegemonic will to empire, the disciplinary state, neo-conservatism cut with the missionary zeal of Christian zealotry – the sign of absolute security hints of another dispensation, another order of experience. In *The Rebel*, Albert Camus discussed two primary forms of human rebellion: the *metaphysical* rebellion of reason against the sovereignty of god; and the *historical* rebellion of twentieth-century ideologies – fascism and communism – against the indeterminacy of life moderated by the necessities of consensual public judgment and tempered by the ultimate irreconcilability of clashing ideologies. Now that politics surfaces in a new century, the quest for perfect immunity has about it a passionate intensity which is not, we believe, solely attributable to the crisis politics of our era. In the discourse of security do we not hear once again the repetition of a more traditional human refrain with its demand for certainty in the midst of historical indeterminacy? Like its predecessors, the demand for the unconditional of absolute security is doomed to culminate in its opposite – a panic state of absolute insecurity. This fate is more in keeping with the pataphysics of mythology than with the contingencies of power and its oppositions. Similar to all campaigns before it for the cessation of incertitude, the myth of security is circular, not telic. While the sign of teleology would provide an almost religious confirmation, indeed certainty, as to its historical inevitability and moral probity, such reasoning still belongs more to humans than the gods, being itself nothing more than a powerful justificatory rhetoric, internally generated by the demand for absolutism itself. But if not a telic sign, then what of the *circularity* of the sign? In the twenty-first century perhaps we are on a mythological speedway moving beyond the surface skin of teleology and positivism to something more primitive in the history of the sign, namely to the Babylonian concept of the "wheel of history." Not opposites, security and insecurity are part of exactly the same wheel of history, temporary points of spatial distinction distributed across the same cycle of political history. In the demand for absolute security, there is located an imminent sense of vulnerability and insecurity, hoping for, but not really confident of achieving the safe harbor of the secured state, the secured body. In the dialectic of security and insecurity, each term is co-present to the other, each entwined in the same historical predicament, each different angles of emotion on the same common aspiration toward the sovereignty of security in the midst of the contingent and the fleeting. However, if this is true then it is also the case that the dialectic of security and insecurity, while propelled into (media) prominence by the discourse of terrorism, probably is an anticipatory sign of something more foreboding, more darkening of the future of the human species. Could it be that the rhetoric of the war on terrorism may ultimately prove to be a convenient *trompe l'oeil* hiding from view the rapid ascendancy of the *new biometric state*? And perhaps not simply hiding from view, but something more. Is it not probable that the discourse on terrorism is the objective political preparation necessary for setting the stage for the appearance of the biometric state? Here, the dialectic of security and insecurity sets in motion a closed circle of action and counter-reaction: biometric identifiers, full body scanning, data tracking, biogen databases, full spectrum surveillance have real consequence, of calling into existence the specter of terrorism as both their fatal object and ultimate justificatory condition. Not limited to politics, the discourse of the war on terrorism is deeply biological. Dominant markers of the new biometric state, viral war and viral terrorism channel the perception of the anxious body, directing its feelings, anticipating its fears, monitoring its behavior, certifying its trustworthiness, provoking its deepest worries, and limiting its modest ambitions. Once begun, the dialectic of security and insecurity can never be unraveled to its primary origins. Once activated by the war on terrorism, the biometric state quickly justifies in the name of state security a sweeping ideological agenda effecting a decisive change in democratic institutions. In the USA, the new biometric state is established by the US Patriot Act; in Canada by the Anti-Terrorism Act; in Britain, by the Anti-Terrorism, Crime and Security Bill.

Slipping into the bloodstream of the body politic

In the new biometric state, the body, whether collective or individual, is the object of a double anxiety: intense fear about surprise attack from an always threatening, imminently dangerous *external* world; and ideological fantasies concerning the psycho-ontological threat *within*, whether in the form of unidentified political dissidents who have managed to slip undetected as sleeper cells into the bloodstream of the American body politic; or individual bodies of the traveling public which can never be absolutely eliminated as security threats because fantasies of uncontrolled mayhem, destruction, and apocalypse are so indigenous to the production of the spectacle of the nomadic traveler. The sign-system of panic security has its privileged fetish objects – scissors, shoes, belts, nail files – just as much as it has an impossible dream: bringing out of concealment the hidden intentionality of the potentially threatening body by hyper-technological methods ranging from electronic pre-screening to biometric scanning – humiliating, probing, stripping, and imaging. *Maximal preventive deterrence for a guaranteed minimum of public security.*

The state of suspicion

With this, we enter the era of the new biometric state: a form of bio-governance which systematically links primitive collective emotions of fear and anxiety with postmodern technologies of surveillance. While the aim of the new biometric state is to immunize itself from direct internal and external challenges by means of the creation of a *bunker society fused by fear*, its ideological method is to foment in the mass psychology of the population a constant *state of suspicion*, both by reporting any "strange behavior" of others and monitoring our own suspicious thoughts for possible signs of imminent subversion. In the citizens' army of the new biometric state, individuals are thus expected to play the role of the *policeman without* as well as the *policeman within*. Not content with the relative passivity and defensive nature of the bunker state or the state of suspicion, the new biometric state also goes on the attack: it engages in preventive wars as ways of destabilizing potential sources of viral terrorism; and, finally, it becomes a bio-terrorist itself – garrisoning the world; creating zones of extra-jurid-ical, extra-constitutional incarceration; installing secret torture prisons in Iraq, Afghanistan, Diego Garcia; seeking to "Git-moize" the outside world now, and probably the domestic population later. Quite literally, we live now under the terrorism of the sign of (absolute) security. Possessing no definitive limits because of the objectively limitless character of the psycho-logical projections of fantasy, illusion, and anxiety upon which the dream of perfect security is based, the signs of panic security can only expand in the future, exploding in relationship to the perception of imminent danger; taking possession of every orifice of the anxious body, collective and individual. So it is that we enter into the feverish, inventive imagi-nary of panic security where viral war replaces cold war, where the threat of terrorism substitutes for the menace of communism, where preventive security measures presented as protection from surprise attacks are the new political expression of fears of viral invasion, and where Homeland Security is the new Body McCarthyism of the twenty-first century.

The seduction of terrorism

But if the terrorism of the sign reaches its moment of apogee in the desperate search for the state of absolute security, this political totalization cannot be sustained for long. Mythologically, it is in the deepest nature of any sign-system always to seek to cancel itself out, to collapse into the welcoming arms of the sign-slide that is its forbidden, transgressionary side. Power is seduced by chaos; sexual purity by perversion; absolute order is energized by secret dreams of crash; technological prowess is confirmed by its fatal accident; the inversions hinted at by the god of nemesis trace a minimal element of ruin within the otherwise solid spectacle of the absolute referent. As in mythology, so too now in contemporary media history. Consider the following *four* stages of rapidly evolving media rhetoric as panic security shifts from being the universal signifier of a symbolically unified American homeland to the present state of cynical security: that is, as the sign of security reverses from absolute primacy as the universal sign of a deeply unified American population to the contemporary era of fear of terrorism as a pretext for the growth of the high-security state. *First*, under the sign of 9/11, the American political community, supported by international expressions of public mourning, was momentarily symbolically unified by pervasive images of the flag as the universal signifier of the moral desire for absolute security. *Second*, as a symbol of public acceptance and civil passivity before the power of the sign of security, dominant media symbols became those vaunted images of pervasive surveillance at every chokepoint in the system of social circulation. While images of the flag morally ground the sign of security, images of surveillance transform the symbolic exchange of the sign of security into the deepest materiality of culture, society, politics and economy. Here, the sign of security is literally reincarnated as the flesh and blood of civil society. At this point, we are suddenly in a state of viral security, wherein technologies of surveillance attach themselves as probing, invading parasites to host-bodies. However, at some point, perhaps under the pressure of failed foreign military adventures or uncontrollable internal changes in political economy and domestic politics, the sign of security begins to falter as an absolute serial signifier. It cannot totalize the social field. Within the context of the 2004 US presidential election, it runs up against the bedrock resistance of television satire, viral cinematic critique (*Fahrenheit 9/11*, *The Manchurian Candidate*), and increasingly bitter policy divisions among elite planners of the neo-imperial state. Or perhaps, as in the mythological dissolution of all sign-systems which strive for absolute hegemony, the eye of total security, bored with the ease with which it has attained absolute hegemony over civil society, finds itself one day seduced by the until now suppressed signs of its own undoing. For a brief moment, the new biometric state begins to satirize itself. It televises its weakness in classic scenes of the perils of presidential hubris on the stage-set decks of the USS *Abraham Lincoln*. It retreats into air force bases and army garrisons where presidential speeches are presented against backgrounds of curtains of cheering soldiers. The famous political cliché – "You're either with us or with the terrorists" – suddenly appeared to be on the verge of flipping in the public mind: *"Everyone was with Bush, soon they will all be against him."* The stability of the image of security begins to fragment: images of dead soldiers, friends turned into foes, political leaders as war criminals, soldiers as torturers, and still no security. Demands for security begin to be more destabilized, more desperately insecure: Condition Orange, Condition Red, announcements of impending attacks which never arrive: at Christmas, Easter, summer holidays, political conventions, presidential elections. Here, we are present at the *third* stage of the postmodern history of the sign, that point where the political stability of the referent fragments into the language of aesthetic parody. American society splits. The polarities are absolute. The draconian political program of the high-security state is checkmated by the theater of increasingly satirical media. For a moment, the sign stands unmasked: overexposed in its manifest political pretensions, over-manipulated, hyper-virtualized, too cynical. *But not for long.* Quickly the postmodern sign of security restabilizes the political field. Threatened by increasingly popular critiques of the referential integrity of calls for increased security, the sign of panic security reverses field. It goes retrograde. It gets religion. Panic security is literally *born again*. Animated by electoral expressions of genuine fear at the specter of invisible enemies, knowing that the American Gothic requires the continuous invention of imaginary external enemies for its sustenance, and fusing the gap between fundamentalist religion and equally fundamentalist security, panic security reconsolidates itself as the new religion of America. Consequently, the *fourth* stage of panic security is achieved: the sign of security is reborn ideologically. America goes stagnant. It's the new age of the bunkered down yet globalizing state.

Tactics of stereotypy, scapegoating and ressentiment

In each case, political tactics of stereotypy and *ressentiment* are deployed for purposes of scapegoating targeted populations. What emerges is a domestic population mobilized around the thematics of *panic security*: distrust of the threatening Other; belief in the moral necessity of the high-security state; intense anxiety concerning breached (territorial) boundaries; fear about any threat to order; deep psychological receptivity to officially directed campaigns of mass hysteria; and the perceptual division of the world into the until now superseded binaries of good and evil. Confronted with the fluidity, indeterminacy, and mobility of postmodern capitalism, panic security represents a sustained psychological reaction-formation aimed at the resurrection of the binaries.

Moreover, as in the halcyon days of the dotcom boom with its double ideology of facilitation and control as ways of solidifying the popular reception of virtual ideology, the ideological agenda of panic security is also doubly secured: *first*, by facilitating smooth circulation within the system for those members of privileged elites (professionals, military, business travelers, etc.) who, in return for surrendering certain rights to personal privacy, are eliminated in advance as security risks; and *second*, by an ideology of control whereby what was once presented as a special privilege available only to the new elites of the high-security state quickly becomes a practical obligation of political citizenship. Now it is considered a privilege to be a "trusted traveler" in order to facilitate business travel. The business class actually feels privileged – in TV images, business faces become giddy with the status differential of iris scanning and fingerprinting – to give up certain privacy rights to speed up business. Perhaps the "trusted traveler" is the prototype of a new ideology of bio-control. In the near future, could it be that everyone will be obliged to be certified in advance as trustworthy? What was introduced as an experiment in facilitating business travel would thus culminate as a control mechanism over nomadic bodies.

In essence, the ideological apparatus of the new biometric state depends on a twofold moment: *normalization* (whereby one is authorized as a speed body fit to travel through the circulatory systems of the social); and *criminalization* (whereby the act of being certified as a speed body moving through the gateways of the high-security state requires background security investigations, iris scanning, fingerprinting, declarations of loyalty). That the new biometric state is capable of orchestrating the movement of domestic populations as a whole through this double movement of normalization and criminalization depends, in the first instance, on surfacing the "fascist within" which is always immanent to the bourgeois ego.

In the founding ideology of the liberal state, Immanuel Kant may have diagnosed the dialectic of order and freedom as the basic code of power, but with panic security we have achieved the era of *hyper-Kant*. Not so much order and freedom as opposing moments in the chain of liberal dialectics but as deeply commensurable terms in a common language of "enhanced citizenship" which is itself a basic precondition for the new state of panic security. In this case, state security requirements for order at any cost combine with individual demands for freedom of movement within the closed circulatory system of contemporary technoculture. Both demands are affirmative, mutually reinforcing, operating precisely within the same coded territory, each part of exactly the same closed sign-system. The permanently mobilized order of the high-security state is the framework within which freedom of individual aspirations and movement will occur. The "signified" of order mirrors perfectly the "signifier" of individual freedom. With this, the potentially warring signs of (modernist) order and freedom cease to be dialectical, oppositional, Kantian; becoming instead the highly volatile, inexorably liquid, intensely virtual signs of the new biometric state – terrorism and security.

Cold security

Thus begins the era of *cold security* whereby the search for an always unattainable state of security purges its way through the coded passages of the system, setting impossible standards of proof of (security) origin, establishing permanent security garrisons in the portals of power, economy and culture, channeling individual anxieties through the carefully orchestrated gateways of mass media, here refusing entry to immigrants, there hunting down perceived internal security risks: now scapegoating artists, dissidents, activists; in the future, applying the science of biogenetics to the maximal security demands of the high-security state. Based on a language of preventive deterrence, the liquid sign of cold security knows no limits. As the dominant sign-form of the high-security state, cold security freezes the normal circulatory movements of culture and life at the speed of surveillance. Indeed, as the epochal sign of panic security, cold security signifies that the long-suppressed crisis of the bourgeois ego has broken out again. The immediate historical precursor of the collapse of the bourgeois ego supported the triumph of Nazi Germany. Here, the ontology of the "fascist within" formed on the basis of a double psycho-political alliance: fear of loss of class privilege in an era of global economic depression; and anxiety concerning the loss of identity in a crisis-situation wherein the bourgeois ego, having no confidence in the foundational identity of liberalism, quickly follows the fascist path of ethnic scapegoating and charismatic "strong man" leadership. In the new era of cold security, the double alliance necessary to activate the fascist within reappears in historically new form: fear of loss of class privilege in an empire economy which has suddenly been challenged by the until now successfully suppressed resistance of the vanquished; and very real psychological anxiety, particularly in the case of the USA, at the realization that the until now unchallenged belief in the "American dream" as *the* universal signifier has met its limit in a form of viral terrorism that is contemptuous of American claims to sovereignty in the theater of freedom. Consequently, while there may be no actual security crisis, there is most definitely a crisis of panic security: a cold crisis of contagious proportions where security and terrorism are the mirror of power in the postmodern state, both only superficially antagonistic, both always requiring the other's presence as the necessary sign of its own existence, authorization, violence.

III. Postmodern intimations and post-human realities

Specter of the unrepresentable

Postmodernism always has about it the specter of the unrepresentable. To the realism of the social it replies with the hyperrealism of the death of the social. To the cynicism of power it responds with the kynicism of critical imagination. To the noise of propaganda it counterpoints with the creative aporias of a poetry of silence. To the fictions of the socially constructed self it speaks only of the paradoxes of the non-self. To the confident language of presence it looks beyond the binary of absence in order to think into the space of impossibility: that strange, third zone between presence and absence, identity and difference where tangible signs are to be found in the language of indifference, irony, and incommensurability.

Consequently, it is only an ironic confirmation of the unrepresentability of the postmodern moment that its first exponents, from Baudrillard and Barthes to Lyotard and Irigaray, would each in turn have their philosophical rebellions against the language of representability turned against them in the end. A wandering prophet of Hannah Arendt's sense of the "not-being" of contemporary nihilism, Baudrillard is in the paradoxical position of enjoying a resurgence of his purely *theoretical* critique of referential logic in the midst of a militant global power that, in actuality, demands the acquiescence of recognition for its ruling referents. Baudrillard's fate is equivalent to the paradoxical character of postmodern theory itself: the sharper the critique, the more blunt the political counter-reaction. So too with Roland Barthes, who went to his death with melancholic reflections on the simulacra of memory and image, but whose literary fate is to be resurrected again and again as an ethnographer of mythologies. Did Lyotard really succeed in teasing out the trace of libidinal pleasure in the texts of Marx? Or has this unacceptable Lyotard – the mischievous, ribald, carnivalesque Lyotard of *Libidinal Economy* – been quickly silenced in favor of the representable Lyotard – the Lyotard of *The Postmodern Condition*. So too with Irigaray, the author of incomposable texts, particularly *Speculum of the Other Woman*, who can only hint now of the luminous trace of ruins in the thought of Plato, of Heidegger, of the speculum of the history of ideas.

But if the intellectual spearheads of the postmodern moment cannot finally materialize either philosophically or politically the essence of their rebellion against the prison-house of the language of the real, this does them no dishonor. While the legacy of representational logic is the darkness of ideology in ruins, the fate of the unrepresentable is to be precisely that: a fluid, indeterminate, highly relativistic moment in history which having staked its claims against the rhetoric of cynical power and cynical truth immediately fades away as an unrepeatable, and certainly unrepresentable, singularity.

Perhaps in speaking of the postmodern moment we have already departed from the strict sphere of epistemology and gone beyond the aesthetics of singularity. Perhaps the very name – the *postmodern moment* – evokes memories of another way of living, another order of space-time. In rehearsing the hyper-logic of the postmodern are we not ultimately drawing into presence two orders of existence which until this moment had thought themselves at a fatal remove, namely mythology and science. Mythologically, postmodernism hints at a longer struggle in the history of the cultural imaginary. Its informing spirit has about it the stubborn recalcitrance of those other thinkers of the unrepresentable: Nietzsche, Artaud, Genet, Spinoza. Not for them the perspectival simulacra of power; not for them the recitatives of a mode of truth-saying that camouflages itself behind the mask of power; not for them a mediocre exit of the animal spirits of the imaginary into the grand signifiers of the theater of representationality. Postmodernism is *mythological* because it is, and has been, nothing less than a form of radical metaphysics, a poetic meditation on the possibility of a way of being that would seek to avoid the polarities of becoming and existence. It's the desert howl of the post-human hermit; the anti-Medusa of the ancient gods of love; the philosophy of the madness of reason which speaks only in honor of irrationality, the surprised silence surrounding that irrecoverable moment of recognition and abandonment when the unredeemed urge to justice follows upon the unresolved demands of the imagination – wild philosophy, wild theory, wild bodies, wild speech, wild minds. And postmodernism is *science* when the modernist temples of Newtonian absolute space and absolute time are finally swept away by a new metaphysics of the physical universe: one which speaks fluidly, poetically, incommensurably, relativistically about the changing "fabric of spacetime"; about "worldlines," "double-cones of light," time which bends and reverses, space which shrinks and expands; about how objects actually slow down when riding the beam of light at its point of maximal acceleration: an Einsteinian science, a postmodern science, which confirms that the specter of postmodernism has departed the space of literature only to become the habitus of quantum mechanics. Is it possible that postmodernism is that electrifying moment when the scientific energies of Einstein's special theory of relativity light up the unrepresentable language of mythology, making of our mythic past a poetic gateway to our quantum future? If this is the case, as we believe it to be, then the leading figures of the postmodern moment, from Artaud and Nietzsche to Baudrillard and Irigaray, are less thinkers in the traditional sense than something much more spectral. They are brilliant "worldlines" whose thought bears faithful resemblance to new scientific theories of "wormholes," those dense, swirling eddies of immense gravitational pressure scattered across the galaxy where other deep space objects, and why not thinkers too, go to have their imaginations instantly transported to other places, other times.

Postmodern worldlines

If postmodernism has become the world we live and breathe and dream, it is due to the fact that social existence is organized today according to the principles of relativity theory. Electronic culture moves at the speed of light. Information technology rides the beam of (fiber-optic) light into the densest structures of finance, culture, society, and politics. In the virtual economy of global capitalism, time routinely folds backwards as the speed of futurist projects routinely *reverses* into archived databases. What captivates attention and seduces popular imagination are less bureaucratic orders of control than the black holes of intense points of energy – in entertainment, sports, politics, crime – that suck everything into their singularities, expelling it into white holes of scattered attention, distracted culture, bored bodies.

Born under the sign of Einstein's overthrowing of the absolutist conception of space and time, postmodernism is the leading cultural manifestation of the most pervasive, and radical, insights of contemporary science. It is that point where relativity theory with its provocative insights concerning *four-dimensional* experience – the impact of the velocity of light in bending space and time into a unitary space-time fabric – escapes the mathematical algorithms of physics, becoming an essentially astronomical theory of culture, society, politics and economy. Similar to science in its epistemological separation of theoretical and experimental physics, postmodernism's first expression may have been deeply theoretical, from eloquent theoretical challenges to representational logic in art and architecture to radical political theories of the death of the author, society and power itself – but its lasting valorization always awaited experimental confirmation. Which is the role of *electronic culture* in the unfolding mythology of the postmodern moment. The Net specifically, and digital culture generally, is a brilliant experimental simulacrum of postmodern relativism. In his famous CTheory article, "Why the Web Will Win the Culture Wars for the Left,"[4] Peter Lurie eloquently argued the same point, noting that the Net is immanently postmodern: *a blast of life as information* which is, by its very (electronic) nature, highly relativistic, multi-dimensional, fluid, perspectival, where only contradictions are true, where only that which is simultaneous is also historical, and where the liquid flows of *light-through space* and *light-through time* often reverse course, seeking futures in the past and memory archives in the sunrise of data. And not just the Net in a narrow sense but the spectrum of electronic connectivity is coded by the postmodern moment, from remix music and streamed video to the cut-ups of "turntabilism" and the explosion of recombinant imagery in arts and entertainment. While postmodernism may have been "born posthumously" as a spectral sign that could only be experienced fully in the future, that future – the actually existent present of the postmodern moment – is coeval with the special theory of (cultural) relativity that is electronic culture. Ironically, the framing of the full spectrum of the social by relativistic codes of postmodernism explains why strictly theoretical discussions of postmodernism have so quickly disappeared. It is the nature of any discourse that has triumphed to immediately render itself invisible: frameworks are directly experienced, but only knowable at one remove by a sideways (theoretical) glance which manages to capture a trace of the postmodern moment as it disappears on the horizon of digital culture. In a curious Einsteinian paradox, the absence of discussion of postmodernism today probably confirms its ineluctable presence as one of the core codes of twenty-first-century life.

The Rings of Saturn

Why the immense fascination with the Rings of Saturn? Simply a fascination with technological prowess in navigating from the near-time of earth to the deep space of Saturn, or awe at the sheer beauty of the amazing ultraviolet optics of those perfectly formed rings circling a gigantic gaseous planet? Perhaps. Or maybe it's what astronomers immediately announced as the perpetual lure of deep-space travel to Saturn: namely that in exploring this gaseous planet at the distant edge of the solar system we are actually time-traveling to our past, to an earlier earth history when gaseous space had not yet congealed into earthly matter.

Or could fascination with the Rings of Saturn have its origins less in scientific or historical reasons than in a mode of world-attentiveness that is subliminally mythological? Are the Rings of Saturn really an astronomical story of our past or future? After all, we do know this about those concentric rings horizoning Saturn against the cold darkness of the void of space: first, that their incredible aesthetic symmetry follows from, and perhaps is almost preordained by, the normal laws of gravitational physics. The Rings of Saturn crystallize in the always night-time sky of deep space the immutable theorems of quantum mechanics having to do with gravitation, velocity, and the chromatics of light. In the artificial form of our techno-logical prosthetics – ultraviolet cameras, deep-space exploration vehicles – we find ourselves deeply linked to the fate of Saturn by a common scientific framework. Consequently, while our earthly gaze upon the Rings of Saturn can express astounded surprise at the elegance of its aesthetic symmetry, there is another part of human consciousness which finds itself oddly comforted by this preternatural gift of astronomical confirmation of the magic of science. But there is also something more to the seduc-tion of the Rings of Saturn; this having more to do with dark futurism as the dominant mood of earthly space-time. From a strictly observational viewpoint, the famous Rings of Saturn are permanently frozen signs of decay and ruins, splayed out orbits of lost worlds. In this account, the rings are most probably the remains of lost moons which, having at some point in the recesses of the past been imploded by proximity to the immense gravi-tational pressures of Saturn, now circle its sky in thin, flattened ice sheets stretching indeterminately into the darkness. Not really only a fable of our lost past of perfect aesthetic symmetry, the Rings of Saturn evoke a more primal, and quintessentially human, emotion: namely an ineffable tension between symmetry and decay. Consequently, looking towards the Rings of Saturn we can find a mythological story of presence and loss, aesthetics without and ruins within; but is it really so different from another story, a story this time of the tension between postmodern intimations and post-human realities as the *Rings of Earth*? Once again, the astronomy of light-through space and light-through time lights up the cultural imaginary to reveal a more abiding story of the strange entwinements of *our* past and future.

Notes

1 Arthur Kroker and Marilouise Kroker, "Theses on the Disappearing Body in the Hyper-Modern Condition" in *Body Invaders: Panic Sex in America*, edited and introduced by Arthur Kroker and Marilouise Kroker (New York: St. Martin's, 1987) 20–1.
2 Ibid. 21.
3 Ibid. 32.
4 Peter Lurie, "Why the Web Will Win the Culture Wars for the Left: Deconstructing Hyperlinks" in *Life in the Wires: The CTheory Reader*, edited and introduced by Arthur Kroker and Marilouise Kroker (Victoria: NWP/CTheory, 2004) 269–76.

Bibliography

Barthes, Roland. *The Pleasure of the Text*. Trans. R. Miller. New York: Hill, 1975.
Barthes, Roland. *Image/Music/Text*. Trans. S. Heath. London: Fontana/Collins, 1977.
Baudrillard, Jean. *Seduction*. Trans. Brian Singer. New York: St. Martin's, 1990.
Baudrillard, Jean. *Symbolic Exchange and Death*. Trans. I. Hamilton. London: Sage, 1993.
Deleuze, Gilles and Félix Guattari. *Anti-Oedipus: Capitalism and Schizophrenia*. Trans. R. Hurley et al. New York: Viking, 1972.
Deleuze, Gilles and Félix Guattari. *A Thousand Plateaus: Capitalism and Schizophrenia*. Trans. B. Massumi. Minneapolis: U of Minnesota P, 1987.
Einstein, Albert. *Relativity: The Special and the General Theory*. Trans. R.W. Lawson. New York: Three Rivers, 1961.
Girard, René. *Violence and the Sacred*. Trans. P. Gregory. Baltimore: Johns Hopkins UP, 1986.
Heidegger, Martin. *The Question Concerning Technology and Other Essays*. Trans. W. Lovitt. New York: Harper, 1977.
Hirschman, Jack (ed. and trans.). *Antonin Artaud Anthology*. San Francisco: City Lights, 1965.
Irigaray, Luce. *This Sex Which is Not One*. Trans. C. Porter. Ithaca, NY: Cornell UP, 1985.
Irigaray, Luce. *To Be Two*. Trans. M.M. Rhodes and M.F. Cocito-Monoc. New York: Routledge, 2001.
Kroker, Arthur. *The Possessed Individual: Technology and the French Postmodern*. New York: St. Martin's, 1992.
Kroker, Arthur. *The Will to Technology and the Culture of Nihilism*. Toronto: U of Toronto P, 2003.
Kroker, Arthur and David Cook. *The Postmodern Scene: Excremental Culture and Hyper-Aesthetics*. New York: St. Martin's, 1986.
Kroker, Arthur and Marilouise Kroker (eds). *Body Invaders: Panic Sex in America*. New York: St. Martin's, 1987.
Kroker, Arthur and Marilouise Kroker (eds). *Body Invaders: Sexuality and the Postmodern Condition*. London: Macmillan, 1988.
Kroker, Arthur and Marilouise Kroker (eds). *Life in the Wires: The CTheory Reader*. Victoria: NWP/CTheory, 2004.
Kurtz, Steve and the Critical Art Ensemble. Available <www.caedefensefund.org>.
Lyotard, Jean-François. *La Condition Postmoderne*. Paris: Minuit, 1979.
Lyotard, Jean-François. *The Differend: Phrases in Dispute*. Trans. G. Van Den Abbeele. Minneapolis: U of Minnesota P, 1988.

Mann, Steve. Available <www.eecg.toronto.edu/mann/>.

Nietzsche, Friedrich. *On the Genealogy of Morals*. Trans. W. Kaufmann and R.J. Hollingdale. New York: Vintage, 1967.

Nietzsche, Friedrich. *The Will to Power*. Ed. Walter Kaufmann. Trans. W. Kaufmann and R.J. Hollingdale. New York: Vintage, 1968.

Smith, Marquard (ed.). *Stelarc: The Monograph*. Cambridge, MA: MIT P, 2005.

lawrence grossberg

AFFECT AND POSTMODERNITY IN THE STRUGGLE OVER "AMERICAN MODERNITY"

This essay is part of a larger effort to describe the context of contemporary politics as a struggle to establish a new "American modernity," against the "liberal modernity" which came into existence during the twentieth century and reached its pinnacle at mid-century. I argue that this is "a hegemonic struggle against hegemony," and depends in crucial ways on an historical crisis of knowledge.[1] But this is at best incomplete as an understanding of the contemporary context of politics, and it poses as many questions as it answers. The question of "what's going on" seems ever more pressing.

It is by now common to read characterizations of the US population as socially and politically divided into two "camps," that the contemporary political culture is being built around a frontier of sorts. But that is not all that can or should be said about the social and everyday realities of people's lives. The existence of any such frontier, moreover, has to be reconciled with the hegemonic nature of the struggle as a "war of position," that is, the fact that it is characterized by all sorts of shifting social and political alliances. My assumption here is that the contemporary political struggles are constructing a frontier across the terrain of sensibilities rather than across the sorts of relations and processes (class, ideology, morality) we are used to considering.

I. An affective politics

The idea of a sensibility is an attempt to describe the organization of people's affective lives. Psychologists often use "affect" to refer to attention, and to volition or will. Freud used it to refer to desire, and some feminists have taken it up to talk about emotional life. What is it that binds all of these together?

It is easy enough to accept that human experience is sensual and cognitive. To say it is sensual is to acknowledge that we are embodied and, as such, we interact with and are oriented within the material environment, including our own body; to say it is cognitive acknowledges that we necessarily interpret and make sense of the world and of what happens to us in that world. Experience is organized by (culturally produced) structures of intelligibility or maps of meaning ("ideologies"). But human experience also has a certain "feeling" to it. Affect points to the complex set of dimensions or aspects that seem to be involved in such a feeling. We relate sensuously to "things" in the world; we perceive them in particular ways. We understand what they are and have certain beliefs about them; they may have moral or political connotations. But none of this captures what it feels like to have a certain experience. That is because experience is more than sensuousness and cognition. That something more – affective state – has both a quality and a quantity. Consider quantity: you don't just pay attention; there are degrees of paying attention. You don't just believe or desire something; you believe it or desire it with some almost measurable intensity. You don't just feel emotions; it is always possible to ask: "How angry, sad, happy, etc. are you?" and the appropriate answers are suggestions of quantity. An affective state provides – it is – the color, texture or tone – what musicians would call the timbre – of our lives.

The same object, with the same cognitive meaning, will be experienced very differently depending on the way you are attending to it, on your emotional state, or your mood. Affect is what actually connects us to the world, what anchors us in our experiences and into particular places, activities and things in the world.

Affect describes the states and structures in which our passions are defined and organized. It is the organization of what we care about, of what matters to us and how it matters, of mattering maps. Just as much as we are socialized into a world of meaning, and our individuality is defined through our negotiations with and among the different socially constructed maps of meaning and intelligibility, so too we are socialized into a world of affect, and our individuality is defined through our negotiations with and among the different socially constructed mattering maps. Such mattering maps direct people's investments in and into the world. They tell people where and how and with what intensities they can and/or should become absorbed in the world and their lives. These are the places where people anchor themselves into the world, the locations of the things that matter. There are not only different places marked out (practices, pleasures, meanings, fantasies, desires, relations, values, etc.) but also different forms and qualities of investment (ways they can matter) and different purposes that these investments can serve.

Mattering maps also define the connections that enable us to move among such places. They define a certain organization of stability – of identities and identifications – in people's lives, by defining the sites at which people can, at least temporarily, find themselves "at home." It is through affect that the relationship of belonging – the feeling that something (including myself) belongs here and not there – is established and organized. Mattering maps are structures of belonging. The investment in any one site also opens up the possibility and sometimes the apparent necessity of investing in other sites. Mattering maps also define the possibilities of mobility, of whether and how one can move between and among different investments, and even how one can change and reorganize the investments. They establish the relations and distances among the different parts and moments of peoples' lives.

Affect is also about energy, the production of energy that opens up and closes off possibilities. Mattering maps tell people how to use and how to generate energy: by investing energy here, additional energy is created over there.[2] Affect enables people to navigate their way into and through various moods and passions, and it enables them to locate themselves within particular emotional and ideological histories. It is by finding the right places on the mattering maps that people can feel like they have some control over their lives and the world, and that they can find the passion necessary to imagine and enact their own projects and possibilities.

However, affective investments and mattering maps can never provide their own justification. Consequently, affect always demands that something else, some other authority (perhaps an ideology of values), legitimate its particular organizations or maps – legitimate the fact that these places, differences and relationships – and not those – matter. Who or what has that authority – the power to shape one's mattering maps and hence one's identity – is defined and determined, paradoxically, only within the mattering maps themselves. Only at particular places within our mattering maps can that authority be asserted. That is, within their mattering maps, people authorize others – individuals, groups, activities, songs, etc. – to speak for them, as spokesperson, surrogate, representative and conscience. People give authority to that which they invest in; they let the objects of such investments speak for and in their stead. They let them organize their emotional and narrative life and identity.

I suggest that we will better understand the current struggle over modernity if we see it as an affective struggle, a hegemonic struggle that is being fought with affectively constituted tactics, for affectively defined stakes. Of course, politics has always been partly about affect, if only in the form of emotion, but the balance between a cognitive politics (imagined as either rational or ideological) and affective politics is changing.

The contemporary hegemonic struggle is a "mood politics," challenging old mattering maps and offering new ones shifting the structures of identification and belonging. What is at stake is what does and what should matter to us as a nation and as individuals. What are often erased in such a struggle are the relations between mattering maps and the political and economic conditions that make them possible. The latter – real questions of economic impoverishment and exploitation, and ideology – are left to what Linda Kintz describes as a "strategic but passionate vagueness."[3] The new right understands that "the cultural work of reconstructing the passions and emotions is precisely where political belief is formed, where the collapse of absolutist religion into politics occurs – in those places where things are felt before they are thought or believed."[4] Affect also helps explain the unity of the new right as a core hegemonic bloc. The unity of the various fractions of the new right (certainly more successfully than any alliance of the left) is built on "a passionate symbolic cohesion."[5] It is affective long before it ever gets around to questions of ideology.

The new right is attempting to restructure people's everyday lives by reorganizing their affective lives, their mattering maps. This cannot be fought out in entirely ideological terms because it involves the very possibilities of authority, of who or what has the right to speak for others, to stand in their place, to construct their mattering maps. Thus it makes sense that the new right would present the crisis of America as a crisis of authority – not merely that specific figures and sites of authority have been challenged but that the very authority of authority has itself become suspect. The new right struggles to strategically reconstruct authority in certain dimensions, places and times, but also to disinvest the very possibility of authority from other sources and sites. So even as new authorities appear – e.g. capitalists and certain sorts of moralists, the common folk, etc. – the new right has to mobilize resentment against those who will now be painted as holding religion and morality, or motherhood, or markets, or America itself, in contempt.

Marketing passion as the belief in belief itself is not the same as playing to people's fantasies, because it makes the actual content of the commitment secondary; the simple fact of affect itself is a solution. One example of this is the contemporary discussion of education policy over the last decade, which seems to copy the attitude of an advertising campaign that said "Where there's a will, there's an A." Unfortunately, education is not simply about trying. A full-page newspaper ad sponsored by Wachovia Bank following a local golf tournament asked: "What can Sunday's winner teach us about educating America?" and it answered its own question: "Passionate people make things happen."[6] It did not comment on whether passion was sufficient to win a golf tournament or whether it made any difference what sorts of things were made to happen. In the end, affect – and new mattering maps – replaces the complex individual, economic, material and social determinations of educational success. This new affective politics has also established a whole new set of educational authorities, although it is not clear on what basis their authority is built (but there I go again, speaking as a liberal, looking for some sort of credentials), while at the same time negating the authority of teachers and educational scholars to speak.

In fact, that is how more and more political campaigns – both electoral and issue specific – are now organized. Campaigns are planned, tested and run just like any other marketing campaign. Show different focus groups a variety of arguments, appeals, slogans, etc., and "perception analyzers" will construct "values maps," which have little or nothing to do with values. They measure "average emotional response"; by hardwiring the participants they measure the intensity of autonomic nervous response. The higher the score, the better the appeal. For example, "a thousand points of light" had an extraordinarily high score. The problem is that there is no way of knowing what the people being tested think the slogan (or appeal) means. But that's okay because, say those who develop and champion these techniques, understanding is "unmanageable" and "uncontrollable."[7]

Another example: commenting on the success of the National Rifle Association, Grover Norquist says: "Sixty-five percent of the American people are for 'reasonable' gun control. But in terms of intensity, only four percent of the American people care about guns – they hate gun control."[8] This 4 percent apparently can determine political results!

In 2001 the Washington Post reported that the political director of the National Association of Manufacturers urged its lobbyists "to be 'dressed down' so that 'a sea of hard hats' could ... help buttress Republican arguments that the [tax cut] plan helps blue collar Americans."[9] Karen Houppert, reporting on conservative anti-feminists' efforts to recruit on college campuses, states it nicely: "What ... all the ... organizations courting campus conservatives know is that the way to counter 'statistically challenged' progressives is not with better statistics ... but with good stories. Passion motivates."[10] The fact that an event is a ruse need not change the affective success of the appeal any more than knowing what is coming in a movie stops the emotional response. This helps to explain the practice of "the big lie" because sometimes repetition may augment affect.

Finally, one can understand the new right's desire to continue to represent itself as the underdog or victim of the all-powerful liberalism; after all, it provides a powerful sense of marginalization, resistance and identification. But now, even corporations represent themselves as victims. An ad by the Washington Legal Foundation (described as an "advocate for freedom and justice") suggests that business has become the target of a McCarthyite witch hunt: "It seems that everywhere you turn these days, you can hear the never-ending campaign to criminalize honest, ordinary business activities. … Government officials too often turn to criminal prosecution for minor … problems instead of using far more appropriate administrative or civil remedies."[11] A little reflection would be more than enough to dismantle the argument of this ad, but it is not about analysis and reflection; it is about trying to produce a certain affective relation between business and "the people."

No doubt, the ability to perform politics affectively depends upon both the techniques and the help of the media and popular culture. Those involved in politics (including politicians) have learned to use the resources of popular culture in their efforts to remake people's mattering maps and to reorganize the possibilities of authority, and the media have incorporated the more successful of these efforts (e.g. Rush Limbaugh, talk radio, reality television, Fox news). Their populism, for example, is so entirely affective that it never actually threatens the power of the media themselves. And because they are such masters of affective communication, they are often able to transcend their supposed niche audience and actually bring together very diverse audiences. Even those last places where one assumes there has to be some limit on affect – the news and advertising, since both are supposed to include some information – have totally succumbed to the appeal of affect. For example, the significance of "branding" is precisely that information is entirely erased in the effort to create an emotional or affective context of some product (including politicians or political positions) so that they can claim a specific place on people's mattering maps.

An affective politics attempts to redefine what matters to people, and the lines that pull them from one place that matters to another. It tries to make substantive differences over any issue less important than, even inconsequential compared to matters of style, timbre, and appeal, that is, compared to affective dimensions. Thus, it makes perfect sense not only that people do not know what is at stake in the issues (or what the differences between the competing positions are, echoing the practices of advertising) but also that, in many cases, it does not seem to matter. Affective issues – how positions "feel," how they are located within broader mattering maps, where one invests authority (if not trust), who sounds more reassuring, more like us – are determining. The fact that the president cares about education, and that investment is linked to all sorts of other popular appeals (responsibility, fairness as objectively measured, science, etc.), overwhelms the need or the ability actually to question the specific proposal. Serious political discussions around complicated issues – which is likely to elicit both pessimism and a complicated and no doubt expensive demand for action – are almost guaranteed to be not only less visible but also less acceptable; they are described in media culture as "comedowns," a quick way to ruin an increasingly rare good time. Affect denies content and it makes political questions into little more than billboards or signposts of people's affective lives. So we end up with a struggle over the particular places that carry some weight on our mattering maps, places that pull people's discourse, actions and lives in certain directions and away from others.

II. The struggle over mattering maps

I want to describe three tactics in the new right's efforts to transform the mattering maps of various groups of people: affective disinvestment, affective magnets, and affective epidemics. The first, affective disinvestment, attempts to weaken if not eliminate people's concern with particular sorts of issues and activities. To put it simply, what happened to the passionate interest in the 1990s in the failures of the US healthcare system, failures that by the decade of 2000 have worsened? Or what about the concerns around corporate corruption and market failures? What happened to the demand for both justice and rectification? After all, it isn't supposed to happen this way: if you work hard, you are supposed to get what has been promised to you. Promises, whether they have been made by corporations or by the government, no longer seem binding, although they continue to hold people to the promises they made. But in fact neither justice nor restitution seems likely, and it is the result of the fact that the passion was never manifested, at least not in any public, sustainable and politically viable form. Where did the anger – and the hope and the fear – go? Finally, it seems that everyone I talk to complains about insurance companies: they take your money for years and when you eventually make a claim, they are likely to cancel your policy or, even worse, to declare bankruptcy. What have they been doing with the money? Rather than putting it in escrow (saving it for a rainy day), they have invested it. They pay out the profits in dividends and salaries and then, when there are no profits to be had, they renounce their responsibility to those whose money they have been investing. An oversimplification to be sure, but it is the story that I have been told over and over again, but the obvious – political – ending never comes. Where has the anger gone? Apparently, it has been redirected at lawyers.

The second strategy, affective magnets, involves particular socially significant markers around which people's mattering maps can be reorganized. The specific magnets function as stable sites of identification that reorganize and redistribute the arrangement of affective sites on our mattering maps. If affective magnets are about the places, the assumed stabilities, on our mattering maps, the third strategy – affective epidemics – is about the paths of mobility and the proliferation of affective investments. The site of an affective epidemic suddenly appears at all sorts of other sites. Often, affective epidemics are defined by empty sites that can be constantly redefined. These mobile sites are invested with intensities disproportionate to their actual worth. An affective epidemic, once set loose, can displace every other possible investment, as in moral panics.

Two of the most obvious affective magnets operating in the contemporary context are the child and the family; the two often come together in a notion of "family values." As Burlein puts it, "Children are the site whereby authority can be made to seem possible again, believable, even natural, or at the very least necessary."[12] Similarly, the family is established as the site of a new authority, even as new authorities are legitimated by their relation to the family. Both have a kind of emotional familiarity, and their appeal as affective magnets is enormously intuitive and difficult to fight in our society. Both are sites around which the new right is attempting to reorganize our investments and activities. Around each, especially the child, an incredible series of moral panics have been produced over the past twenty-five years, a never ending series of emergencies and instabilities: satanic ritual abuse; child abduction, molestation and murder by strangers; pedophilia; child sex offenders; child pornography; sexual solicitation over the Internet.[13] There are other affective magnets at work today – for example, markets, choice, and freedom.

One of the most obvious examples of an affective epidemic is the war on drugs. How can an entire generation, many of whom used drugs in their youth, suddenly support a highly charged and misinformed, highly costly and ineffective war on drugs? Given the large numbers of people who have used drugs, why is it impossible to admit it in public (especially, but not only, for politicians and teachers)? Drugs can be blamed for anything, anywhere. The epidemic is not only a matter of drug use (all drugs apparently being equal and equally bad). To make matters worse, there is apparently an infinite number of drugs: new ones are invented all the time and old ones come back to haunt us. They are everywhere and anything bad that happens is likely to at least raise the suspicion of drugs. But that is not all – they are responsible for much of the violence in the world (including, in some cases, terrorism), and for the collapse of inner cites and the rise of youth gangs. Almost every social problem, accident, and crime in this country can be and often has been, at some point, tied to drugs, if not in reality then in the popular imagination. It is an epidemic that will destroy us, and everything we stand for, if we do not defeat it first, no matter what the cost. Both evidence and success are irrelevant.

Affective epidemics are more difficult to establish and sustain than affective magnets, but a very good example of the attempt to let loose another one is the "war on terrorism," which may replace the epidemic that was built around the notion of crime, which had been effective for most of the life of the new right, despite the fact that people did not always perceive themselves to be in danger.[14]

I also think that the new right has been trying to create an affective epidemic around the notion of pleasure itself. In other words, they are waging a war on pleasure, if only because pleasure seems to stand in direct opposition to the kind of affective discipline that the new right is trying to install in people's everyday lives in the name of social order and the production of wealth. Every particular society demands a kind of affective harmonization between individuality (as the locus and definition of freedom) and the structures of social control, between what we colloquially call desire and sacrifice. Such a discipline describes that balance between a demand for happiness and its affective opposite, resignation or acceptance of one's lot. It maps out a logic of calculation of the costs of seeking pleasure and happiness against the price to be paid in pleasure's affective opposite, humiliation. Humiliation seems to have become, over the course of the past decades, the new dominant structure of feeling of everyday life, the bottom line of the new right's affective discipline. It is the threat constantly held over our heads, even as we seem to demand to be its witness in ever more disturbing ways. What used to be bullying has now become the mechanism for entertainment on reality programming (and it has filtered down already into children's programming). Humiliation is about knowing one's place and accepting it, about recognizing that one cannot move beyond one's already defined affective territory.

That the new right is challenging what had become the affective discipline of liberal modernity, especially in the postwar years, with its emphasis on freedom, happiness and pleasure, is often obvious in the ways the new right talks about the 1960s, the counterculture and especially feminism. It is not just a matter of politics but of the ways in which these movements have empowered the celebration of all sorts of pleasures and the assumption that everyone is supposed to be happy, against the demands of both personal responsibility (morality) and social responsibility (religion). By constructing an epidemic around pleasure, suggesting that the "craving" to satisfy individual desires and pleasures is responsible for the decline of American society, the new right is constructing a particular structure of discipline, one that might reasonably be called "denial." And yet this flies in the face of the market as an affective market, which pulls against any form of denial.

III. Divesting electoral democracy

Many commentators have observed the eerie similarities between the contemporary moment and the period around the turn of the twentieth century, when liberal modernity was just emerging. They have also noted one absolutely crucial difference: while the turn of the twentieth century was defined by complicated articulations of resistance and opposition (and it was out of this struggle that liberal modernity arose), the present moment seems to be characterized by the absence of any effective opposition to the directions being charted by the new right. In fact, it is commonly said, there is very little sense of political engagement in the present struggle, except from the right.[15] Both popular and academic observers have noted a growing "indifference" to politics in this country. Common wisdom suggests that people have lost their faith in political action and in their roles as citizens, in their capability or perhaps the desirability of influencing the direction of political change. This depoliticization appears as a loss of commitment to a common social purpose, an agreed upon social good and a collectively imagined social future. Its most visible expression is found not only in declining voter participation – although the USA has rarely had consistently high voter participation, the decline that we have witnessed over the past four decades is the longest sustained downturn in the country's history[16] – but also in such things as the anti-tax movement (for the refusal to pay taxes is a statement of the individual's refusal to share in the costs and responsibilities of government) and in declining expectations of what the government can and should do. Consider, for example, a recent ad for Office Max: it opens with a view of a struggling young couple who can't afford school supplies. We then discover that the woman is a teacher who has to buy the supplies for her own classroom. We see her buying school supplies, presumably in an Office Max; and then we see her husband also buying supplies. They look at each other romantically. The ad ends with a voiceover telling us that Office Max will donate an unspecified percentage of what you spend to your local school. There is no suggestion that, just maybe, the problem here is the declining government and public support for education.

In fact, there are at least two aspects or dimensions to this disinvestment of politics in the contemporary USA. The first is often described as a disengagement from politics altogether; it is not merely that people appear to lack any interest in political activity but that they actively avoid political activities and discourses. Even in the heated 2004 election, a frighteningly high percentage of people still did not vote. Politics and concern about government are receding as a crucial or even viable part of public life. We might say that we are witnessing "the disappearance of politics" or, better, a growing disconnection between people's everyday lives and the domain of politics, between the popular and the public so to speak. Governmental politics is receding as a viable and active site at which the individual invests and inserts him or herself into public life.

This development is particularly disturbing if, as Thomas Mann said, "in our time, the question of man's destiny presents itself no longer in religious terms but in political terms."[17] The result is often a sense of inevitability and an expanding culture of powerlessness. Things are the way they have to be and there is nothing we can do about it. Most of the real problems are not really political but just the facts of life and we have to learn to live with them. Or "it's just the changing times, there's nothing you can do about it." As Paul Krugman writes, "an influential body of opinion has reacted to global warming and the emergence of an American plutocracy the same way: 'It's not true, it's not true, it's not true, nothing can be done about it.'"[18] And on the other side, politicians are either ineffective or they will do what they are going to do, so, for example, the same tax cut is good in a boom and a recession.

Now there is one sense in which any honest observer of the political culture has to stand up and protest that this declaration of political disinvestment is simply false. There are many people – on both the left and the right – who are politically active and engaged. In fact some have claimed that there has been more political activism on university campuses over the past decade than there was in the 1960s. It may be too hard to accurately measure either moment to worry about the actual comparison. Suffice it to say that the claim is not, prima facie, absurd. Many people continue to give politics, and particular political issues, a privileged place on their mattering maps. Does this mean that we can now ignore the claim of disinvestment? I do not think so for two reasons. Its truth lies in its reference to a very different group of people, what we might call the mainstream or center of US society. And second, even if there is a lot of political activity and opposition, little of it is invested in people's relation to the state. Political opposition, since the rise of the new right, has increasingly been located outside of the citizen's relationship to the government. It is this fact that still demands some explanation.[19]

The withdrawal from politics is a withdrawal from the public and collective participation in the determination of the shape and direction of state/governmental policies. Such policies, at least as politics was understood in liberal modernity, aim at the realization and enhancement of the common good, through acts of participation that are seen to be constitutive of democracy itself. The affective withdrawal from – and transformation of – politics may still not be appropriately described as apathetic; it is more active than apathy suggests. At the same time, it is not accidental that such disengagements from politics are constantly being described and defined, in the public arena, as apathy. At the very least, this puts the blame on the people as individuals rather than on the political system itself. Still, we must go further if we are to get an adequate sense of the contemporary indifference toward politics. There are many explanations that have been given for the abandonment of politics, and for the appearance of what Ralph Nader has called "under-citizenship." No doubt all of them contain some truth. I want to consider five broad accounts of what has happened to politics as a public and political responsibility.

The first account says, basically, that people's disengagement from politics is the expression of a healthy skepticism or even realism. For example, one might suggest that it is, in fact, a rational response, under rational choice theory, as measured by comparing the small expected utility or benefit of voting (or of any political action for that matter) against the costs – in time spent reading, going to meetings, traveling to polls, etc.[20]

There are other ways of expressing the same basic outlook. Castoriadis observes that "the most conspicuous feature of contemporary politics … is its insignificance."[21] Or in other words, "politicians are impotent … They no more have a programme. Their purpose is to stay in office."[22] Putting it bluntly: even if you could organize, you probably wouldn't change anything, and even if you did succeed, your success would probably be corrupted, and even if it were not, everything is so complicated, there are so many other issues, that it probably wouldn't mean a lot anyway.

Another common version of this impotence blames changes in our political system itself. Whether or not these changes are intentional, the political parties are not only consolidating their power but also transferring control of the government from the people to corporations. Elections are determined not by popular will but by money and the media (which depend on the increasingly continuous electoral process), and present the illusion ("false consciousness") through public opinion polls that the country has some interest in this process and actually supports the choice between the candidates. The media empty politics of content at best, and misrepresent not only people's interests but the truth as well. Such arguments, increasingly common these days, are very suspect. It is nice to explain away these problems by assuming either that the majority of people are too stupid to understand that they are being manipulated or that, even if they did realize it, without access to other information, there is nothing they can do about it. It is nice – but very undemocratic – to think that if people only knew what I know, they would obviously agree with me. It is also, I might add, not a very good way to start a discussion to try to convince people to join one's side or at least form an alliance.

A second account of the new culture of politics asserts that people are basically too scared and insecure to get involved in politics. Under the sign of the "risk society," a number of commentators have argued that contemporary experience has become so uncertain, so insecure, so unsafe, so vulnerable, so precarious as to make politics seem all but impossible.[23] Economic insecurity makes people acquiesce to policies they do not support.

The third account suggests that we are confronting the collapse, disappearance or impoverishment of civil society, social life and the political sphere.[24] On this view, something that used to be there is now lacking: political alternatives, a public-moral vision that can bind together the fabric of collective political life,[25] political hope ("We live in the disappointed aftermath of a politics that aspired to change the human predicament in elemental ways, but whose hopes have resolved into heavy disillusionment"[26]), a political community, consensus, or mediating communal and institutional political structures and agencies.

Most powerfully, this lack is understood to involve the relationship between the public and the private realms, either through the deconstruction of the line separating them, or through the dismantling of "the bridges between private and public life ... or to put it differently ... there is no easy and obvious way to translate private worries into public issues, and conversely, to discern and pinpoint public issues in private troubles."[27] One of the great advances of modernity was to create and separate the public and private realms, thereby allowing the private life to remain relatively free of politics. But increasingly it seems that private life has replaced politics. As a result, "the sole grievances aired in public are sackfuls of private agonies and anxieties ... the public has become the 'territory' where private affairs ... are put on display."[28] As we have given up a notion of the common good, traditionally private concerns rush in to fill all of the space of the public – whether on television or in the changing functions of police forces. Private life seems to have become the locus of value and privilege.[29] As the public sphere has been evacuated, traditionally public functions are redefined as "private" matters in the double sense of domestic/familial issues and market services; state functions are recast as service industries open to privatization (including everything from power and water to prisons and education), and public concerns are displaced into questions of familial responsibility and morality.

A fourth view of the changing political culture asserts that the market (and technology as something intrinsically tied to the market) has replaced politics; business has become the locus for value, self-expression and self-determination. It is under the sign of business and markets that we now imagine and forge our destiny. Who needs something as negative and stultifying as politics when all the limits on possibility have been removed in the "new economy"?

From another perspective, the celebration of the market as the new politics expresses the mistrust of both the bureaucracies and the claims to expertise (which were supposed to bring impartiality and knowledge, respectively, to decision making) that people have come to associate with government.[30] As a result, the market magically appears to be both less morally compromised and more rational and efficient than the institutions of politics. Interestingly, if the appeal to the market appears to cleanse politics, the replacement of politics by the market apparently cleanses the market as well. For example, while the public found the image of corporate bean-counters weighing the costs of repairs vs. lives absolutely unacceptable, the image of using such cost–benefit analysis to make decisions about the environment, or health policy, or worker safety seems less objectionable. Business thus becomes the site of our political hopes and struggles.

Fukuyama offers an interesting variation on this argument. Rejecting the view that civil society has collapsed, he asserts instead that what we are witnessing is the result of "moral miniaturization: while people continue to participate in group life, the groups themselves are less authoritative and produce a smaller radius of trust."[31] This "miniaturization of community and morality" is a result of the belief that most people and public institutions have become more selfish and less trustworthy. As a result, "most middle class Americans don't believe in anything strongly enough to want to impose their values on one another, and therefore have no motive" for serious political involvement.[32] This is not very different from the third account above, but Fukuyama connects this argument to a vision of capitalism as the new politics by asserting that we must turn to capitalism for norms. While most critics of capitalism have argued that capitalism tears down traditions and values, and undermines stable social norms, Fukuyama proudly asserts that "capitalism is a net creator of norms and thus a net moralizing force in modern societies."[33]

A final account invokes the role of liberalism itself, and of the critique of liberalism from the left. Fukuyama, for example, blames liberalism itself for the divorce between the people and politics; it has produced its own crisis in that liberalism is about tolerance and tolerance is the death of passion:

> In a situation in which all moralisms and religious fanaticisms are discouraged in the interest of tolerance, in an intellectual climate that weakens the possibility of belief in any one doctrine because of an overriding commitment to be open to all the world's beliefs and "value systems," it should not be surprising that the strength of community life has declined in America.

Without any real convictions, the good liberal "knows better than to risk his life for a cause."[34]

On the other hand, there are those who would lay the blame at the doorstep of a more radical left that, since the 1960s, has been engaged in a sustained attack on liberalism. If the demand of a national liberal politics is precisely that one subordinate all prior, local and competing identities in order to claim the position of citizen as an agent of change, the left attempted to deconstruct this apparently unified political subject. In so doing it not only put the claim of communitarianism (group identity and loyalty) before that of citizenship but also challenged the right of the state itself to act as an agent of change in the name of its supposedly unified and undifferentiated subject-citizens. In its place it put what one sympathetic critic calls "the drudgery of identity construction," which "look[s] limitless and never likely to end."[35]

IV. The production of indifference and the postmodern frontier

There is probably some truth in all of these accounts. And yet all these accounts avoid the possibility that the growing indifference and disengagement from both state politics and a sense of politics as a project aimed at the realization of some public good are being produced as a crucial part of the contemporary hegemonic struggle over modernity! It is not merely an accident of history or the unwelcome result of other historical events, but a somewhat intentional attempt to make politics, at least as it was understood in liberal modernity, "disappear." I want to propose that the disappearance of politics, then, not only defines the end of a certain hegemony but of hegemony itself. It opens a new conception of politics that is connected in new and somewhat surprising ways with morality, religion and the market.

Eliasoph recognizes that people "have to learn how to connect their personal lives to political issues,"[36] and that contemporary institutional power is making politics "invisible and always 'out of place' in public."[37] Recognizing that "people are not born apolitical," she then poses the question of "how people convince themselves [and each other] to care or not to care about politics ... [how they] learn to make the heavy burden of powerlessness feel natural and freely borne."[38] Her only answer is that "apathy takes work to produce."[39]

Let me use an analogy here. Suppose that you were trying to sell a product, say a particular brand of soda. You hire an advertising and marketing company, which puts together a massive campaign that lasts for well over forty years. Now suppose that the only consistent result was a steady decline not only in your sales but in the total sales of sodas. Would you not end the marketing campaign and fire the advertising company? The most visible effect of political discourses over the past four decades has been a radical disinvestment of governmental politics (or at least a general belief among the population that there is such a disinvestment). Yet there are absolutely no signs that the various institutions of politics are bothered by these trends, or want to change the discourse. Doesn't it seem reasonable to assume that they actually wanted to produce these effects? Otherwise, why would negative campaign ads continue even though it is clear that they have little impact on undecided voters and merely reinforce many people's skepticism and cynicism about the political process itself?[40]

One of the most powerful political strategists of the new right, Lee Atwater, Reagan's campaign manager and one-time Chair of the Republican Party, admitted as much in an interview in the *New York Times*. Not surprisingly, the *Times* missed the revelation in his statement that "Bull permeates everything." Instead, it blamed the situation – the failures, the lack of vision, the apathy – of contemporary politics on the high cost of campaigns, the decreasing intelligence of the media's political coverage, and negative campaigning. But Atwater himself dissents from this too easy vision of culpability: "If you want to look at a solid trend for the last 15 or 20 years, it is that the American people are cynical and turned off about all the institutions, and politics is one."[41] In fact, I would add, politics is the first and most important one.

The only way to make sense of the behavior of the variety of actors and institutions involved in state politics may be to realize that they are not trying to challenge or undo the growing cynicism and indifference of the nation; in fact, they are using every political and cultural means at their disposal to actively encourage this disengagement, to augment it and to make people conscious of the fact that they (and their neighbors) are cynical and uninvolved. Politicians blame this on liberalism and relativism, even as they speak the languages of liberalism and relativism whenever it is politically efficacious. Political media are constantly bemoaning the popular vision of politics as irrational, superficial, sold-out and dishonest even as they maintain that this is how it has to be, given the world within which politics is operating. Politicians are constantly accused of being slaves to public opinion polls, despite the fact that, increasingly, they approach such polls, and even the desires of the people, strategically as tools.[42] When they follow the people, they are democratic, when the other side follows it, they are slaves to public opinion. When they do not follow it, they are principled and brave leaders, when the other side does not, they are hypocrites putting their own false moralities ahead of the common wisdom of the people. And, all along, they are interpreting public opinion and the popular will to fit their own rhetorical and tactical needs; unlike the common criticism, politicians no longer take the content of such polls for granted, seeing them instead as more opportunities for political articulation.

Politicians no longer hide the disparity between their rhetoric and actions or, perhaps more accurately, they happily assert that their rhetoric should count more than the actions. It is not bad enough that so many politicians are blatantly dishonest; they now spend more time seeking out and publicizing scandalous behavior than reforming the institutional conditions of such behavior. What was a scandal yesterday need not be one today. If there is no scandal today, we can happily admit that just the accusation works almost as well. What is or is not scandalous seems increasingly to be a matter of rhetorical posturing. George Bush stages a phony drug bust outside the White House to coincide with a speech defending the war against drugs, with little objection. And his son, George W. Bush, uses (and later rewards) mid-level campaign workers to pose as "ordinary citizens" demanding a halt to the recounting of votes in Florida. These "dirty tricks" are noted and then passed over in the media.[43] Congressional republicans gleefully and publicly change the rules – and the moral standards – to protect and enhance their power. Politicians today seem proud to have been sold to the highest bidder and to be the most cynical users of marketing techniques. They no longer hide their financial scaffolding, nor do they dissimulate the fact that they are running advertising campaigns.[44] And when, in those rare moments, they admit some embarrassment at their own behavior and talk about reform, they do so knowing – and making it visible enough for most people to see – that the reforms, if they do come off, which is unlikely in the long run, will actually be insignificant.

I do not mean to sound nostalgic for some long-gone era when politicians were honest; quite the contrary. If it is nostalgia, it is nostalgia for a moment when politicians were still insecure enough about their power (and their relation to a public) that they knew they had to hide the dishonesty and hypocrisy. It is as if politicians – and the new right in particular – learned the lesson of the Grand Inquisitor, whom Sloterdijk describes as "a prototype of modern (political) cynics. … His bitter anthropology prompts him to believe that human beings must be and want to be deceived. Human beings require order, which in turn requires domination, and domination requires lies."[45] What the Grand Inquisitor could not imagine was that, eventually, the people would know and accept the fact that they are being and have to be deceived. Such a politics can only end "in a collectively dispersed rage of anxiety against modernity,"[46] which is, paradoxically, exactly what the new right wants in its struggle to deconstruct and reconstruct modernity.

There is another side to this erasure of politics. For in constructing both the image and the reality of an apathetic citizenry, it is absolutely vital that one erase any sense of a vital culture of civil and political activism. So we have to be careful not to accept on face value the totalizing assertions of apathy and withdrawal. Despite the claim that civil society and the public sphere have been evacuated, there are lots of spaces of civic attachment and social involvement. That they may not look like earlier sites of attachment – PTOs rather than PTAs – should not be taken necessarily as a sign of decline.[47] I have already pointed to the lie that denies a vital culture of a wide range of political activisms in this country (and globally). And the contemporary possibilities and imaginations of activism (including from the right) are not so dominated by preconceptions of where the appropriate sites are or what the social identities of the activists (and those they address) are supposed to be.

This is accomplished in a variety of ways, for different sites of activism. Extremists on the right (including militia, various religious sects, etc.) are simply ignored or dismissed as conspiracy theorists. (More mainstream new right activists are always presented as if their actions were not actually a political struggle but operating in the realms of culture and morality.) Images of left activism are usually simply erased or trivialized (as nothing to be taken seriously). There is in fact little actual coverage of the real political activism on campuses in the national media, for example, although there is a great deal of concern about the supposedly radical political culture that liberal professors and students have imposed on campuses. Sometimes, of course, activism is taken seriously and presented as a radical conspiracy presenting a serious threat (rhetorically linked to terrorism) to our very way of life and everything the country stands for. Even feminism and anti-racism, rather than being co-opted or incorporated, are sometimes constructed by the new right as a fundamental threat to our way of life.[48] The coverage of the anti-globalization (or global justice) movement nicely demonstrates this strategic schizophrenia. On the one hand, the coverage of the anti-globalization protests usually presents them as having little relevance to the actual conditions or system of our national politics. This is significantly different from the way in which the media covered the movements of the 1960s and 1970s, and not only because there was still something of a residual liberal presence in the media and government. On the other hand, we are presented with a sensationalized image of violent anarchists that, like their terrorist comrades, do threaten the peace of the world and the health of the nation. Recently, this schizophrenic approach to oppositional politics has drifted from activism to institutional politics, as was evident in the coverage of the Brazilian elections at the end of 2002 and the Venezuelan national strike in early 2003.

Insofar as the left appears incapable of achieving even the most temporary alliance or unity, it can continue to be denied any real presence as an activist political force in the national popular imagination. The coverage of the anti-Bush movement fueling the democratic presidential campaign in 2004 is the exception that proves the rule! Perhaps that is because one of the projects of the liberal modernity of the twentieth century was to move political agency into the arena of state politics and, in that way, harness popular dissent and resistance. Maybe one of the unforeseen results of the attempt to depoliticize people's relation to the state has been to reestablish the importance of that other politics and to reaffirm the vitality of popular dissent.

Still, the depoliticization of public life is an ongoing production. Not only is disengagement being constructed as the rational response, but the fact that large segments of the population are increasingly "apathetic" is presented as a fait accompli. Critics and commentators have, I believe, avoided this conclusion only by – mistakenly – assuming that the existence of political commitment is a matter of knowledge rather than affect. The irony is that everyone assumes they know it but that the rest do not. But then politicians know that people know what is going on ... The sorts of explanations I discussed above – the destruction of the civil sphere, the celebration of the private, the growing sense of living under the sign of risk and insecurity – too often have the effect of closing off the recognition that this indifference is a crucial product of the very political culture it has come to characterize. People are almost forced to retreat into a more limited and private universe, to give up any assumption that one's commitments carry some responsibilities with them, and to evacuate the public political sphere and politics.

But this still leaves open the question of why disinvestment seems to be such a reasonable option. How has it become so inextricably woven into the affective disciplining of everyday life in the USA? To answer these final questions, we have to take a detour and understand that these political sensibilities were constructed out of the larger contexts of lived experience and popular culture in the USA. They were not invented by the new right; they were not, in the first instance, political sensibilities but popular sensibilities.

These affective sensibilities can be located in the broader cultural contexts that developed in the USA over the past fifty years and, more specifically, they can be connected to the emergence of a certain affective postmodernity as one dimension of those contexts. This postmodern logic describes a change in the relation between affect (mattering) and meaning (content). This change does not define everyone's experience; it does not describe all of anyone's experience. The particular relation it describes has probably existed in other times and places, to varying degrees. In fact, the reason it becomes important in the postwar culture is precisely a matter of degree – of the frequency, importance and intensity of its appearance across the experience and culture of certain key segments of the (primarily youth) population. It cannot be assumed to be abnormal as if there were some single and universally normal ways in which mattering maps are supposed to connect to maps of meaning. I do think, however, that this postmodernity has become a crucial, if not dominant, part of what Raymond Williams called "the structures of feeling" of US society. And its centrality in the cultural life of the nation has had significant consequences elsewhere, including, I shall suggest, in the political culture of the new right and the contemporary struggle over modernity.

I use "postmodernity" to refer to the increasingly distant and precarious relations that exist between the available mattering maps and the available maps of meaning. The latter tell us how to make sense of our world, and define one plane of our experience or everyday life. They illuminate the meanings, relationships and values that are available to us to organize our lives. They define the possible objects and sites of our affective investments. Mattering maps, on the other hand, define the necessary and possible organizations of our investments in the world. Obviously, any sense of coherent experience would seem to demand some relationship between these two sets of maps.

Postmodernity names the historical appearance of an expanding series of ruptures or gaps between the meanings, relationships and values that socially organize our existence and identity, and the possibilities for affectively investing in them. This goes beyond a sense that it is difficult to make sense of one's affective relations, or to put one's total faith in some ideological meaning. It points to the fact that it is increasingly difficult to locate places where it is possible to care about something enough, to have enough faith that it matters, so that one can actually make a commitment to it and invest oneself in it. It is an inability to locate any meaning as a possible and appropriate source for an impassioned commitment, or to find any legitimation for such a commitment. It is a dissolution of the anchoring effect that articulates meaning to affect. It is not that nothing matters, for something has to matter, but there is no way of choosing or of finding something to warrant that investment. It is as if we had to speak about our lives with stories that cannot work, to use languages that are unable to make sense of our lives.[49] People can no longer trust their common sense, even as they are compelled to live it, and for that very reason they live it all the more aggressively. This is, in fact, exactly Ann Burlein's description of Rush Limbaugh: he "establishes a passionate belief in the very things he admits he is constructing."[50]

Sloterdijk describes this as a "universal diffuse cynicism":

their psychic apparatus has become elastic enough to incorporate as a survival factor a permanent doubt about their own activities. They know what they are doing, but they do it because, in the short run, the force of circumstances and the instinct for self-preservation are speaking the same language, and they are telling them that it has to be so.[51]

Postmodernity defines a popular attitude in which people know exactly what they are doing and they do it anyway. (This is the exact opposite of Marx's definition of ideology: people don't know what they are doing but they are doing it anyway.) One cannot legitimate one's actions on the basis of ignorance or false consciousness (I know cheating is wrong and I would not have done it if I knew I was cheating, but I did not know). The postmodern sensibility says: "I know cheating is wrong and I know I am cheating, but that is the way things are, that is what reality is like. One knows that life, and every choice, is a scam, but the knowledge has become so universally accepted that there are no longer any alternatives. Everyone knows everyone cheats, so everyone cheats, and if I did not, I would in effect suffer for being honest."

One can only make choices with a certain detachment and irony, being aware that no choice is any more legitimate than any other. The postmodern sensibility is located in the space between "nothing matters (and what if it did)" and "it doesn't matter what matters as long as something matters." I have called this sensibility "ironic nihilism" or authentic inauthenticity. It might also be called impassioned apathy. It assumes that distance is the only necessity, because that is what allows you to refuse any claim or demand that might be made on you, even as you answer such claims or demands all the time. This sensibility defines an ironic nihilism in which distance is offered as the only reasonable relation to a reality that is no longer reasonable. Investments are always self-consciously temporary and ironic. After all, if every possible site of investment (a location on a mattering map) is equally suspect and ultimately false, then every commitment is nothing but a pose. And then all one can do is to invest in any particular pose without denying that that is all it is.[52]

There are, I think, at least two different ways of living such a sensibility. Let's call them cynical inauthenticity and sentimental inauthenticity. In fact, these describe two of the most common attitudes of American popular culture. Cynical inauthenticity asserts that there are no grounds for distinguishing the value of possible commitments. One simply commits oneself, temporarily, to whatever seems to work at the moment, and one has to be willing to give it up whenever it stops working. In that sense, differences don't actually matter. Sentimental authenticity asserts that the fact that something matters makes it different (and is therefore the only source of difference). One simply celebrates the magical possibility of making a difference (against impossible odds, the more impossible the better) by the sheer quantity or intensity of one's commitment. So whatever happens, one never gives up because it is the very fact that one cares so much about something that makes it matter (not what it actually is).

If the former defines a kind of nihilism for pleasure, the latter describes nihilism with a happy face.[53] The former embraces instability and inauthenticity, the latter pretends to like them (but what difference does it make after all). The former – cynical inauthenticity – can only passionately reaffirm its own relativism and is likely, ultimately, to lead to some form of the organization of pessimism, some form of political disengagement and even apathy. The latter – sentimental inauthenticity – actually has to constantly negate, by the very force of its will, the very cynicism and relativism that are located at its foundations. This difference between these two forms of strategic response to postmodernity has constituted a kind of frontier within the very heart of popular culture and everyday life. This postmodern frontier defines not the choice of whether or not to live within postmodernity, relativism and cynicism, but of how to respond to this increasingly common affective popular sensibility.

Finally, I want to return to the question of how this postmodern sensibility has been articulated into the new right's struggle to establish a new modernity. I have described this struggle as a hegemonic struggle against hegemony, and suggested that it works in part by establishing an affective frontier within society itself.[54] I want to suggest that the construction of a political culture of depoliticization is a product of the new right's strategic efforts to bend, to its own ends, a frontier that was already reconstructing the possibilities of popular consciousness outside of the political arena. That is to say, the new right is articulating two frontiers – one popular-cynical and the other moral-political – to produce a powerful new reconfiguration of the very possibilities of politics in modernity. The politics of the new right enacts its struggle against politics as usual (hegemony) at the frontier of postmodern affective culture. In taking up and redirecting the very sensibility and practice of a popular culture it simultaneously renounces and mimics, the new right articulates that popular affective frontier to its own morally constructed frontier, transforming the nature of both frontiers and, in the process, remaking the possibilities of a politics derived out of the feelings of powerlessness and hopelessness that seem to be our common inheritance. It is this articulation of the two frontiers that explains how it is that, increasingly, contemporary cultural products like Hollywood films can be, simultaneously, politically crucial and ideologically irrelevant.

What we now have is a doubly articulated frontier that offers three possibilities for a livable political position, even as it seems to divide the population into two opposing camps. The first position describes, not surprisingly, the position that the new right claims for itself; it connects what I have called sentimental inauthenticity with the affirmation of a moral and religiously defined sense of politics. That is to say, the new right's affirmation of its own absolute political investment, not only in politics but in the absolute rightness of its own political struggle, has now to be understood as a response to the same postmodern uncertainty that the rest of the population feels. Sentimental inauthenticity responds to that uncertainty by over-investing in whatever content has been chosen, as if the affirmation of belief itself, as if the very quantity of affect invested, can magically overcome the contradiction inherent in the very position (but isn't that the very function of faith in the postmodern world?). On this side of the frontier is the simple fact of belief and commitment (without requiring one to actually live the values embodied in the object of one's faith). On this side is the celebration of fanaticism (believing in something "too" strongly). One does not have to live the Christian life to be a Christian fanatic. One does not have to live the principles of American democracy to be a patriot. And one does not have to actually believe in open and fair competition to be a fanatic supporter of the free market. As Ann Burlein puts it, the new right "performs religion as the possibility of protest and passion."[55]

The second position is that of withdrawal itself, of the renunciation of politics in favor of cynical inauthenticity. Here, to put it simply, society acknowledges and accepts that the very recognition of postmodern inauthenticity is sufficient to legitimate the abandonment of the social and political field. The renunciation of the possibility of politics as a locus of human agency or of meaning becomes a new common sense. Anyone who celebrates the impossibility of a political solution is a realist and, as such, can be admitted into the kingdom of god (the vision of a uniquely American democratic capitalism), if only because they have not prevented it from coming into existence. Embracing such a depoliticized relation to reality means that one is acceding to whatever changes are being produced by others occupying a different position along the frontier. Often, this detachment can allow people to take up the beliefs of those in the first position as temporary commitments, as affective magnets, epidemics, etc. The withdrawal from politics does not place one outside of the political, and the refusal of agency can become a new form of political agency. In this way, the new right attempts to construct a new popular vision of the nation and a new national popular that can embrace not only those who actively commit to its struggle but also those who grant it hegemonic leadership either explicitly or by withdrawing entirely from the field of struggle.

The third position on the frontier is most interesting and important for it tries to construct the impossibility of political opposition, which is, by the very definition of the frontier, self-contradictory. This third position offers possible ways of refusing to fall into either a postmodern moral absolutism or a postmodern apathy. The first denies the lived reality of the postmodern frontier but this appears increasingly problematic. By locating such a political commitment on the frontier, the new right tries to make political opposition into a dream divorced from any reality. Anyone who actually talks about serious problems and their solutions in purely political terms is a dreamer, not to be taken seriously. We have been there and done that, after all, and seen that it has failed. Such a politics is the groundless and even dangerous work of the imagination.

The second possibility is to embrace the postmodern frontier as cynical inauthenticity, without abandoning the political field. But the inevitable result, according to the new right, is that one has nowhere to go but into an impossible and amoral (immoral?) relativism that fundamentally undermines the very possibility of any value (and hence, of any real politics). The new right has, to some extent, succeeded in identifying both of these possibilities with the continuing affirmation of liberal modernity. The result is that, indirectly, the two possibilities are collapsed into a single untenable and unlivable position. The new right's reconfiguration of this frontier produces a reversal by which social concern is translated, simultaneously, into selfishness, special interests, a childish refusal of reality and a dangerous relativism. This reversal locates any political opposition to its own struggle on one side of the frontier in such a way that it can never cross the frontier to do battle with the enemy but is always fighting its own windmills.

Thus, precisely by repoliticizing the social relations and cultural practices of everyday life at the affective postmodern frontier, the new right is effectively redefining and redistributing the possibilities and forms of political action and subjectivity. It empowers people only so that it can ultimately disempower them; it rescues politics only so that it can ultimately negate it in the name of a morality/religion that is never lived!

Notes

1 See my *Caught in the Crossfire: Kids, Politics and America's Future* (Boulder: Paradigm, 2005). This piece draws upon – summarizing and amending and sometimes quoting (without marking the specific passages) – chapter 9 of that work.

2 Think of how dancing often seems to generate the energy necessary to continue dancing or of how particular emotions can exhaust one.

3 Linda Kintz, *Between Jesus and the Market: The Emotions that Matter in Right-Wing America* (Durham, NC: Duke UP, 1997) 10.

4 Ann Burlein, *Lift High the Cross: Where White Supremacy and the Christian Right Converge* (Durham, NC: Duke UP, 2002) 235.

5 Kintz, *Between Jesus and the Market* 4.

6 Ad, *News & Observer* 12 May 2003: 11A.

7 Over the past decade such techniques have become increasingly widespread and sophisticated.

8 Dick Dahl, "The NRA Sees Room to Grow as Faithful Adjunct to the GOP," *The Nation* 4 Nov. 2002: 17.

9 Juliet Eilperin and Dan Morgan, "Something Borrowed Something Blue," *Washington Post*, 9 Mar. 2001: A16.
10 Karen Houppert, "Wanted: A Few Good Girls," *The Nation* 25 Nov. 2002: 16.
11 Ad, Washington Legal Foundation, "Defaming Free Enterprise," *New York Times* 13 May 2002.
12 Burlein, *Lift High the Cross* 15.
13 Judith Levine, *Harmful to Minors: The Perils of Protecting Children from Sex* (Minneapolis: U of Minnesota P, 2002) 12.
14 In 1996 sixty-six percent were not too worried or not worried at all that they would be victims of crime.
15 Obviously, this was written before the anti-war and anti-Bush campaigns of 2003 and 2004.
16 Thomas E. Patterson, *The Vanishing Voter: Public Involvement in an Age of Uncertainty* (New York: Knopf, 2002).
17 Jedediah Purdy, *For Common Things: Irony, Trust and Commitment in America Today* (New York: Knopf, 1999) xxii.
18 Paul Krugman, "Plutocracy and Politics," *News & Observer* 14 June 2002.
19 It may be useful, following Eliasoph, to distinguish among the variety of political attitudes and positions that are collapsed into the general claim of a growing apathy and cynicism. Eliasoph, for example, identifies four distinct types of people who have disinvested politics; she calls them cynics, volunteers, private people, and "activists." See Nina Eliasoph, *Avoiding Politics: How Americans Produce Apathy in Everyday Life* (Cambridge: Cambridge UP, 1998).
20 Titus Levi, personal conversation.
21 Zygmunt Bauman, *In Search of Politics* (Stanford, CA: Stanford UP, 1999) 4.
22 Ibid.
23 Bauman, *In Search of Politics* 52.
24 Robert Putnam, *Bowling Alone: The Collapse and Revival of American Community* (New York: Simon, 2000).
25 Michael J. Sandel, "Political Economy of Citizenship," *Atlantic Monthly* Mar. 1996.
26 Purdy, *For Common Things* xxii.
27 Bauman, *In Search of Politics* 2.
28 Ibid. 3.
29 Yet Sloterdijk: "For over two hundred years, we have been observing a permanent, though always contested, movement of the private into the public sphere." What other people see as the private replacing the public, I see as a consequence of the growing affectivity (and separation from meaning) of everyday life and politics. Peter Sloterdijk, *Critique of Cynical Reason*, trans. Michael Eldred (Minneapolis: U of Minnesota P, 1987) 106.
30 See John Clarke and Janet Newman, *The Managerial State: Power, Politics and Ideology in the Remaking of Social Welfare* (London: Sage, 1997).
31 Francis Fukuyama, *The Great Disruption: Human Nature and the Reconstitution of the Social Order* (New York: Free, 1999) 49.
32 Ibid. 89.
33 Ibid. 253.
34 Francis Fukuyama, *The End of History and the Last Man* (New York: Free, 1992) 307.
35 Bauman, *In Search of Politics* 20. There is a slightly different – and I think stronger – argument about the left's contribution to the current crisis. Put simply, this argument suggests that the left has undermined its own credibility because it has been making the same arguments over and over again as if they were new, and as if they explained

any and every problem, no matter how new it may seem. After a while, the very repetition of these arguments, so predictable and so apparently ineffective, seems to undermine the power of the left itself.

36 Eliasoph, *Avoiding Politics* 260.

37 Ibid. 17.

38 Ibid. 234.

39 Ibid. 6.

40 Mathew A. Crenson and Benjamin Ginsberg, in *Downsizing Democracy: How America Sidelined its Citizens and Privatized its Public* (Baltimore: Johns Hopkins UP, 2002), make a similar suggestion – that the disinvestment of politics is being produced, although they do not necessarily see it as strategic.

41 M. Orestes, "America's Politics Loses its Way as its Vision Changes the World," *New York Times* 18 Mar. 1990: A16.

42 James W. Carey, personal conversation.

43 Carol Rosenberg, "Newspaper: Bush Gave Plumb Jobs to Recount Supporters," *News & Observer* 14 July 2002: 4A.

44 How else can one explain the public use of fronts which are intentionally but also publicly self-misrepresentational? An example would be the Racial Privacy Initiative movement in California, sponsored by a group deceptively called the American Civil Rights Coalition.

45 Sloterdijk, *Critique of Cynical Reason* 189.

46 Ibid. 483.

47 Cf. Putnam, *Bowling Alone*.

48 Cf. Todd Gitlin, *The Twilight of Common Dreams: Why America is Wracked by Culture Wars* (New York: Holt, 1995); the trivialization of the anti-globalization movement, or its construction as terrorists, is significantly different from Gitlin's description of the incorporation of the anti-war and new left movements.

49 It is not merely a re-creation of the split between thought and feeling so commonly blamed for all the ills of Western society.

50 Burlein, *Lift High the Cross* 206.

51 Sloterdijk, *Critique of Cynical Reason* 3, 5.

52 One might think about the ease with which G.W. Bush legitimated or tried to legitimate the invasion of Iraq in 2003. Bush cycled through reasons; whenever one seemed to fall apart, another appeared. The one that kept reappearing – the presence of weapons of mass destruction – kept appearing despite the fact that there was no evidence and that it was publicly demonstrated that the administration's presentation to the United Nations was filled with errors, misrepresentations and lies. In fact, Bush's presidency has reached a certain pinnacle of postmodern sophistication. See, for example, Franck Rich, "The Jerry Bruckheimer White House," *New York Times* 11 May 2003, for a discussion of Bush's having turned national politics into a movie production.

53 Reality television is a rich field of postmodern production. Among the most appalling examples are the bachelor/millionaire series. The latest is extraordinary for its overt cynicism. The woman who convinces the bachelor to marry her will win a million dollars, although the bachelor does not know it. Sounds like prostitution to me.

54 I take the notion of a hegemonic frontier from Ernesto Laclau and Chantal Mouffe, *Hegemony and Socialist Strategy* (London: Verso, 1985).

55 Burlein, *Lift High the Cross* 28. Burlein also suggests that this frontier may have a second – economic (neoliberal) – existence: "A different model of abstract nationalism requires a different kind of American frontier, a speculative financial one: entrepreneurial frontier" (150).

ernesto laclau

HETEROGENEITY AND POST-MODERNITY

When the theme of post-modernity emerged a few decades ago within our political and philosophical horizon, it was associated with a variety of dimensions. In that sense, it was more the reflection of an epochal new perceptual field than a precise theoretical stand. Theoretical attempts at capturing its meaning did not, however, take long to come forth. They were many and greatly differ from each other, but one, however, had pride of place from the beginning: I am referring to what, in Lyotard's canonical approach to post-modernity, was called the "crisis of grand narratives." From *The Postmodern Condition* to *The Differend* Lyotard elaborated a theoretical perspective whose central tenet was that, while the founding discourses of modernity had been centred in the postulation of a universal subject and in the notion of an ultimate ground of the social – as epitomized in the classical philosophies of history – the contemporary scene would be characterized by the breaking up of such a subject and such a ground and by the proliferation of a plurality of language games whose interconnections do not lead to any kind of mutual compatibility. *Ergo*: irreducible *differends* are at the very root of social interaction. Heterogeneity would thus be constitutive. The following reflections have been written in the conviction that, while the dialectic between the homogeneous and the heterogeneous is indeed far more complex than it was conceived in the past – and it is at the root of the epochal change which we are referring to – such a complexity is far from necessarily going in the direction of the pure disposition and multiplicity that mainstream post-modern approaches presuppose.[1] This means that such dispersion and multiplicity is only *one* of the developments that the breakdown of a fundamentalist grounding makes possible. I would even say that to conceive of such a breakdown in terms of a "crisis of grand narratives" is extremely misleading and short-sighted. A widening of the theoretical horizon which makes other possibilities visible becomes necessary. This should question whether the movement from "modernity" to "post-modernity" can still be conceived in terms of "break."

Let us start from a passage by Frantz Fanon that, prima facie, nobody would associate with post-modernism:

> The *lumpenproletariat*, once it is constituted, brings all its forces to endanger the "security" of the town, and is the sign of the irrevocable decay, the gangrene ever present at the heart of colonial domination. So the pimps, the hooligans, the unemployed, and the petty criminals ... throw themselves into the struggle like stout working men. These classless idlers will by militant and decisive action discover the path that leads to nationhood ... The prostitutes too, and the maids who are paid two pounds a month, all who turn in circles between suicide and madness, will recover their balance, once more go forward, and march proudly in the great procession of the awakened nation.[2]

Apparently, we are in the antipodes of anything resembling post-modernity. There is a strong revolutionary (anti-colonialist) appeal to a will supposed to be the absolute ground of the (new) nation; there is the postulation of a sharp frontier separating that nation from the colonial order; and there is the attempt at creating an absolute subject of the emancipatory project. However, if we take a careful look at the discursive operations through which those effects are obtained, we immediately see that the worm of post-modernity is already silently eating away the certainties of classical modernity. For what we have in Fanon's text is the attempt at reading emancipation *by other than modern means*. There is, first, the appeal to an absolute exteriority vis-à-vis the colonial order. He is not appealing to the internal contradictions of colonialist society (to people whose antagonism would result from the *inside* of that society) but to *total* outsiders, to people who are *uncountable* within the order of the city. This means that between "insiders" and "outsiders" there is no common measure. So we have a *differend* in Lyotard's sense. This shows a sharp differentiation between Fanon's discourse and the "modern" attempts at conceiving antagonisms as subsumable under the category of "contradiction," which proceeds through dialectical retrievals – e.g. through the contradiction between forces and relations of production. For the latter there is no radical "outside" (A is opposed to B, only to be reabsorbed in a new stage, C, in which the antagonism between A and B reveals itself to have been only the prelude to a higher positivity superseding both). History is here a purely internal affair. So we are within the most classical parameters of the "modern" project. The true "outsiders" – the "peoples without history" of Hegel, the *lumpenproletariat* of Marx – can be ignored as being purely external to the main line of historical development.

For Fanon, on the contrary, to be a total outsider becomes the precondition for the emergence of a revolutionary subjectivity. This is the reason why the *lumpenproletariat*, unceremoniously brushed aside by Marx and Engels as agent of any possible radical change, becomes, for Fanon, the very axis of the revolutionary process. There are two aspects worth under-lining here. The first concerns the very nature of the discursive operation in which Fanon is involved. In order to be a purely internal process, any succession of reversal and retrievals, if it is going to be truly dialectical, has to reduce the opposition between A and B to that between A and non-A, so that (1) the essence of B is exhausted in its being non-A, and (2) there is in the essence of A everything needed to explain its transition to B as its necessary opposite. Now, in Fanon's argument the opposition colonialism/anti-colonialism also has the external form of a dialectical opposition A/non-A, but with this crucial difference: that there are not the internal contra-dictions of the colonial order – the inside of the colonial order – which explain the emergence of the anti-colonial subjects, but the total exteri-ority of the latter vis-à-vis the former. That is the reason why Fanon has to appeal to total outsiders (hooligans, prostitutes, petty criminals) whose lack of any *positive* location within the community puts them in a position of total heterogeneity in relation to the latter. For these subjects, being anti-colonialist is the alpha and omega of their social identity. Thus, this identity becomes fully political.

At this point we find a first sense of heterogeneity which is resolutely post-modern: B is heterogeneous vis-à-vis A, not because it is the dialec-tical (and so retrievable) opposite of A but because it is *unrepresentable* within A. Lacan's radically anti-Hegelian notion of the Real is, perhaps, the clearest expression of the logic of this unrepresentability. (Recent attempts to edulcorate the Lacanian notion of the Real by domesticating it through Hegelian dialectics entirely miss the point.)

But there is a second aspect that we have to take into consideration. We have approached Fanon's discursive operation to Lyotard's *differend*. We cannot, however, do so without making clear that, in the case of Fanon, the radical character of the *differend* moves in directions which Lyotard would have never recognized as his own. For Lyotard, *differends* are sources of an irreducible plurality, while for Fanon the effect is exactly the opposite: that irreducibility is at the root of a sharp frontier separating the anti-colonial subjects from the colonial order. We are beyond modernity because there is no objective movement which reduces the two poles of the antagonism to a deeper homogeneous logic, but this does not lead to any simple separation between them but, on the contrary, to a close imbrication. This explains the meaning of our assertion, at the beginning of this essay, that the language games which it is possible to play out of the systematic de-grounding associ-ated with the notion of "post-modernity" are wider and more differentiated than notions such as "multiplicity" or "dispersion" can capture. If there is something inherently post-modern it is the displacement in the relation between homogeneity and heterogeneity, not the simple replacement of one by the other. And this displacement is perfectly compatible, as the example of Fanon shows, with the continuation of "grand narratives" of a different type. Homogeneity can be achieved, even at the level of global narratives, out of an original heterogeneity. What has changed is that the homogeneous has ceased to be a ground and has become the horizon of a social construction. That is why the notion of "break" does not adequately apprehend the type of mutation that is involved in this substitution of paradigms.

This, however, also explains why even the heterogenization of the dialectical operation that Fanon performs cannot be the only game in town within the post-modern horizon. Fanon's rigid opposition can only maintain its sharpness as far as the relationship between the colonial order and the marginals located outside it is one of *total* exteriority. This, however, can be achieved only by exaggerating out of all proportion the degree of internal coherence of the colonial order. If such an order is, on the contrary, seen as criss-crossed by points of rupture and many types of antagonisms, an externality will emerge *within* that order, so that the anti-colonialist struggle will not be limited to the total marginals (to the *lumpenproletariat* in the sense given to this term by Fanon). But something more will also happen: the internal fissures of the colonial order will call into question its ability to bring about "order" *tout court*. In that case the anti-colonial movement will have not only a *confrontational* but also a *reconstructive* dimension. If we incorporate into the picture these two additions – expansion of the points of antagonism to the interior of the communitarian space and inherence of the reconstructive dimension to any project of radical change – a consequence clearly follows: there is going to be a constitutive contamination between the internal and the external, between the homogeneous and the heterogeneous. Heterogeneity is constitutive as far as it is not a *natura naturata* emerging out of a homogeneous *natura naturans*, but the primary terrain within which homogenizing logics operate. And the latter do not proceed from a terrain different from that of the heterogeneous: as this terrain is essentially uneven, some of the heterogeneous elements will be able, at some point, to carry out hegemonic/homogenizing operations. So there is no fixed frontier dominated by an entirely stable opposition between "insiders" and "outsiders," but a displacement of frontiers which constantly renegotiates the relations between internality and externality – a "war of position" in the Gramscian sense. *My* "post-modernity" – providing that we want to stick to the term – is grounded in the constitutive character of this undecidable contaminating game. It rejects both the notion of a homogeneous foundation and its symmetrical opposite: an uncontaminated heterogeneity.

The perspective concerning heterogeneity which we have just outlined also has important consequences for the way we approach the question of the discursive apprehension of collective identities. We can say that, while modernity privileged a predominantly *conceptual* grasping of the social, today we are moving towards an alternative vision, one that privileges the moment of *singularity* as that which resists universality and which, thus, cannot be captured by purely conceptual means. The reason for this is clear: conceptual thought moves itself within the terrain of the homogeneous, of that which reduces diversity to an underlying unity. It is important to realize that homogenization, conceived in this way, in not incompatible with particularism: the only requirement is that the transition between particularities take place through purely conceptual means, that is that particularities be conceived as part of a wider whole which explains and gives sense to all of them. The terrain of homogenization presupposes, from this point of view, the presence of a unique field of representation. What is specific of essentialism is not uniformity but universal representability through conceptual means. This is the reason why "singularity" means something entirely different from "particularism."

Where does this difference lie? In the simple fact that, while the differences constituting particularities can still be represented conceptually as expressions of a universal ground, this does not happen in the case of a true heterogeneity. The heterogeneous demands constituting a chain of equivalences opposed to a repressive power do not tend spontaneously – without a political construction – to coalesce with each other; they are not expressions of an aprioristic ground constituting and giving meaning to all of them. Here we have something crucially important: in the same way that true particularism is not incompatible with an essentialist grounding, true heterogeneity is not incompatible with some forms of political totalization. The only thing that the latter requires is that, the heterogeneous being constitutive and irreducible, such a totalization does not function as a necessary ground. In other words: the empty signifiers – to use our terminology – which totalize and give hegemonic universality to an equivalential chain, cannot consist in a minimal formal content shared by all the links of that chain, a content which, although minimal, would still be conceptually representable. So if it entirely escapes the conceptual, in what does it consist? The answer is: in a *name. The name as the ground of the thing, this is the precondition of a true singularity.*

It is here that contemporary thought has made considerable advances. Let us give one example. For analytic philosophy in its early stages, a name refers to a thing only through the conceptual mediation represented by the descriptive features associated with that name. This is the descriptivist approach to be found, in its most classical expression, in the work of Bertrand Russell. This approach has been decisively undermined in recent years by the anti-descriptivist school led by Saul Kripke. Names do not refer to objects through conceptual mediation but constitute primal baptisms. So in naming we are dealing with true singularities. If we are, however, going to associate singularity and heterogeneity, one more step has to be taken, and it was actually taken by Lacan, for whom the unity of the object (of the primal baptism) is only the retroactive effect of the act of naming it. At this point singularity and heterogeneity come together: the name becomes the ground of the thing. The equivalential chain is still heterogeneous, but the act of unification is compatible with such a heterogeneity, because it is of a nominal and not of a conceptual nature. The essentialism of the discourse of modernity starts being left behind, but what replaces it is not mere dispersion and fragmentation but a reconstitution of collective identities as singularities. And this singularity is not incompatible with a universalism of a hegemonic type, for which universality is not a ground but a horizon.

This transition can be seen clearly reflected, among other traditions, in the history of Marxism. At the beginning, the discourse asserting homogeneity is overwhelmingly dominant. The simplification of social structure under capitalism would eliminate all heterogeneity, and the final act of history would be a simple showdown between the capitalist class and the proletariat. On top of that, the general laws of capitalism and the stages associated with them will be repeated in all essential respects in every society. Any singularity is reduced to the epiphenomenal expression of a process which, in all its essential determinations, is fully universal and conceptually apprehensible. The lowest ebb in this curb was the Marxism of the Second International and its two most characteristic thinkers: Kautsky and Plekhanov. Very soon, however, a series of dislocations within this model of historical change started tarnishing its neat outlines: the difficult articulation between workers' political and economic struggles; the evident fact that social structure under capitalism, far from becoming more homogeneous through proletarianization was becoming more heterogeneous and complex every day; and, especially, the phenomena associated with combined and uneven development, which made possible all kinds of non-orthodox combinations between agents, stages and political tasks. This leads to consequences for which all our previous analysis has prepared us to understand: any kind of emancipatory subject, being the combination of a heterogeneity of antagonistic positions which no logic of history can explain, has to result from a political articulation and not from an aprioristic objective process preceding and explaining it. That is, those subjects are *singularities*, in the sense that we have given to that term. That is why

Gramsci gave such a central role to the category of "hegemony" and spoke of "collective wills" rather than "classes" as objective locations. Both Mao and Togliatti called themselves "communists." Their obvious political differences, however, should be explained by the fact that the chains of equivalences that the signifier "communist" tried to unify were entirely different in both cases. Thus, the signifier "communist" does not express a common conceptual content underlying both projects but functions instead as a name – i.e. it constitutes a historical singularity. While the traditional notion of an "International" – either socialist or communist – was still very much dominated by a "modern" outlook, the actual history of socialism is nothing but the history of the breaking up of that postulated uniformity in which the various local parties were conceived as sections of a homogeneous international army. The irruption of this irreducible moment of heterogeneity follows point by point the transition from modernity to post-modernity as we have described it. Needless to say, the proliferation of points of rupture and antagonism in a globalized world makes the heterogeneous nature of social actors even more visible, and also makes any kind of link existing between them increasingly dependent on political articulations.

There is another dimension, however, which it is important to incorporate into our analysis. Privileging the constitutive nature of heterogeneity and presenting homogenizing logics as always operating within that primary heterogeneous terrain has led us to invert the traditional relations of priority between concept and name. The name is not the transparent medium through which the concept shows itself but, instead, any concept is only an abstract determination within the more fundamental homogenization of the heterogeneous that the name brings about. This, however, presents a new problem: which, among the heterogeneous elements, is going to function as the name of the equivalential series? For if we said that it is transcendentally predetermined which this element is going to be, we would be reintroducing through the window what we had expelled through the door: the homogeneous would still be functioning as a ground. If the heterogeneous is really constitutive, the unifying operation carried out by naming can only proceed from the very interiority of the heterogeneous field. This is the point where psychoanalysis shows all its ontological potential. Let us consider the Freudian category of "overdetermination." In a process of condensation one element expresses a chain of associations with other elements which are absolutely heterogeneous between themselves. And there is no aprioristic determination of which this element is going to be, only a purely personal history determines it. So we are in the terrain of singularity and naming.

In what does this process of (unconscious) privileging of one element as the overdetermined/overdetermining one consist? Freud's answer is clear:

in the process of investment that he calls *cathexis*. But cathexis is something belonging to the order of *affect*. I will describe in a moment how this logic of cathexis/investment operates. Before that, however, we should stress the important point that what we have just stated means that affect is not derivative but constitutive. If the decision giving the overdetermining role to a particular element were to be taken a priori, the affective dimension would be entirely derivative: it would not constitute the object but would be a secondary aspect accompanying something which had been fully constituted outside the cathectic investment. But if we assert that cathexis is constitutive, it necessarily determines the very identity of the object. So we have a second inversion of priorities. The first was that between concept and name; now we have a second, displacing affect from the secondary position to which rationalistic essentialism had relegated it. Both inversions are, actually, dimensions of the same process through which heterogeneity becomes ontologically primary.

The psychoanalytic exploration of affect leads us to the same blending of universalism and particularism that we had found in our discussion of the homogeneity/heterogeneity relationship. This can be seen most clearly in the Lacanian conception of the *objet petit a*.[3] As is well known, the aim of every drive is, for Freud, death, in the sense of a return to a mythical earlier state of inanimation or inertia conceived, by psychoanalysis, in terms of the primordial mother/child dyad. This, however, does not lead to destruction owing to the fact, in Copjec's words:

> (1) That there is no simple, complete drive, only partial drives, and thus *no realizable will to destruction*; and (2) the second paradox of the drive, which states that the drive inhibits, as part of its very activity, the achievement of its aim. Some inherent obstacle – the *object* of the drive – simultaneously *brakes* the drive and *breaks it up*, curbs it, thus preventing it from reaching its aim, and divides it into partial drives.[4]

So a certain partial object is invested with the role of representing an impossible totality – impossible because it is no more than a retroactive assumption. In her other essays[5] Copjec relates the logic of the *objet petit a* to that of the close-up in film: the latter is not a part which could simply be added to other parts, but a part which is the whole – i.e., it functions as the name of the totality, in the sense in which we have previously used the category of name. This point is crucial: not only is affect constitutive of the object – without which we would only have a mere dispersion of heterogeneous elements – but we also find that the homogenizing role that affect plays operates through a very specific pattern: the investment of an object with the role of representing the totality. To put it in Lacan's terms: sublimation consists in elevating an object to the dignity of the Thing. It does not take long to realize that this is what, in political analysis, we have called hegemony: a relation by which a partiality becomes the name of a totality with which it is entirely incommensurable. So the privileging of naming and the relation *objet petit a*/hegemony constitute two fundamental displacements in the transition from modernity (grounded in the transparency of the conceptual medium and in the fullness of being) to a certain post-modernity. For the latter, the failure of totality in its process of self-constitution does not open the way to mere multiplicity but to a different way of articulating the particular and the universal – what we have called singularity – by which the totality is very much present as that which is absent, and only shows itself through partial objects which become its actual *names*.

Various other displacements dominate the transition that we are discussing, but there is one in particular that we should refer to: the elevation of rhetoric, from the marginal and subordinated role that it occupied within the traditional classification of humanistic disciplines, to a constitutive role within the terrain of a general ontology. The condition for this displacement is the increasing recognition of what, in psychoanalytic terms, has been called the *materiality of the signifier* and the concomitant enlargement of the field of operation of the figurative at the expense of the literal. Our discussion on naming already announces this displacement. Let us consider the matter carefully. "Materiality of the signifier" does not mean privileging the phonic over the conceptual substance, simply because linguistic analysis is concerned with form and not with substance. "Materiality of the signifier" means the interruption of the one-to-one relationship between signifier and signified and, as a result, the emergence of something that is constitutively unrepresentable within the process of signification. This can happen at various levels: through incompatible equivalential chains that exercise structural pressure on the same signifier and thus cut its links with any precise signified; through contradictory associative chains operating at the level of what traditionally has been called the signified; through the unevenness of the investments that cathect the various links of the signifying chain, etc. In all cases "materiality of the signifier" means subversion of the Symbolic by the Real. Let us just consider the investment involved in the *objet petit a*. Being the object "elevated to the dignity of the Thing" and being the "Thing" is only a retrospective illusion; the investment cannot be considered as a "normal" process of representation in which the identities of both representative and represented have a direct form of expression. (Whether there is any process of representation that follows this transparent pattern is something we could doubt, but the discussion of this issue would take us too far away from the main topic of this essay.) The investment of the *objet petit a* is one in which what is invested is a non-existing fullness, and so the object becomes the name of an absence. In that case, however, what we have is a figurative meaning that occupies the place of a non-existing literality. This figurative meaning is well known in classical rhetoric: it is called *catachresis*. Once we reach the conclusion that the logic of the *objet petit a* – and, in politics, that of hegemony, which is identical – is not a marginal one but is the very condition of objectivity, we immediately see that the categories of a fundamental ontology necessarily have to be rhetorical.

This contamination between rhetoric and ontology cannot, of course, proceed without producing internal displacements within the categories that had traditionally defined their respective terrains. From the point of view of ontology its "rhetorization" necessarily puts into question any notion of a hard transcendentality – i.e., any sharp division between the transcendental and the empirical. What we have said about heterogeneity and naming already makes this crystal clear. The necessary steps, in this change of perspective are, first, the enlargement of the notion of discourse to cover the whole field of objectivity – a movement that was possible once linguistic formalism had broken the necessary links of linguistics with the conceptual and phonic substances. The second is the "ontologization" of the linguistic categories – i.e., their generalization as a pure relational logic. The third is the analysis of how the emergence of the unrepresentable within the field of representation alters the system of those relations. This is the point where, finally, ontology meets rhetoric, not as an external addition but as something required by the very logic of the ontological categories. Rhetoric, however, in order to be equal to the task, also has to change its internal structure. To give just one example: if the representation of the unrepresentable is constitutive of objectivity, catachresis cannot be one figure among others but becomes synonymous with the very principle of rhetoricity. And many other displacements within the rhetorical field become equally necessary.

I hope that my argument in this essay makes clear how I see the relationship between modernity and a possible post-modernity: not in terms of a break with the past but as an enlargement of the terrain within which that past operated. Very few – if any – of the categories of modernity have to be simply abandoned. The task as I see it today is not one of dismissal but of redefining fields of operation. Democracy as conceived within the modern outlook, for instance, should not be dismissed but seen as one among many other forms of democratic arrangement that we see today as possible within our globalized world. Several of the categories of modern metaphysics could be maintained, although their status should be redefined: they no longer function as grounds but as horizons. And, as should be clear, this essay is an argument against any radical opposition between universalism and particularism, although the forms of their combination that we are advocating clearly transcend the horizon of modernity. To put it briefly: a transition governed by displacements, not a sharp cut in which we would function as the gravediggers of modernity.

Notes

1 These issues are discussed more thoroughly in my book *On Populist Reason* (London: Verso, 2005).
2 Frantz Fanon, *The Wretched of the Earth*, trans. Constance Farrington (New York: Grove, 1968) 130.
3 I have discussed this matter in chapter 4 of my previously mentioned book. My discussion is inspired largely by Joan Copjec's book *Imagine There's No Woman: Ethics and Sublimation* (Cambridge, MA: MIT P, 2003).
4 Copjec, *Imagine There's No Woman* 34.
5 See especially Copjec, "Narcissism, Approached Obliquely" in *Imagine There's No Woman* 48–82.

fredric jameson

POSTSCRIPT

This representative collection of thoughts on postmodernism or postmodernity allows us to observe the fortunes and the multiple trajectories of an idea about which the principal question asked used to be whether it existed in the first place – is there such a thing as postmodernity? Isn't it just a more "radical" version of modernity? – but about which people now seem to be asking whether it is still with us and whether it has not already ended and been replaced by something else. The now classical version of this query takes the form of the Bush government's affirmation that "after 9/11 nothing is the same any more," which is to say, in our present context, that postmodernity also ended on that date, being replaced by one does not quite know what.

These confusions have at least one merit, namely to underscore the fact that in its most fundamental acceptation, postmodernity functioned first and foremost as a periodizing concept, one only later hijacked for a variety of other purposes and uses of which the present collection gives us a rich sampling. Thus, we can here distinguish between approaches which see postmodernism as a kind of philosophy or philosophical stance; those which see it as a social phenomenon, including cultural and political values and deeper phenomenological experiences; and those, finally, which grasp it more narrowly as an aesthetic or even one artistic style among others.

All these approaches are perfectly proper, of course, and give us many insights into the new system, if that is what it is. But if that is what it is – a system, perhaps one of an as yet unauthorized kind – the insistence on each focus in the absence of the others risks missing the nature and dynamics of the totality. Meanwhile, the thematic approach, being in some sense additive, threatens to leave important thematizations out, as I will show in a moment.

Finally, every one of these inquiries tends to be governed by a slippage in which we move insensibly from a historical description to something closer to an ethical judgment or a moral choice. If postmodernism is a philosophy, then what is implied is that it is still a conceptual option, that we can take it or leave it; dig in our heels with the traditionalists or celebrate the new dispensation with all the enthusiasm of neophytes. These choices then tend to be exercised according to the extremes of moral revulsion or delirious euphoria (an alternation, indeed, which I once – characterizing it as the "waning of affect" – identified as one of the distinguishing marks of postmodernity in the first place). But these passionate convictions (or opinions) do not quite seem to correspond to what happens to whole populations whose subjectivities and mentalities are slowly or rapidly transformed by the coming of a new historical and social moment.

Indeed, it might be better to see the seemingly philosophical issues as so many symptoms of change, rather than as a set philosophical position. I enumerate the stereotypical features as follows: the death of god, or of values; relativism; the end of grand narratives; anti-utopianism or the commitment to the heterogeneous and its "singularities"; postmodern feminisms and even post-humanisms; and so forth. Surely these are less signs of the dawning of some great new postmodern Truth than they are psychic phenomenological or reactive thoughts which demand some deeper explanation. But perhaps philosophy always tends to reify its data, as though its conceptual materials were somehow self-sufficient, if not indeed themselves the deeper causes of all the other changes.

With sociological or cultural perspectives, as for example with Grossberg's analysis of "cynical reason," we are on firmer ground, at least to the degree that the phenomena in question here are less likely to project some mirage of autonomy and more likely to inspire a restless search for fuller descriptions. Still, the old American tradition of the "culture critique" (the culture of narcissism, for example) does carry the danger of its own specific "culture-and-personality" reifications with it. And perhaps this is the place to regret that even on this social or cultural level the contributions are mainly Americano-centric and scarcely address the "alternate postmodernities" of other parts of the world. Perhaps, as several contributors suggest, it is best to ground such analyses in the movement of affect, whereby this cultural and social moment can be most conveniently distinguished from older modernist ones, than in anything too redolent of the old centered subject, even the old centered cultural subject.

With aesthetics we reach a terrain in which once again some of the methodological confusions can be dispelled: for Venturi's intervention demonstrates, if anything could, that it will not be very useful to think of postmodernism as some mere style or stylistic craze. (It might not be uninteresting, however, to follow his suggestion of mannerism on into a general inquiry into changing forms of collective and historical taste.) I've tried to suggest that a simple distinction between postmodernism as a certain style and postmodernity as a historical or periodizing concept might be useful here. (One might also want to add a new third to this potential triad, and speak of "postmodernization"; but I'll come to that in a moment.)

At any rate, at this point one begins, perhaps ungratefully, to think of all the other kinds of postmodern phenomena which might have been suggestive here but whose absence is certainly damaging to any picture of the whole. McKenzie Wark has usefully supplied a candidate for collective agency (in the hacker) but it is one which then demands completion by a host of other levels. Postmodern space is certainly a candidate; and postmodern politics too. Postmodern religion is certainly on the agenda, demanding (in my view) a rigorous demonstration of the postmodernity of so-called religious fundamentalisms.

But perhaps we can limit the enumeration to the most glaring omission, that of the economic infrastructure. Surely there is today a postmodern labor process which has had a profound effect on traditional or industrial working classes: something that leads on at once to what I termed postmodernization above, namely the signal role of cybernetic production in current postmodern technology, something for which the still current expression "post-Fordism" or "flexible production" would now seem a little inadequate.

But the other dimension of these transformations, that of business itself and the corporations, surely brings us up against that central phenomenon of postmodernity in general which is finance capitalism as such, as it has been reinvented in the informational age. Once we mention this key missing player, then at once the fundamental possibility of redefining and re-analyzing postmodernity today presents itself: it is simply globalization as such which is the other face of postmodernity and offers the most reliable access to all its other embodiments. Even postmodern philosophy might well have offered new features for analysis had it been confronted with this historically new and unparalleled reorganization of the global context in which its own new thoughts are being conceived.

But who knows? Maybe "globalization" itself is as outworn a slogan as "postmodernism," and has long since been left behind by new theoretical fashions. That would not be as disastrous a development as it might seem for those of us who have spent some time and energy working within the seemingly now outworn paradigms. There is a simple methodological rule for dealing with such problems: turn the problem into its own solution; read the new fashion (the ever more rapid changeover of theoretical labels) as itself yet another symptom of the postmodern process it was supposed to have supplanted. At any rate, whatever the changes in nomenclature, we can be sure that the third stage of capitalism, as it is expressed in globalization and postmodernity alike, will still be with us for a bit longer.

INDEX